GRETZKY

GRETZKY

From the Back Yard Rink
to the Stanley Cup

Walter Gretzky
and Jim Taylor

McClelland and Stewart

McClelland and Stewart Limited
The Canadian Publishers
25 Hollinger Road
Toronto, Ontario M4B 3G2

Canadian Cataloguing in Publication Data

Gretzky, Walter
  Gretzky: from the back yard rink to the Stanley
Cup

ISBN 0-7710-8438-2

1. Gretzky, Wayne, 1961–   2. Hockey players –
Canada – Biography.   I. Taylor, Jim, 1937–
II. Title.

GV848.5.G73G73 1984   796.96′2′0924   C84-099172-X

Printed and bound in Canada by John Deyell Company

Avon Books ISBN: 0-380-69888-9

Distributed in the United States by Avon Books,
a Division of the Hearst Corporation,
1790 Broadway, New York, NY 10019.

CONTENTS

For Phyllis

FOREWORD

Wayne Gretzky has a getaway place, fifteen minutes from the back yard where he learned to skate and a million miles from the National Hockey League he dominates. To see him there is to understand, a little, how a seventeen-year-old kid could jump headlong into the fast-lane lifestyle of superstardom and surface with his values intact.

This book is about some of those reasons – reasons named Phyllis and Walter and Kim and Keith and Glen and Brent and Grandma; about the house on Varadi Avenue with the back-yard rink and indoor pandemonium; and about the farm with the Nith River running through it where a kid could raft and canoe and fish in the summer and skate in the winter, and where the grown-up kid can return, when time allows, to take a deep breath and recharge his batteries with the people and things that really count.

I guess we really started to write the book on June 12, 1983. I was sitting in a motel room in Brantford, Ont. (pop. 74,800), just down the road from Paris (pop. 6,200) and Canning (formerly Mudge Hollow and about twenty houses big), waiting for this man named Walter Gretzky whom I'd never met and wondering whether I'd checked into a funny factory.

It was the morning after the third annual Wayne Gretzky Celebrity Tennis Tournament. The previous afternoon model Cheryl Tiegs had wandered in to shake a hand I swore I'd never wash again, Burt Reynolds was said to be interested in playing in the tournament next year, and every time I started to mention to Wayne's Director of Marketing, Michael Barnett, that I'd flown clear across the country to talk to Walter about the possibility of writing this book and was there any chance I would ever actually *see* the guy, the phone would ring and Michael would be listening to endorsement proposals for Wayne involving figures so big they looked like telephone numbers.

"Right after the tournament dinner I'll try to bring Walter over," Michael said. "Wait up."

No Walter. Not that night, nor all the next morning. Finally, I phoned his home. "Couldn't Michael reach you?" he asked. "I'm coming over to get you in an hour."

He arrived – a short, wiry man of forty-four with dark hair and darting movement – and popped me into the car. "About the book . . ." I said.

"Yeah, we've got to talk about that," he agreed. "But first we've gotta get over to the park. Keith's playing ball."

It was a day for frying eggs on your forehead. We climbed the concrete steps of the ball park, searching in vain for a spot of shade. Two or three of Walter's friends were there. We talked baseball. "Second base," Walter said. "That's Keith, No. 13, playing second."

Over in another section of the near-empty stands a slender blond kid lounged bare-chested with his buddies. He turned, waved, and a boy about nine approached him hesitantly with pencil and scrap paper. "That Wayne," Walter sighed. "You know, of all the sports he loved ball most of all. Look at him. He just loves to come home and be with his friends . . . ."

We picked up Keith, Walter turned on the car's air conditioning, and we sat back to enjoy the cool. "Walter," I said, "the way I thought we could do it is . . . ."

"Wayne's heading for the farm with Eddie," Walter said. "We'll pick up Glen and Brent and head out there, then come home where we can talk."

We gathered at the farm – Keith, sixteen, Glen, fourteen, Brent, eleven, Michael Barnett, Wayne and goaltender Eddie Mio, at that time with the New York Rangers. It was like stepping back fifty years to a better, quieter time: twenty-five acres of rolling farmland, the old farmhouse with the copper boiler at the back for catching the rainwater, and the red barn whose sides had been falling off until Walter and his brother Ed ran cable through the loft and literally bolted it back together.

Wayne's grandmother, Mary Gretzky, who lives there with her daughter, Ellen, discussed the tomatoes she'd planted and served soup so good you knew the vegetables were home-grown. Everyone went down-river by canoe to fish, Walter with his ever-present movie camera at the ready, and thus able to record for posterity the moment when Mio fell into the river. When they got home Wayne grabbed the watering can from his Grandma's hand and strode slowly down the rows dripping water into the parched earth. Then he was back to dig out a tennis racquet and a nerf ball from the car. "Okay," he hollered, "let's play a little ball!"

Sides were chosen, coats and T-shirts thrown down for bases. The world's highest-paid hockey player lashed a shot to the outfield. Glen took one step, threw himself headlong for a one-handed catch inches off the grass and rolled over in triumph. "Watch," Walter said. "They'll play for a while, then the argument will start and I'll have to step in and settle it."

It was 8 p.m. by the time we headed back. "Meet you at the Kalico!" Wayne yelled as the other car took off. "Best foot-long hot dogs in the world!"

"The Kalico Kitchen," Walter explained. "In Paris. The kids love it. Wayne's eaten there as long as I can remember. We'll just stop for a bite." The book had not yet been mentioned . . . .

We sat in the Kalico, gabbing and munching hot dogs and knocking back milk shakes. There were the usual nudges as customers noticed Wayne, but they didn't stare.

9

Why stare? He was one of theirs just as he was one of theirs in Brantford, where the sign you read coming into the city says: "Welcome to Brantford. Home of Wayne Gretzky." One request for an autograph and we were gone, headed for the house on Varadi Ave., where Phyllis Gretzky was catching a moment's solitude after a weekend mob scene in which there were more house guests than beds. Walter and I settled down on the porch with a beer.

"Uh, the way I see the book," I said, "is that it should be a . . . ."

Suddenly the porch was full of people: Michael Barnett, his associate, Rod Proudfoot, Wayne and a couple of his Brantford buddies. The talk was of old games and coaches and friends and girls, and all at once it was 2:30 a.m. and my plane left in eleven hours.

Walter looked over at me. He did not look good. He has an ulcer and lives with a more or less perpetual headache, the result of an accident at work while installing underground telephone cable. He was slapped across the head by part of the gear, leaving him deaf in one ear. Running the tennis tournament had worn him to a frazzle and he'd pulled a groin muscle lifting something earlier in the day. "Let's go into my office where it's quiet," he said. "We should talk about the book."

We went into his office.

"Do you want to write the book?" I asked.

"Oh, yeah."

"Do you want to write it with me?"

"Yeah, I feel comfortable with you. It should work out fine."

"Okay, let's do it."

End of discussion. Nine hours later I was flying home, thinking about an old-school man and a family raised on old-school values. And understanding, a little, why The Great Gretzky is almost always smiling.

Jim Taylor, May, 1984.

Chapter 1

ME, CRYING? MUST BE THE CHAMPAGNE

"There's no in-between for me. I'll be one of the heroes in this series or I'll be the goat."

– Wayne Gretzky, May 13, 1984.

The vultures were circling. The 1984 Stanley Cup final between the Edmonton Oilers and the New York Islanders was tied at one game apiece, but Wayne Gretzky didn't have a goal or even an assist. He'd struggled in the quarter-finals against the Calgary Flames and now, for the second straight year, the Islanders were cancelling him out in the final. Was he a seasonal sensation and a playoff fade-out? A lot of people didn't mind suggesting it.

"Is a pattern emerging?" asked columnist Trent Frayne in the Toronto *Globe and Mail*, after the Oilers had upset the Islanders 1-0 in the opener in Uniondale. "Does it begin to appear that in games where the checking grows tougher, playoff games in which home teams struggle for survival, Wayne is not quite the runaway express he is during the season when goals, goals and more goals are now the way of life?"

Two nights later, again playing on their home ice, the Islanders rebounded to whip the Oilers 6-1. Suddenly, it was a disaster, and Wayne Gretzky was the target.

"Gretzky had a miserable night with just two shots and no points," the Edmonton *Journal* reported. "In two games in the Stanley Cup final series Gretzky has more penalties than points. He took a hooking penalty on Paul Boutilier in the third period, the only way he could make the final summary. Two-game totals: five shots, no goals, no assists. In the past six playoff games against the Islanders, Gretzky has no goals and four assists. In the past eleven meetings with the league champs, including league play, he's managed just two goals."

Even general manager and coach Glen Sather was critical. "You have to skate," he told reporters who questioned him about Wayne's health and the fact that he wasn't scoring. "You can't stand still. You can't wait at centre. You have to come back deep. You're a sitting duck to get hit standing still.

"Wayne is perfectly healthy," he concluded. "That (a bruised shoulder that kept Wayne out of six league games) was three months ago. Right now Gretzky's feelings are the only thing that's hurting."

It probably bothered me more than it did Wayne. That was my son they were talking about. I've heard a lot of it over the years, but you never get used to it. Wayne just shrugs and says, "You're only as good as your last game."

He'd had the shoulder problem, he'd had the flu, he *hadn't* been as consistent as he'd have liked to have been – but when I picked up the paper, he was still leading the playoffs in scoring and had been almost from day one. The Oilers, whipped in four straight by the Islanders in the 1983 Stanley Cup final, had gone into Uniondale this time and gotten a split in two games on New York ice. Under the new playoff format, they played the next three games in Edmonton. Sweep those, and the cup was theirs without leaving home.

Unless they were pulling for the Islanders, people should have been delighted. When they filled Northlands Coliseum in Edmonton and watched the Oilers trounce the Islanders

7-2, to go up 2-1 in the series, they should have been ecstatic.

They weren't.

These were the Islanders their team was facing, the Islanders of Bryan Trottier and Mike Bossy and goalie Billy Smith, who had won the last four Stanley Cups, and who had humiliated the Oilers in the last cup final, and who were now trying to finish off their "Drive for Five" to tie the Montreal Canadiens of 1955-56 through 1959-60 for most consecutive championships. Edmonton fans put up banners and bought "I Hate New York" T-Shirts – but they were still uneasy. They knew what might happen if the Oilers had to go back to New York for the last two games. To win the Stanley Cup, they had to win the next two at home – and Wayne Gretzky wasn't scoring.

Wayne was more puzzled than surprised. If the team was winning, what difference did it make who was getting the goals? But he knew people wouldn't think that way. When you've set scoring records at figures once thought impossible, when you've been in the National Hockey League for five seasons, won the Hart Memorial Trophy as the league's most-valuable player in each of the first four years, and were odds-on favourite to make it five when the media votes were counted in a few weeks, and when you've become the biggest attraction the league has ever known, then you're going to be the focal point win or lose. For Wayne it had been that way since he was ten. Why should it be any different now?

In 1981-82, he'd had the greatest season in the history of the NHL. He'd set records for most goals, most assists and most points. But then the Oilers had been upset by the Los Angeles Kings in the first round of the playoffs, and he began to hear and read the charge that would stay with him until the Oilers went all the way: "He's a fine player, all right, but he can never be called a great one until he leads the Oilers to a Stanley Cup title. He can't prove his greatness until he wears that championship ring."

It was such a stupid argument. If you accept it, then Gilbert Perreault is not a great player because the Buffalo Sabres have never won the Stanley Cup in the fourteen seasons he's been there. Brad Park will surely be in the Hall of Fame some day, but in his great years with the New York Rangers and later the Boston Bruins they never won a Stanley Cup. Were they saying Brad Park wasn't a great hockey player?

Wayne tried his best to ignore it. Through the years he'd come up with his own philosophy about personal criticism: "I've taken the roses, I'll take the thorns," he said, over and over again. But when the Oilers stormed through the Smythe Division and Campbell Conference playoffs to the cup final in 1982-83, only to have the Islanders slap them aside in four straight, it was something he couldn't escape.

Hockey magazines zeroed in on one thing: the Oilers with Wayne Gretzky weren't winning the Stanley Cup. The Islanders with Bryan Trottier were winning it every year. For the writers it was a natural: "Gretzky or Trottier? Who's Really the Greatest?" The answer was always Trottier, the reason always the same: Gretzky has the scoring records, but Trottier has four Stanley Cup rings. It isn't fair to either of two great hockey players who respect one another so much.

Now he had a chance to get the monkey off his back once and for all. Beat the Islanders twice in the next four games – better yet, beat them in the next two right there in Edmonton – and the Oilers would have the Stanley Cup. They'd all be wearing championship rings. But he hadn't scored on the Islanders. Even in the 7-2 win he'd had only one assist. And management apparently was disappointed in him. There'd been the suggestions in the press that he was hanging back.

But Wayne chose to remember something else. When the criticism over his scoring slump was at its highest, assistant coach John Muckler had taken him aside for a brief talk.

"Wayne," he said, "don't worry about not scoring so far.

Just make sure that when you do get a goal for us, it's a big one . . . ."

He carried that thought with him through the day of Game Four, a game that was pivotal in that it would either put the Islanders on the ropes or force the Oilers to win at least one more in New York. When you score, make sure it's a big one . . . .

While all this was going on I was sitting at home in Brantford becoming a nervous wreck.

The quarter-final series against the Calgary Flames had been bad enough. I'd bought a satellite dish during the season so I could pick up more Oiler games. During the playoffs, that allowed me to watch the western network games. What I saw scared me stiff. Wayne had always been good on his skates, with quick moves and great balance. Now, when he tried a quick turn, he was falling down without anyone even touching him. When he did get hit, he seemed to have no strength to resist. There was no jump, no drive. He just wasn't Wayne.

The Oilers had taken a 3-1 lead in the Calgary series. They should have won it in four straight, but they blew a 4-1 lead in the second game and wound up losing 6-5 in overtime. When you've got a team down like that and can't finish it off, sometimes it gets up and starts kicking back. The Flames lost a couple of close ones, 3-2 and 5-3, then won 5-4 in Edmonton, and had a chance to tie the series on home ice two nights later.

I couldn't stand it anymore. Ever since he turned pro, Wayne has played better when his mother and I were watching. Maybe it could make a difference. Phyllis and I hopped a plane west – and got to Calgary in time to see the Flames win 5-4 in overtime on a goal by Lanny McDonald. Now the series was down to one game in Edmonton, winner take all.

Wayne had had the flu. So had some of the other Oilers,

including Paul Coffey, the defenceman who does so much to trigger their offence. That explained the lack of strength. But why was Wayne falling so much?

"What skates are you wearing?" I asked him.

"The new ones," he said. "The old ones are pretty battered up."

"Why don't you go back to the old ones?" I suggested. "You've lost weight. I think your feet are slipping inside the boot and it's affecting your balance."

I also asked him if he'd noticed that the puck was slipping off his stick. Three times in the sixth game he'd stolen the puck – and left it behind as he turned quickly to go up ice. He had to reach back and get it again, which cancelled the breakaway. Yes, he said, he had noticed. "The stick's either too long or too short."

"Which part of the stick are you losing the puck off?" I asked. "The heel or the toe?" "The heel," he said, thinking back. That meant the stick was just a shade too long. Wayne agreed and said he'd get it cut down a little before the seventh game. Then he loaded up on antibiotics and went to bed.

I'm not claiming the two suggestions made the difference. But hockey players are a bit superstitious. When they're hot, they like to keep the routine exactly as it's been. (Around 10 p.m. the night before the game, for instance, Wayne called his marketing man, Michael Barnett. "Better bring the record over," he said. Once before a key game, he'd played a song called "Rock This Town," off an LP by a group called the Stray Cats, and had had a big night as the Oilers won. There wasn't a bigger game all season than this one. No sense taking chances. Michael brought the LP over and Wayne got his fix of Stray Cats.) The old skates had been comfortable. He'd played well in them. If he *thought* the shorter stick was better, maybe it would be. Games can be won and lost in the head as well as on the ice.

That night when the Oilers came out for the warm-up, the first thing I did was look at Wayne's feet. He was wearing the old, battered skates. He scored a goal, assisted on two others, and stayed on his feet as the Oilers won 7-4. It was his best game of the series. Now we had only one problem: would the skates last through the playoffs?

We called the Daoust skate people in Montreal, just in case. Wayne endorses their product and they make all his skates. We asked for a pair in the old pattern, but a tiny bit smaller to allow for the weight loss. Maybe the old ones would last – but this was no time to take chances.

After the close call with Calgary, the Oilers weren't about to relax or take anyone lightly. They blew past the injury-riddled Minnesota North Stars in the Campbell Conference final in four straight. But it was one of those years where there always seemed to be a near crisis, and this series was no exception.

The Oilers took the first game 7-1, with Wayne getting a goal and three assists before being crashed into the boards by defenceman Lars Lindgren behind the Minnesota net with 4:21 left to play. At first it was said to be a bruised cheek, then a wrenched back. It turned out to be a bad blow to the jaw. He was back two nights later to score the winner in the second game, which ended 4-3 – but Grant Fuhr, the goalie who'd been so hot through the playoffs, came out of it with a hyper-extended elbow.

It was one of those times when you bless the fact that you have two good young goalies, not just one. Andy Moog replaced Fuhr in the third game, a wild one in which the North Stars scored five straight goals in the second period – three on the same power play, as Dave Lumley took a major for spearing Dino Ciccarelli – to build up a 5-2 lead, only to have the Oilers roar back with six straight. Wayne had two goals, one on a penalty shot, plus an assist. He also assisted on a late goal by Jari Kurri in the fourth game, which the Oilers won 3-1.

They were in the Stanley Cup final. Better yet, they were in against the Islanders, who'd lost the first two games of their series to the Canadiens in Montreal, then won the next four. All through that series reporters had been asking the Oilers which team they'd rather face, and the players were saying the polite things about respecting both teams. That was true – they did respect both of them. But there's no doubt which one they wanted in the final. Billy Smith had laughed at them. The Islanders had humilated them. They wanted another shot at New York, and they wanted it badly.

The Oilers went into the final as underdogs, which suited them just fine. If people wanted to believe they were the same team that had gone out in four the last time, so much the better. They knew they weren't.

For one thing, they had a cup final under their belts. They'd lost it, but they'd been there. They knew now what they'd be facing. And they had a few extra things going for them – extra homework, and muscle up the middle.

Shortly after the season opened, Sather made a trade with the Pittsburgh Penguins to get centre Kevin McClelland, a six-foot, 180-pounder who didn't score much, but was very strong and relished the tough going. Then, late in the year, Sather moved Mark Messier from left wing to centre. Messier, one of the league's best skaters and an outstanding goal scorer, has enormous upper-body strength. Now the Oilers had strength at centre as well as the scoring and play-making of Wayne and Ken Linseman.

The homework was with videotape provided by Roger Neilson. In his years as head coach in Toronto, Buffalo and Vancouver, Neilson had acquired the nickname "Captain Video" for his expertise at using and breaking down video-tape to scout and prepare for other teams. It hadn't been a good year for Roger. He'd been fired as head coach by the Vancouver Canucks, hired to coach the Los Angeles Kings, and fired by them at the end of the season. But when he phoned and offered his services to Sather to help the Oilers in the playoffs, Sather jumped at it.

Every team uses videotape for preparation these days.

The Oilers' assistants, Muckler and Ted Green, had been working with it all season. The difference now was that the Oilers had someone working with it all the time. Roger simply parked in his hotel room and went over tapes until his eyes bugged.

When it came time to play the Islanders, the Oilers had done their homework. Neilson had prepared separate tapes showing the Islanders' forechecking, their backchecking, how they came out of their own zone, how they killed penalties and how they ran their power play. Then he gave the Oilers a separate segment on each Islander, showing individual habits and style of play.

Out of all this, together with the normal workload of their own practices, came the game plan they thought would beat the Islanders. One of the keys: hit Bryan Trottier at every opportunity. Nothing illegal. Nothing flagrant. Just hit him.

Roger remembered the year the Maple Leafs had beaten the Islanders in a playoff round. Darryl Sittler had bumped Trottier throughout the series. Some of the Oilers who'd been on the Canada Cup team with Trottier recalled coach Scotty Bowman telling Trottier to quit worrying about hitting back and to concentrate on the puck. The theory now was that Trottier is such a great player, so competitive, so strong and determined, that when he's hit, you can sometimes knock him out of his game by getting him preoccupied with retaliation. And if they could get Trottier off his game, that might go a long way toward cancelling out Mike Bossy, because Trottier was the guy who got the puck to him for that devastating shot.

The plan seemed to have merit, particularly since the third, fourth and fifth games would be played in Edmonton where the Oilers had the last line change and could keep either McClelland or Messier against Trottier. If only the Oilers could get a split in those first two games in New York and then go home . . . .

In the first game it worked beautifully. McClelland, obtained for his strength and checking, scored the only goal in as close and tight and exciting a game as you'll ever see. "We knew everything they were going to do!" Wayne said when he phoned about 1:30 a.m. "Everything!" But the Islanders didn't win four championships by folding. They had a lot of people hurt. Their pride had been stung at home. They met the challenge in the second game as you might expect from champions. Trottier scored fifty-three seconds after the opening face-off. Big Clark Gillies, the forgotten man during the season, got a hat trick. It ended 6-1 and the Oilers were never in it.

When the Oilers responded in turn by trouncing the Islanders 7-2 in the first game in Edmonton, the skeptics had one question answered. This was going to be no blow-out series. This was going to be a dogfight. But that Gretzky! The Islanders had a special way to stop him. They must have. They'd done it last year and they were doing it again. If he didn't get going . . . .

Wayne shut it out of his mind, or tried to. The morning of the fourth game he was on the phone again. "You know, the Islanders don't do anything special to me, Dad," he said. "What happens is when I pass off to a winger, the guy checking me stays right with me so I can't get back into the play. So you watch: tonight I'm gonna give it a Gilbert Perreault."

I knew what he meant. Wayne has respected and admired Perreault since he was a little kid. He knew how Perreault could hold on to the puck and keep it until he'd manoeuvered himself into position for a shot. He was saying that tonight he wasn't going to pass off right away. He was going to hold the puck a little bit longer and try to shake off his check before he passed, so he'd be open for the return. And as he took to the ice, he had Muckler's message uppermost in his mind: "When you score, make sure it's a big one for us . . . ."

It was. At 1:53 of the opening period, Dave Semenko got the puck off the boards in his own zone. As he headed for it, he'd seen Wayne breaking up the middle, so he flipped the puck down-ice. He couldn't have passed it better. There was Wayne, all alone, breaking in on Billy Smith. This time there was no question. He deked once, Smith went for it, and Wayne parked the puck in the other side of the net.

Northlands Coliseum exploded. It was his tenth goal of the playoffs, but his first in twelve games against the Islanders. The monkey was dead. He'd beaten Smith, put the Oilers ahead. By the end of the second period, it was 6-2. At 14:11 of the third, he stole the puck and beat Smith again, this time unassisted. The Oilers were within one win of the cup. Saturday night they could do it at home.

The whole family moved to Edmonton – Phyllis, Kim, Keith, Glen, Brent and me. Phyllis and Kim left on Wednesday night and I brought the boys out on the early flight Saturday. We arrived; our luggage didn't. Phyllis had to bundle the kids downtown for some new gear. I borrowed a jacket and tie from Wayne, who gave it to me on one condition:

"When you come into the dressing room after the game tonight," he said, "take the jacket off first and leave it outside. Otherwise it'll get caught in the crossfire."

"What crossfire?" I asked blankly.

"Champagne, Dad,"he said. "Champagne."

I felt a lot better then. He was confident. They were going to do it. It reminded me of something that had happened earlier in the playoffs. I'd seen a picture of someone lifting weights and had told Wayne he'd better start doing some weight work. "Why?" he asked.

"Otherwise," I said, "you'll never be able to lift that Stanley Cup."

"Don't you worry, Dad," he said. "I'll get it up there, all right."

Tonight, with luck, he'd get his chance.

That afternoon, a few hours before the game, I talked to Wayne one last time. He was very nervous, he said. No one wanted to go back to New York. They had to end it tonight. *He* was nervous! My ulcer was killing me. But Wayne fixed it in a hurry once we got to the rink.

The Oilers had Moog in goal for the big one, an announcement that sent a restless little wave through the crowd. Fuhr had sprained his shoulder in the third game. Moog had finished that one and had played a solid Game Four. He was a good goalie. He'd proved that before. On a lot of teams he'd have been No. 1. But it wasn't that Fuhr was merely not starting this one. He wasn't dressing. He'd been scratched. The back-up goalie, if one was needed, would be Mike Zanier, a youngster from Trail with no NHL experience, let alone Stanley Cup play. For the crowd, it wasn't a good opening.

It didn't take the Oilers long to show how tight they were. Forty-seven seconds after referee Brian Lewis dropped the puck, they took a bench minor for too many men on the ice. But they weathered it, and it seemed to settle them down. At 12:08, with Lewis holding up his arm to indicate a delayed penalty to the Islanders, Wayne took a lead pass from Jari Kurri, raced in on Smith while being pressured from behind, deked and put it past him. Five minutes later, with a drop-pass from Kurri on a three-on-one break, he beat him again.

It was the beginning of the end for Smith. Trailing 2-0, Islander coach Al Arbour replaced him with Roland Melanson to start the second period. As Melanson took his warm-up, the crowd, remembering the scene of a year ago when Smith had done so much to frustrate the Oilers with both his play and his mouth, got theirs back. "BILLEE!" they roared. "We want BILLEE!"

Thirty-eight seconds into the period, it was 3-0 on a power play goal by Ken Linseman with Wayne and Charlie Huddy drawing assists. Now the Oilers could smell blood. At 4:39, Kurri scored on a power play, from Paul Coffey and Glenn Anderson, to make it 4-0. Up in the stands, the cheerleader with the specially designed hat let flames gush out the top of his head. The Islanders were tired. The injuries to their defence were beginning to take their toll. It was over. The Islanders were done.

But not quite yet. Never, ever count a champion out. The Islanders stormed out for the third period and in less than a minute it was a hockey game again. Pat LaFontaine scored at thirteen seconds and again at forty-five seconds. Now it was 4-2, the Islanders were pressing and the Oilers were starting to run around in aimless pursuit, as they'd done in the second game. Actually, if the Islanders hadn't missed a couple of open corners, it could have been 4-3 a minute or so later.

The Oilers settled down, with Moog making some excellent saves under great pressure. Then, with 3:15 left, Pat Flatley smashed into Moog, who lay motionless on the ice. Flatley got a penalty for it, but if the Oilers had to shove the inexperienced Zanier into a situation like this . . . .

Moog got up. Around the rink you could hear one long, massive sigh of relief. He held the fort again until, with twenty-eight seconds left and the Islander net empty, Dave Lumley got the puck after a face-off inside the Edmonton blue line, and shot it clear down-ice into the open goal to make it 5-2, and put the Islanders down and out for good.

What can I tell you about that moment? Fans jumped the boards. There must have been fifty balloons on the ice. Police couldn't escort the people off fast enough. Finally, referee Lewis shrugged and dropped the puck for the face-off, balloons or no balloons. The game ended in bedlam with Moog struggling under a mob of Oilers, two fans unfurling a large banner reading "BRING ON THE SOVIETS!" and Wayne holding on to his stick for dear life as souvenir hunters fought to wrestle it away.

One fan did get past his defences, leaped up and threw himself into his arms. It was Brent. If anybody was going to hug Wayne on the ice, it was going to be his little brother. Wayne skated around for a minute, holding him with one hand, waving with the other. If you looked closely, I think you'd have seen a tear or so. And he wouldn't have been the only one.

Then he saw the Stanley Cup. They'd rolled the red carpet out onto the ice and the cup was right there on a table in front of John Ziegler, president of the NHL.

Wayne took off as though he had jets. If Mr. Ziegler had a speech planned, he never got a chance to give it. Wayne gave him a bear hug, then swept the cup aloft as his team-mates swarmed around him. He couldn't skate with it. There were too many people – players, fans, photographers shoving for position to get shots of Wayne, and of a tearful Mark Messier, who'd just learned that he'd won the Conn Smythe Trophy as the most valuable player in the Stanley Cup playoffs. It was one big lump of humanity moving slowly around the ice while the fans in the stands went crazy.

When I finally got into the dressing room, it was wall-to-wall people. It took me a while even to get close to Wayne. I saw Phyllis first, although I hardly recognized her. We hadn't been sitting together – at hockey games we never do unless we have to – and she'd got there before me, just in time to take a fizzing champagne bottle right in the kisser. She was drenched from head to waist. In a minute, so was Wayne's jacket. I'd forgotten to take it off as he'd instructed. Tough!

Finally, I got through to him. A while later he'd be phoning his Grandma at the farm in Canning, and waking the entire night watch at the Brantford fire department to share the celebration with a family friend, Bryan Wilson. The kids would be crowded around and the party would go far into the night. But just for a second there, it was like there were only the two of us in the room.

He's had a lot of big moments in his career, a lot of personal triumphs and awards, but I'd never seen the look of pure joy that was on his face just then – a face streaked with sweat, champagne and tears.

24

We hugged, then pulled back and gave each other a silly kind of grin. "Way to go, Weiner," I said, and watched the crowd sweep him away.

It didn't matter. There'd be plenty of time later. The Oilers had the Stanley Cup and people were already talking dynasty. The plan had worked; the Islanders had been stopped. They'd had a lot of injuries, but over the five games Trottier was held to a goal and three assists and Bossy to three assists. For all his supposed problems, Wayne had finished with 34 points, just four shy of the playoff record he'd set the year before.

For me, one thought kept running through my mind: there'd be no more of that "He can't be called a great until he wears that Stanley Cup ring." The Oilers had the cup, and he'd have the ring, and no one could ever take it away.

Chapter 2

OKAY, WHO STOLE MY LUCKY GARTER BELT?

"I've never felt pressure like this. Never."

– Wayne Gretzky, Jan. 26, 1984.

In the 1983 NHL All-Star game, Wayne scored four goals in the third period, set three records, tied one, and won another car. In the 1984 game, he missed two breakaways, scored one goal, played about twenty-five per cent as well as he can, and didn't win anything. But it was one of the greatest performances of his life.

He shouldn't have played that game at all, any more than he should have played the three league games before it. Ten days earlier, on his first shift in a game in Los Angeles, he'd been checked cleanly, fallen against the boards and felt something give in his right shoulder. A bruise, he thought at first. As the days went by and it got worse, the Oilers thought it might be a slight sprain – painful, but it would clear up.

Two days after the All-Star game, they x-rayed it. The shoulder wasn't bruised and it wasn't sprained. It was separated. A "Class 1" separation, they called it, which is the least serious on a scale of three. It still meant he'd played four league games and the All-Star game with a separated shoulder.

There were a couple of reasons. As far as the All-Star game went, I don't think you could have kept him out of it with a gun. He was captain of the Campbell Conference team. Six other players, including Mike Bossy and Bryan Trottier of the Islanders, were already out with injuries. The NHL was in a sweat. Now it was going to hold its All-Star game without the league scoring leader and biggest draw? No chance. It was a question of responsibility. Besides, Wayne wanted to play. He loves that All-Star game. It's like a gathering of gunfighters in the Old West. If you're voted among the best, you've got to be there to prove it.

There'd be no proving it this time. He knew that, too. But he was determined to play, determined that he wouldn't make any token appearance. Glen Sather, coaching the Campbells, said later, "Before every shift I asked him if he was okay, if he wanted to go on. He just kept saying yes." He played hurt. Each time he came off the ice, you could see on his face just how much it hurt. It was obvious he couldn't do half the things he normally does as a matter of course. To score on the breakaways, all he needed to do was lift the puck. He couldn't do it. But he took his regular shift, worked the power play and killed penalties. They lost, 7-6, but I've never been more proud of him than I was that night in New Jersey.

As for the three league games before that – well, he could have sat out. Maybe he should have, because despite what he was telling reporters it was hurting a lot. To make it worse, he'd hurt his left hand trying to put an ice pack on the shoulder. He'd taken the glove off during a practice, and with the bare hand resting on top of the boards at the Edmonton box, Ken Linseman had vaulted the boards to get on the ice and landed on it. Linseman felt badly, but it was just one of those freak accidents. "If it's anybody's fault, it's mine," Wayne said. "I shouldn't have had the hand there in the first place and I should have been watching what was going on." In other circumstances the Oilers might have insisted he sit out a game or two. But, you see, there was the matter of the Streak . . . .

Wayne headed into the 1983-84 season about ten pounds heavier, convinced that it could be his best year yet. Considering what he'd accomplished so far, that could have been considered foolish optimism.

In four NHL years, he'd set twenty-four league records and held a share of ten others. He'd won three straight league scoring championships, setting those goal, assist and point records along the way. If his 1982-83 season record (71 goals, a league-record 125 assists and 196 points) wasn't considered spectacular by some, it was only because he'd reached the point where he was being measured only against himself. So he got 196 points – big deal. It was only the third-highest season point total in history, and the two up above both belonged to him. Heck, maybe he was slowing down!

It's something that's always puzzled me, something that's going to make it harder every season for Wayne to collect the league's major awards, whether he deserves them or not: a lot of the people doing the voting don't measure him by the normal yardstick. Dick Chubey, hockey writer for the Edmonton *Sun*, admits it. "When we vote for the three stars in a game, sometimes Wayne will get three points and not get a vote," he told me. "That's a big night for most players. From Wayne, it's just a night we've come to expect. Wayne competes with Wayne."

Fans apparently feel the same way. In the hockey pools that spring up all over the country at playoff time there are usually special Gretzky rules. If you draft Wayne, you count only his goals or his assists, or you count only half his points. But Wayne still likes to have goals. Some of his personal records and some of the league's team records, he thought, were within reach. Four games into the season, with the Oilers 4-0, he suggested one to a friend over breakfast.

"You know," he said, "this team could average six goals per game for the season."

"There something funny in that peanut butter?" the guy asked. "One or two shutouts, a couple of low-scoring games and you're done."

"No, seriously," Wayne said. "All it would take would be a few seven-goal games."

"C'mon, Wayne! A few seven-goal games? Don't be silly."

Wayne just looked at him. "We've already got two eights," he said gently.

Before too long they also had a ten and an eleven and a thirteen against the New Jersey Devils that was to haunt Wayne all season. In one four-game span they beat Washington 11-3, Pittsburgh 7-3, Winnipeg 8-4 and Quebec 7-4. Thirty-three goals in four games. Defensively they left a lot to be desired, and they lost their first two meetings with the Islanders, which was becoming a bit of a psychological problem after losing four straight in the 1983 Stanley Cup final. But fire power they had to spare. At the All-Star break, after 52 games, they were averaging 5.78 goals per game. And Wayne was flying, leading the league in goals with 61 (which put him one game behind his pace of 1981-82 when he set the record with 92), in assists with 92 and in points with 153 – which put him 68 points ahead of his winger, Jari Kurri, who was in second place.

The only smudge on the '83-'84 season so far was what came to be known as The Mickey Mouse Caper. But that was a dandy . . . .

It started November 19. The New Jersey Devils were in Edmonton. Their starting goalie, Ron Low, was an ex-Oiler and a personal friend of Wayne's. The Devils were sitting in last place in the NHL and that night they showed why. The Oilers won 13-4. Wayne scored three goals and had five assists. And later in the dressing room, he did something he'd never done as a pro before: he opened his mouth and put his skate in it.

"They're putting a Mickey Mouse operation on the ice," he told reporters. "They'd better start getting some better personnel. It's ruining hockey!"

It wasn't the smartest move he could have made. He spoke in a fit of anger because he felt sorry for Ron and for Chico Resch, who replaced him in the Devils' net as the score mounted. The next day he apologized, but the damage was done. The quote made all the papers. New Jersey officials more or less suggested that they'd run their team and Wayne could please concentrate on his. (In a matter of days they also fired coach and general-manager Billy MacMillan, one of three coaches to get chopped that season after getting blitzed by the Oilers. The other two: Tom Watt in Winnipeg and Roger Neilson in Vancouver.) "I shouldn't have said it," Wayne admitted later. "But I can't win. For three hundred and sixty-four days of the year I keep my mouth shut and reporters say I'm dull. One day I say something and everything hits the fan."

The sequel, though, was an interesting example of what Wayne does for the league. The Devils and the Oilers were to play again January 15 in New Jersey's Byrne Meadowlands Arena. The fans, Wayne understood, would be waiting. There was even a rumour that the Devils themselves were organizing a Mickey Mouse Night. It later was denied vehemently by Max McNab, the club's vice-president and director of hockey operations. "We wanted no part of that. Our feeling is that Wayne is a quality young man who has fifteen or twenty microphones stuck in front of him every day and as far as we know that's the first mistake he ever made. He apologized, and as far as we were concerned it was over."

New Jersey fans, however, were not so forgiving. They turned up by the hundreds wearing Mickey Mouse shirts and ears with "99" or "Gretzky" written on the ears. They shouted and booed and hooted at the Oilers, and waved signs saying things like "The Devils Mickey Mouse? Gretzky's Goofy!" and "Glen Sather Presents Gretzky and Mou-skate-teers!"

It was all good fun. Wayne went on TV and apologized again. The Devils played very well, before losing 5-4.

Wayne didn't score, but he got three assists. And the place was packed. All he'd done, really, was help create another full house.

There was one record Wayne didn't talk much about. He'd have looked foolish. But in the back of his mind was the thought that a 100-goal season was not entirely out of range. His assist and total points records were logical targets. And there was another one that intrigued him. He held the league record of thirty consecutive games in which he collected a point or more. Was it possible, he wondered, to get a point in *all eighty* games in a season? Now *that* would be a Streak.

It's not the kind of thing you go after. Not at first, anyway. But as the games went by and he passed the 30 mark, people began to wonder. The Streak became a hot topic for discussion. As he ran it to 40, it really caught the imagination. Sportscasts began to open with "Wayne Gretzky got his point last night as . . . ." And there were some curious side-effects.

The Daoust skate people had just produced a skate with a blue and orange boot – the Oiler colours – that they feel is really going to be big. They wanted Wayne to start wearing it, which would give it all kinds of publicity leading up to the National Sporting Goods Show in Montreal, two days before the All-Star game. Now, they didn't want him to wear it, for fear the Streak would end the game he put on the new skate.

It was the same thing with the Titan people. They had a new stick called a Turbo injected with plastic that they felt would revolutionize stick-making. Wayne had had it for weeks, just testing it in practice, and he loved it. Titan wanted him to start using it – but not while the Streak was on. They had the same fears as Daoust. If it happened to end the night he tried the new stick, the publicity could really backfire.

They needn't have worried. As long as the Streak was going Wayne wasn't going to change *anything*. That's why trainer Barrie Stafford was so concerned about the garter belt . . . .

As garter belts go it wasn't much. Just standard hockey issue, the kind you use to hold up your socks. It was ratty and old and torn. The button you slip the garter clip over had fallen off. Actually it was a mess – but Wayne had been wearing it every game through the Streak. There'd been close calls, too. On January 11 in Game 44 in Chicago, he batted down an attempted clearing pass at the Edmonton blue line, fought off a check all the way down-ice, and fired the puck into the empty net with two seconds left on the clock. There'd been other one-point games, too. So when the button went on that lucky belt, he took a dime, slid it into the slot for the button and hooked the snap over that. There was no way he'd throw that belt away.

In Los Angeles, he got two third-period assists, one on a short-handed goal in a 6-3 win. With three days off before their next game in Vancouver, the Oilers rested in Palm Springs. The shoulder was sore, but the Streak was at 49 and he was two goals shy of another personal target – 60 goals in 50 games.

They got to Vancouver, started to dress for the game – and the lucky garter belt was gone. Barrie was frantic. Someone had stolen the belt, probably in Palm Springs. If Wayne wore a new belt and the Streak ended . . . .

"Relax," Wayne told him. "It'll be all right." He was a nervous wreck himself. They'd looked everywhere. His lucky belt was gone and his shoulder hurt and the Canucks were always tough in their own building.

The new belt worked – that night. The Oilers came from behind in the third period to go up 5-4, and Wayne scored his 60th goal on the empty net on a pass from Glenn Anderson. That night he had two goals and two assists. The Streak was at 50 – but the shoulder was hurting a lot more than he let on. He'd taken a couple of good hits on it, fallen on it twice. The Vancouver crowd booed every time he touched the puck. In fact, it only cheered him once: when he was hit late in the second period, doubled up and barely made it back to the bench. It wasn't a cheer for Wayne. It was a cheer because he was hurt. Oh, they love him in Vancouver.

He was playing down the injury. For public consumption he was saying things like, "It's okay. People have played with a lot worse. The Streak? Yes, there is a certain amount of pressure, but . . . ." In private the next morning it was a different story.

"You know, I look back now at when I was going for Maurice Richard's record and then Phil Esposito's and I remember there was a strain, but there's no comparison to what I'm going through now. When I was chasing them, I could miss a game or get blanked one night and I was still in it. This one there's no missing. The Streak is getting to me. Maybe I'm thinking about it more than I should. I don't know what it's going to be like the day I wake up and say, 'Hey, it's finished. I've got to start all over again.' "

And that shoulder?

"I've missed only one game in my pro career," he said. "You've got to play hurt in this league. But I don't know. If it wasn't for the Streak . . . ."

The Streak lasted one more game. The Oilers blew a 3-0 lead at home and settled for a 3-3 tie against, of all people, the Devils. Wayne got his 61st goal early, but saw limited action after that and gave the puck away in his own zone to give the Devils their chance for the tying goal. He was there, but he wasn't Wayne Gretzky. And the next night, the Kings came to town and shut him down in a 4-2 victory. After 51 games, the Streak was over.

In one sense Wayne was upset. But deep down there was a little sigh of relief. The pressure was off now. The Stanley Cup chase was still on, which was the important thing, and the point and assist records were well within reach if he could get healthy. To do that he'd have to sit out. There was no help for it. He had no way of knowing how many games he'd miss. All he could do was massage the shoulder and wait.

The waiting lasted six games. For a guy used to playing every game and logging a large chunk of ice time, it was agony.

The Oilers weren't just without Wayne. Kurri was out, too, with a groin pull that would cost him sixteen games and hamper his effectiveness when he returned. For one game it didn't look as though the Oilers needed either of them. Pat Hughes erupted for five goals in a 10-5 win over Calgary. Then they dropped five straight, including a 5-3 loss to an Islander team without Trottier, Bossy and four other regulars.

There were some suggestions in the Edmonton media that maybe the Oilers couldn't win without Gretzky, which made Wayne feel awfully uncomfortable. But when he and Kurri got back in the line-up February 15, he went on a tear.

He celebrated his return with two goals and two assists against Winnipeg. And in a three-game, four-day span he scored ten goals, two against the Pittsburgh Penguins in Edmonton, then back-to-back four-goal games in St. Louis and Pittsburgh. (There was an interesting sidelight to the game in Pittsburgh. Over the previous twenty-nine home games, the Penguins had averaged 6,866 fans. For Wayne and the Oilers they drew 15,838.) I really thought that he had a shot at his point record and maybe the assist record, too.

Then everything just seemed to fade. Maybe it was because Sather was leaning more and more toward four lines – preparing for the playoffs and trying to give his gunners a rest. Whatever, Wayne didn't seem to be getting as much ice time as he'd had in the past. And over the last six games of the regular season, all the guns seemed to run out of bullets.

In that stretch, Wayne had four goals and six assists – not bad, but not terrific. Glenn Anderson had one four-goal and one two-goal game, but was scoreless in the other four. Mark Messier had two two-goal games and was shut out in four. Jari Kurri, still bothered by the groin injury, had two goals and two assists.

Any thought of personal record-breaking ended right there. At that, Wayne came close, considering the six games out. He finished with 87 goals, 118 assists and 205 points – 5 goals, 7 assists and 7 points shy of his league records.

There was neither time nor reason to be disappointed. The Oilers hadn't quite averaged the six goals per game he'd predicted, but they'd scored a record 446 and upped their all-time league per-game average to 5.8. In Wayne (87), Anderson (54) and Kurri (52) they had the first one-team, 50-goal trio in NHL history. And they were primed for another run at the Stanley Cup, a run that would end with balloons on the ice and tears in the eyes.

For Wayne, and for all of the Gretzkys, it would provide a fairy tale ending to an unbelievable story – a story that began six years earlier on a private jet plane heading out of Vancouver, on a trip that would change all our lives . . . .

Chapter 3

WRITE $825,000, WAYNE. I'M TOO SCARED TO HOLD THE PENCIL

"I know he can out-think and outsmart the others and his skating is not that bad. But turn pro at seventeen? He'd get killed!"

— Howie Meeker, Brantford *Expositor*, May 3, 1978.

There was lightning, I remember that. The rain was bouncing off the windows of Nelson Skalbania's private jet, the storm was flaring up outside and Phyllis and I were sitting there staring at each other and wondering what in the world we'd just done.

We weren't jet-set people and never would be. We were Phyllis and Walter Gretzky of Brantford, Ontario, with five kids and a house and a mortgage and a job at Bell Canada. But here we were, being flown out of Indianapolis, the only passengers on a private Lear jet making a special flight so that I could get to work for Monday morning, and down below we'd left our seventeen-year-old son, Wayne, in a strange city where he didn't know a soul, to start playing professional hockey with everybody in North America watching because all of a sudden he was going to get all this money. Every time you picked up a newspaper or turned on a radio or TV you heard that he might have triggered a war. He was by himself, and he was seventeen.

I don't know how he felt down there, but in that plane my stomach was churning. Had we done the right thing? Had Wayne? Would he be happy in Indianapolis? Except for July and August he'd been away from home for three years, but never more than a couple of hours away. This was another *country*. What about school? What about a home life? What about a million other things?

We were still thinking about it when we landed in Toronto and drove home to Brantford. The next day I was back repairing teletype machines. It had been one crazy weekend . . . .

I guess everyone who follows sports knows about Wayne Gretzky by now. The scoring records, the trophies, the new contract running through 1999 to match the 99 on the back of his sweater, the television commercials, the endorsements and the stories about all the money he's making have seen to that. It's been a long time since he could go anywhere without being recognized or having someone asking for his autograph. He'd have to be triplets to attend all the functions that want him. He has an agent, a marketing man, a lawyer, an accountant and a lady to sort through his mail, which runs to more than a thousand letters per week. He's a corporation, a boy who had to grow up awfully fast and who did it without changing or forgetting where he comes from. Of all the things, I'm proudest of that.

And I guess everyone in hockey knows about Nelson Skalbania, the millionaire real estate developer from Vancouver. For a while there he really shook things up. At one point in 1981 he owned the Montreal Alouettes of the Canadian Football League, the Atlanta Flames of the National Hockey League, fifty per cent of the Vancouver Canadians of the Pacific Coast Baseball League, the Calgary Boomers of the North American Soccer League and junior hockey franchises in Calgary and New Westminster, B.C. He'd also tried to buy the Seattle Mariners American League baseball team for $12.5 million and made a try for an expansion franchise for Vancouver in the National Basketball Association.

He's out of sports entirely now and probably glad of it, because on most of them he wound up taking a beating. But when we met him on the weekend in June of 1978, he was just starting to get really serious about sports as an investment, and just reaching the point where people in sports were starting to recognize his name. He'd been making million-dollar deals for years in real estate, but a lot of people don't read the business pages. All of a sudden he was on the sports pages, and he was big news.

I liked him. But he certainly was different. For instance, he was flying around the country making deals so often it was hard for him to reserve a racquetball court at the Vancouver YMCA when he made it home. And he was a racquetball fanatic. So he and another Vancouver businessman named Herb Capozzi played a challenge match in which the loser would donate $5,000 to the cause of the winner's choice. Capozzi showed up dressed as a Roman senator – toga, wreath on his head and everything – and was carried to the court on one of those litters you see in the old movies. Nelson won and donated Capozzi's $5,000 to the Y to build a racquetball court – on one condition: he would have a standing reservation at four every afternoon, just in case he was in town and wanted to play.

In 1975, he bought the Edmonton Oilers of the World Hockey Association, then sold them to the present owner, Peter Pocklington, for cash, two Rolls-Royce cars, Mrs. Pocklington's diamond ring and two Krieghoff prints. At one point he owned four Rolls-Royces (including the one they'd used in making the movie *The Great Gatsby*) three condominiums, a 165-foot yacht, the jet, and this gorgeous house he'd bought for $1.5 million in 1979 (and later tore down to build a new one).

And now he wanted to buy Wayne.

We'd never met, of course. In fact, he'd never seen Wayne play hockey. I'm not sure he knew much about the game anyway. What he wanted was a lever to force the National Hockey League into a merger with the World Hockey Association. The way to get it, he figured, was to break the existing agreement and sign an under-age junior, a player under twenty and thus still eligible to play junior hockey.

And Wayne wanted out. Boy, did he want out.

He'd just finished his first year in junior "A", with the Soo Greyhounds, won the rookie-of-the-year award, scored 70 goals and assisted on 112 more to finish second in scoring to Bobby Smith, whom the Minnesota North Stars had made the No. 1 pick in the NHL draft that year. Wayne had been a legend in minor hockey since he was eight years old, and now he seemed about to pick off junior records the same way.

But there was a hitch. The coach for most of that season had been Muzz MacPherson, and Wayne and Muzz got along fine. Then the team had a few problems and Muzz resigned with about two months left. He was replaced by a man named Paul Theriault. One of the first things Theriault did was to tell Wayne he was going to make him a different kind of hockey player.

Now, if you've seen Wayne play you know that one of the things he does best is anticipate where the puck is going to be. It's something I've tried to teach all the boys: don't follow the puck, go to where it's going to be. That meant that a lot of times Wayne would be where technically he wasn't supposed to be. But the puck would be there with him. That was the part Paul wanted to change. He had a system where Wayne would be at a certain place at a certain time and that was it.

Wayne pleaded with him. "Don't take away what I do

best," he said. "Add to me whatever you want, but don't take away what I do best because that's how I make up for some of the things I lack."

Wayne levelled with him. "If you make me a different kind of a player," he said, "I won't be back next year."

Everybody thought he was kidding. The team started winning and Wayne was in that scoring race with Smith and having a big year, so it never seemed to occur to anyone that he was serious. Even in the off-season, when a lot was being written about what he might or might not do, when he went on the radio with Muzz, who was doing a show by then, and said that he was playing junior to get drafted by the pros "and I'm going to get there by putting the puck in the net, not by playing defensive hockey," the idea that he might actually quit didn't seem to sink in.

Wayne was being careful about what he said. There was some newspaper speculation that he was upset because his grades were down and the Greyhounds hadn't provided the tutor they'd promised. (It was nonsense. Angelo Bumbacco, general-manager of the Greyhounds, would have done anything for Wayne.) There were suggestions that he might want to be traded. And Wayne even said he thought he might be back with the Greyhounds. But I knew differently. I'd taken the phone calls.

He'd called me one night at home shortly after Muzz had resigned and Paul had taken over. "I want you to call Mr. Bassett," he said. "Tell him I'm not going back to the Soo. Call him right now!"

John Bassett Jr., a Toronto man who owned the WHA's Birmingham Bulls (formerly the Toronto Toros) is generally credited with firing the first shot in what escalated to all-out war with the NHL by signing eighteen-year-old Wayne Dillon of the Toronto Marlboros junior team in 1973. Now, in the very year the two leagues had agreed to keep hands off under-age players, he'd gone ahead and signed Ken Linseman, an eighteen-year-old playing for the Kingston Canadians. The way Wayne had it figured, if Mr.

Bassett would sign one under-age player, maybe he'd sign two.

He was really upset. I tried to calm him down and said I'd call Mr. Bassett. Twenty minutes later the phone rang again. "Did you get him?" Wayne asked. "What did he say?"

Now, I had no intention of calling Mr. Bassett. I just let on I had while I tried to settle Wayne down. "Stay in junior," I said. "People change, situations change. You've got three more years of junior. You can play one year as an over-age (each team is allowed to carry one player for one season over the age limit). In four years you can go just about wherever you want and name your price!"

"If I stay here four more years," he said, "I'll *never* play pro. The longer you stay the more fault they'll find. Call Mr. Bassett! *Please!*"

He must have phoned me three or four more times that night, just to see if I'd reached Mr. Bassett. He was just beside himself. Don't forget, this is a seventeen-year-old boy, and at seventeen it's pretty easy to think the world is coming to an end.

It ended up that Gus Badali, Wayne's agent, finally did call Mr. Bassett. The WHA held a meeting and decided to go for it. The league would try to sign Wayne – and the man to try it would be Nelson Skalbania.

And that's how it started: the craziest weekend of my life.

Nelson wanted the whole family to fly to Vancouver the next day, in the middle of the week, and sign Wayne there. Just like that, everybody pack up and go. "Hey," Gus said, "Walter works for a living. He can't just grab a plane and leave his job." So Nelson left $1,000 with Gus for expenses and waited for us to arrive on the weekend.

He had style, I'll give him that. He met us at the airport in a Rolls-Royce and drove us through Vancouver, like royalty on parade, to a big, gorgeous house in one of the city's most posh areas. It was as though we'd stepped into a different world. Nelson didn't put on airs. You'd have thought the Gretzkys were just another group of his rich business associates, flying in to make a deal on an oil well or a hotel chain. When he got out of the car it was smoking. The brakes had seized or something. There was another Rolls sitting in the driveway. "Walter," he said, "take my advice. Don't ever buy a damned Rolls Royce. They're nothing but trouble." I looked to see if he was kidding. He wasn't. "Don't worry, Mr. Skalbania," I said, straight-faced, "I never will." The boys at the phone company would have died laughing.

He was a shrewd man, too. "You folks clean up and we'll see you when we get back," he said, ever so casually. "Wayne and I are going to take a little run."

I knew what he was trying to do. Nelson was a dedicated jogger. He took great pride in his physical condition. He didn't know hockey but he knew stamina. Before he signed this kid he'd find out whether he had any.

Wayne told me about it. Nelson really pushed it. You have to remember that we'd spent four hours on a plane. Wayne naturally hadn't gotten any sleep the night before what with the excitement, and he was absolutely bushed. But in the end he pulled away from him. Nelson must have been impressed. "We ran six miles and he beat me," he told a reporter later, "so I signed him."

For Phyllis and me the whole thing was like some kind of crazy dream. Did people really *live* like this? There we were, driving to his office in the afternoon and he's waving at a building and saying he owns it and maybe it could be part of Wayne's deal. He starts throwing out all these figures, and for me it's just mind-boggling.

Then we get there and he says, "How much is your time and trouble worth for coming out here and signing if it turns out that the two leagues merge and Wayne can't play pro because he's under age and has to go back to junior?"

I'm sitting there trying not to gulp and frantically think-ing about how much I could ask for. I'm just about to shoot the works and say $10,000 when he scribbles out a cheque and hands it to me. It's for $50,000.

"Uh, fine," I said weakly, and off we went back to the house to talk contract. Walter Gretzky, wheeler-dealer.

You see, that's the part that people don't understand. Since Wayne turned pro and things just sort of exploded, I've had to learn to be a little bit of an accountant, a little bit of an agent, and a little bit of a lawyer, because there are always people out there who want a piece of Wayne and if you don't watch every step he can wind up sliced to bits. But that day in Vancouver . . . who were we, talking to this millionaire about more dollars than we were ever likely to see in our lives? We had Gus there to represent Wayne, but this was our son and we were talking about his future. It was scary, particularly the way Nelson was moving at the time.

He already owned the Racers in Indianapolis, but he was negotiating to buy the Houston Aeros or maybe the Quebec Nordiques. He didn't know which team to put Wayne on once he signed him. In fact, right in the middle of the negotiations he phoned some hockey guy in Houston who told him not to sign Wayne because he wasn't that big, or that fast . . . all the things we'd heard before. The guy even named another kid Nelson should sign instead. Nelson thanked him, hung up, and we got back to negotiations.

Well, we finally got it straightened out, but we didn't get around to writing out the contract. That didn't happen until the next day, aboard Nelson's jet. And do you know who wrote up the contract? Wayne did.

It was the craziest thing. Nelson wanted to make the announcement in Edmonton, probably because it was a WHA city. But the deal wasn't signed. Signed? Heck, it wasn't even typed. Nelson dictated and Phyllis and I just sat there in this luxury business jet owned by this bearded millionaire in one of the other seats – a man we'd met only that weekend, a man said to have amused himself during flights in that very plane by playing backgammon for thousands of dollars per game – watching our son write something that was going to make him rich beyond our wildest dreams. It was silly. Things like this didn't happen. Any day now we'd wake up.

But there was Wayne, writing it out in longhand on a piece of ordinary writing paper with a sheet of school foolscap underneath it so the lines would show through. After all, he was writing something that would change his life. The least he could do was keep the lines straight.

The figure that came out in the media was $1.75 million, which was wrong. One of the first things you learn about contracts is that the figures you read and hear about are hardly ever the ones on the paper. The real ones were these:

* The contract was not with the WHA or the Indianapolis Racers, it was a personal service contract between Wayne Gretzky and Nelson Skalbania, under which Wayne "must be prepared to work starting June 11, 1978 with either Houston or Indianapolis." (When someone asked later what would happen if for some reason Wayne wasn't allowed to play, Nelson said, "Then I guess I've just bought myself the world's most expensive racquetball partner.")

* The contract was for four years with an option for three more on mutually agreed terms, with a neutral arbitrator to settle it if there was no agreement.

* There was a signing bonus of $250,000 – $50,000 of which Wayne received when he signed the deal he was writing, the balance when his lawyers okayed the rest of the contract terms.

* The salary was $100,000 in the first year, $150,000 in each of the next two and $175,000 in the fourth.

* The contract was null and void and Wayne kept all the money advanced to him to that point should a merger take place that kept under-age juniors from playing in the league.

That was it: four years worth of hockey for $825,000. In junior "B" the players got $4 for a win, $2 for a tie and $1 for a loss. In the Soo his weekly salary was $25. Now he would earn $3,000 a week. You might call it a substantial raise.

Incidentally, people still ask Wayne how much he was *really* making in junior "A". "You know," (nudge, nudge) they say, "how much extra under the table?" It makes him laugh because he can remember only once when there was something extra. When he was invited to try out for Team Canada's entry in the World Junior Tournament he didn't have a topcoat. Angelo Bumbacco bought him one out of his own pocket. "But you're right about that $25-a-week being a fib," he says, straight-faced. "I wasn't making any $25 a week. It was $24.01. They deducted 99 cents tax."

Anyway, Wayne wrote it all down, he and Nelson signed it, and Gus and I witnessed it. We landed in Edmonton for the press conference, then flew to Indianapolis where we said goodbye to our son.

The press conference had been wild – all those reporters when we got off the plane (because, naturally, there'd been a leak) and even more at the hotel. Holy suffering, there were a lot of them. But flying home to Brantford I wasn't thinking about that. I was thinking of a talk we had had, Wayne and his mother and I, when we had been back in the hotel in Vancouver.

We'd put two conditions on any agreement Wayne might sign: first, that he would live with a family and second that he would go to school until he had completed his Grade Twelve. That meant there would be pressures other than hockey. He'd also have to concentrate on his schooling. It was going to be a heavy load. I wanted to make sure Wayne knew just how heavy, that he wasn't just caught up in the glamour of the whole thing.

"Wayne," I said, "do you know what you're doing? Do you really *know*?"

"Yes," he said.

"You want to be really sure," I told him, "because all the money in the world isn't worth it if you don't know. Are you ready to accept the fact that your life will no longer be your own? I don't want to hear from you in a couple of years that you've got no privacy, or that you can't do this or can't do that. As soon as you sign that contract you have to understand that your life is no longer your own. Because that's the way it'll be, I guarantee it. You're going to miss out on a lot of things people your age do."

"I know that," he said.

I gave it one last shot. "You're *sure*? You're awfully sure? Because if this is what you want, what you really want, then it's fine with us. Otherwise, let's walk away and forget the whole thing."

"I understand," he said. "I know what it's going to be like."

He thought he did. We all thought we did. But we didn't. We didn't have any idea . . . .

Chapter 4

GRANDMA WAS A HECK OF A GOALIE

"It's nice to go somewhere where you're getting spoiled by somebody who's spoiling you because you're their grandson and they love you, and not because you're Wayne Gretzky."

– Wayne Gretzky, 1983.

My mother's shins should be in the Hockey Hall of Fame. They were the first goalposts Wayne ever hit.

He was two years old at the time, using one of those tiny souvenir hockey sticks and a sponge ball for a puck. We'd be at the farm on a Saturday night watching *Hockey Night in Canada* and here would come Wayne, sliding along the pine floor like he was skating, heading for Grandma the goalie sitting there in the big lazyboy chair with a stick the same size as his. He'd whack away at that ball and when it bounced off Grandma or the chair he'd just charge in and keep swinging. He didn't know the rules or the object of the game, but even then he seemed to know about rebounds.

The farm, his grandparents, and *Hockey Night in Canada*. From the very beginning Wayne was wrapped up in all of them, and if there was a better way of growing up I don't know what it would be.

My father, Tony, bought the place in the thirties with money he borrowed under the War Veterans Act: twenty-five acres with the Nith River running through it for $1,500. His roots were in farming.

He was a White Russian, born and raised in a small village in the province of Russia, who'd emigrated with the rest of his family a few years prior to the First World War. When they reached the U.S. they split up, three brothers and a sister stayed in the U.S., three brothers and his mother settling in Argentina. My father lived in Chicago until the war broke out. He wanted to join up, and when he heard that the Canadian army was the best if you were thinking of going overseas he crossed the border, signed on, and served through the war in the European theatre. When he came back, he simply stayed in Canada and eventually bought the farm.

My whole family was born there: Sophie, Eddie, Jennie, Albert, Ellen and me. It was a working farm in those days. We grew cucumbers, which were a big crop at one time, and potatoes and other vegetables which my father would take into town to sell. The farm is in Canning, just outside the town of Paris, about twelve miles from Brantford. Actually it was going to be part of a town site. It was surveyed, the lots were laid out and everybody waited for the railroad to build a depot and put the town on the map. But the railroad decided to stop in Paris instead and Canning remained what it is today, a nice, sleepy little place with about twenty houses surrounded by hills with the river running through it. For us, it was the luckiest break we could get. It gave us all a special place, first to grow up in, then to bring up our own kids. And for Wayne, it's been a lifesaver.

Ask him about it now and his face takes on a different, softer look. You can see him remembering the good times. And when he needs to get away, when all the publicity and the hockey and the demands on his time pile up and he needs a place to be himself, he comes home to Brantford and heads for the farm.

"Sometimes," he says, "I even go there and go for a walk by the river when nobody knows. I'm not a great fisherman, but I like to fish there. I know I'm not going to catch anything, but I can stand there for ninety minutes with absolutely no one around. And I need that. I need it badly."

My father died in 1973. Mother stayed on the farm looking after my sister Ellen, who was born a victim of Down's Syndrome (which people used to know as Mongolian Idiocy). They could move into town, but their life is there. Mother could never sell the farm and if she did it would have to be to Wayne. He couldn't stand to see it leave the family. It's his escape hatch, his refuge from the demands that go with being a hockey star. "When I go out to that farm," he says, "I know I'm going to be happy to see my grandmother and she's going to be happy to see me. And I can be Wayne again."

There was always a special kind of closeness between Wayne and his grandparents. After my father died Wayne was even closer to his Grandma – my mother, Mary. Probably it was because the farm was a second home. We were living in an apartment in Brantford when Wayne was born and bought the house we're in now when Wayne was seven months old, but even then we practically lived on the farm. We'd drive out after supper and spend just about every weekend there. I love to fish and the Nith is full them. I'd fish all day and Phyllis would spend all day in the farmhouse. (Sometimes when I got back she'd barely be speaking to me, but fishermen will understand . . . .) It worked out, though, because until Phyllis arrived Mom couldn't speak English very well, only Polish and Ukrainian. Phyllis couldn't speak either of those, so Mom had to work on her English.

But Mom never forgot her Polish background. Like my father, she came from farming people, village people who had little they didn't grow themselves. You became self-sufficient early in those days, and the lessons you learned stayed with you. The beliefs and the folklore of the Old

Country are in her blood, and if you don't believe in superstitions, think about this: my mother was the only member of the family who knew for certain that Wayne was going to be a big success. She didn't know it would be in hockey, but from the time he was very small she knew he was going to make a lot of money. How? Hairy arms.

When he was a little guy he used to be very, very hairy on his arms and on his back around his spine and neck. It was *long* hair. "You know what that means?" she'd ask us. "When you're young and have a lot of hair on your arms and back that means you're going to be an awfully rich person." Wayne loved it. He'd get up in the morning and check to see if he had any more hair. If he thought he did he'd run to show his Grandma and she'd smile and tell him all over again: "Hairy means money. You're going to be rich."

She was sure of that, but she was also practical. When Wayne was five years old he told her that some day he was going to have a car. From that day on she started putting a little of her pension money aside. In fact, she buried it. And by the time Wayne was sixteen, she was ready.

"I'm going to buy you a car," she told him. "I've got the money buried."

Wayne told her thank you, but he just couldn't let her do that.

"Well," she confided, "I buy you the car, but I know you pay me back."

A year later when Wayne turned pro he bought a car of his own, a new Pontiac Trans-Am he got in Indianapolis, and drove it to the farm. "Look, Grandma," he said. "How do you like my car?" She looked at the car. She looked at Wayne. She looked back at the car. "Now what am I going to do with the $4,000?" she asked.

It was the first and last time she ever buried money. From then on, she dealt strictly with banks.

People have wondered why the boys started in hockey so early. You can just see them thinking: "Boy, did he push those kids! That's a hockey father for you!" Actually, it was the most natural thing in the world. I'd played minor hockey in Paris and Junior "B" for five years in Woodstock, Ont., plus some intermediate later. We had the Nith River frozen over right outside the farmhouse door – and inside that door on a Saturday, *Hockey Night in Canada*.

My mother is a sports enthusiast and an avid fan of the Toronto Maple Leafs. In those days her No. 1 player was Frank Mahovlich. Now Wayne grew up pulling for Gordie Howe and it made for interesting Saturday nights when the Leafs played the Detroit Red Wings. Years later when Wayne realized a lifetime dream and played with Gordie for the WHA All-Stars in a best-of-three series against the Soviet Union, he presented his Grandma with a beautifully framed picture of him and Gordie side by side on the ice in their Team Canada uniforms. He signed it:

Hi Grandma: Sorry it's not Frank, but Gordie will have to do.
   Wayne

Now, of course, Wayne is No. 1 in her affections and the number of pictures she has of him has become one of our family jokes. We store a lot of ours at the farm because the trophy room in the basement at home in Brantford is getting jammed. Ellen and her mother don't want them stored; they want them on the walls. The farmhouse is covered with pictures of Wayne, so many that sometimes when company's coming I'll go out and take some down. But next time I come out, they're back up on the walls. Eat your heart out, Frank Mahovlich.

Anyway, we'd all gather round that TV set in those early days and Wayne would be right there with us, waving that little stick, imitating the players and firing shots at Grandma. He liked it so much he actually burst out crying one night. The game had ended while his back was turned and when he looked at the set he thought someone had changed the channel. Howl? You bet.

That winter his mother got him his first pair of skates. I cut a hockey stick down to size. Phyllis bundled him up in the usual winter outdoor clothing – leggings, snow pants, jacket, toque, scarf wrapped around his face – and he stood there by the door, almost bouncing he was so impatient. But I had something important to do first. I had to load my movie camera. I'm a photography buff. If my son was going to take his first step or his first fall on skates, I wanted it on film.

By the time we got to the river he was about ready to burst. It was a big day for him: first skate and first chilblains when his feet began to warm up back in the farmhouse. But he didn't notice that for long. He was busy coaxing Grandma to sit down in the big chair and play goalie. Skating was fun, but hockey was hockey. Maybe he figured he didn't have much time left to learn the game. After all, in two months – January 26, 1964 – he'd be three years old.

The farm wasn't just a hockey place. It was the kind of growing-up place city kids might dream of.

There was the skating and the hockey in winter, the raft, the fishing and swimming in summer. When he was little, Wayne never let the seasons bother him. It might be ninety degrees outside, but there he'd be in his hockey gear, batting away at that rubber ball. After supper we'd play baseball – me catching, Wayne pitching.

There wasn't always as much time to spend there as he might have liked. The way he plunged into sports from the time he was old enough to go to school, there was hardly a minute for anything else. In public school he played baseball, soccer and basketball and ran track and cross country. He also played for city teams in hockey, lacrosse and baseball, ran track, played golf and did weight training three times a week. He loved the farm, he loved sports, and he found a way to mix the two. Part of his work and play on the farm became training for his sports.

When he was a little guy feeding the chickens, he'd high

jump the wire fence getting in and out. Later he dug a high jump pit. We put some nails in a couple of posts and he went out in the woods to cut a bar. Dug a long jump pit, too. So when he missed track practice because he was involved in another sport somewhere else, he had his own course laid out and would do his training on his own. If there was a scrub ball game after school he'd play, come home to eat, then go back out and train.

There were plenty of weekends when he'd have two sports going at one time. One Sunday he played lacrosse in Chatham, Ontario, and as soon as it was over we jumped in the car and headed for Hamilton where he was scheduled to pitch in a baseball tournament. He got there in time, found himself in a pitcher's duel, struck out nineteen, won the game, and we drove home.

Later, as the other kids were born and things got more hectic, he had to make a choice in the summer, baseball or lacrosse. There just wasn't time to get everything in. Actually, that meant two sports because he could fit in the track on his own. But it meant saying goodbye to lacrosse and that was a shame. He was good at it and he really liked it. But if you ask him about lacrosse today he'll start to laugh and tell you not about the goals, but about the window at the farm.

Wayne had been fooling around with a lacrosse stick, bouncing a ball, trying fancy stick-work, that kind of thing, when the ball got away and went crashing through the farmhouse window.

His grandfather wasn't all that upset. After all, boys will be boys. He made a special trip into Paris to get the replacement glass, and while Wayne and I went fishing he set about replacing the window. My father did a very painstaking job on things like that. Everything had to be just so: the glass had to fit perfectly, the lines of putty had to be perfectly straight. He had done a great job. He was standing back admiring it when Wayne and I got back.

Now, my father made his own wine in the basement.

When the family was picking cucumbers or corn he always made it his job to get the baskets or sacks. He'd get them one at a time because they were in the basement, and that was where he kept the wine. After a hot day, the trip for the glass and the work installing the window, a little nip seemed in order. He threw back the outside door to the basement, disappeared inside – and came back up just in time to watch the lacrosse ball sail through the same window again.

For a second we all stood perfectly still. I don't know who was shocked most, but Wayne knew right away what he had to do. He started to run.

My father let out a roar, picked up a stick and took after him. Wayne is running and laughing and his Grandpa is roaring and we're all standing there not knowing who to pull for. Why was Wayne laughing? Simple. Looking back he could see past his Grandpa. And behind Grandpa, coming on strong, was Grandma. She had a stick of her own. And she was chasing Grandpa.

I guess our back yard is a little bit famous. Just about every book or story on Wayne's life gets around to it: the rink I made in the yard behind the little house on Varadi Ave. in Brantford where Wayne learned to skate and Walter Gretzky built a hockey star. Well, it's partially true. I did put the rink in when Wayne was four years old. But he didn't learn to skate there, he learned on the Nith out at the farm and at public skating on weekends. And I didn't put it in to turn my son into a hockey star. I had a better reason. I did it because my feet were too damned cold.

You see, once we got him on skates the tough part was getting him off the ice. He loved it. He'd bug us to go to the farm or to take him to the park every night so he could skate. He couldn't get enough of it. Well, there was a park with an outdoor rink not far from the house, so when he was three I started taking him there. It was closer to home. It meant when he finished I could get him home faster.

It didn't work. Wayne loved it, but I darn near died. I'd

54

take him to the park and sit in the car waiting for him to finish. The other kids would skate, pack up and go home. Wayne would still be out there. Pretty soon everybody was gone – everybody but Wayne on the ice and this frozen lump in the car that was me. One night as I was thawing out in the kitchen I gave Phyllis the word.

"That's it," I said. "I'm all through freezing my tail off. I knew he wanted to skate at the park. I didn't know he wanted to *live* there. Next winter we flood the back yard and he can stay out there as long as he wants." See? It wasn't ambition, it was survival. Not Wayne's, mine.

I flooded the yard the first time in the winter of 1965 and I've done it every year since. (It hasn't always been easy. One day the sprinkler on the hose broke when I was flooding. Someone had to go to Canadian Tire and ask the salesman where he kept his lawn sprinklers. It was in December. Do you have any idea how crazy you look, trying to buy a lawn sprinkler in December? There was only one way out: I sent Phyllis. She got it all right, but she came home sputtering. "The next time you want a sprinkler you can buy it yourself," she said. "That man thought I was crazy!") It became a neighbourhood playground. We had a light strung from the clothesline, a neighbour turned on the one over his garage, and the kids would stay out there until we had to drag them in. Wayne would even bribe the boy next door with a nickel to stay longer so he wouldn't have to come in.

The second winter we had the rink I tried to get Wayne registered in minor hockey. He was five years old, he was living on the ice and he was bugging me.

"Dad," he'd ask, over and over again, "when can I play on a real *team?*"

"When I get you registered," I'd answer. Well, Wayne didn't know about registration, or how you had to sign up weeks in advance. All he knew was that hockey meant teams and he wasn't on one. So, I tried. Doing it today is easy, because there are leagues for kids five years old. But in those days minor hockey in Brantford started with ten-year-olds. There was no place for Wayne to play. Boy, was he disappointed.

I told him not to worry about it, that practicing fundamentals was the important thing anyway. "You look like you might have a size problem as far as hockey goes," I told him, "but that can be overcome with puck control and concentration."

"All right," he said. That winter he lived on the backyard rink, carrying the puck in and out of pylons made from Javex bleach containers, or any other plastic jug we could find, working on his skating and puck control. Sometimes you had to argue to get him to come in at night.

The following year, a few weeks before the 1967-68 season, we saw a notice in the paper: open tryouts for the major novice team. Just come to the civic centre. Wayne could hardly wait.

When we got there the ice was crammed with kids up to ten years old. Wayne was so tiny he looked lost. I didn't know any of the coaches. I hardly knew anyone in Brantford at that time. So I just turned him loose on the ice with the mob. And a man named Dick Martin, who became Wayne's first coach, ignored his size and his age, looked only at his skating, and signed him up. He was so small that when he scored his one goal of the season (there's a trivia question for you: lowest number of goals in a season by Wayne Gretzky - 1) and his teammates swarmed around to congratulate him, you couldn't see any sign of Wayne.

I remember, though, that in the dressing room after the game, Bob Phillips, the assistant coach, came over to congratulate him. "That's only the first one, Wayne," he said. "There'll be lots more after this." He had no idea how right he'd turn out to be.

That's where the trip started, really, the trip that would take Wayne all over North America and then all over the world: on a family farm outside of town and a little back-yard rink, surrounded by people who cared. And before you knew it there was Kim and Keith and Glen and Brent and we were going in fifty-seven different directions at once. It's been great and it's been hectic and it's not likely to slow down for a long time yet, and there aren't many minutes of it we'd trade.

You know, I've still got that piece of film we took that day on the Nith. There's this little bundle of clothing stumbling, picking himself up, taking a couple of strides and falling again. It's a long way from the farm, 99. A long, long way.

Chapter 5

WE'RE NOT RAISING STARS, WE'RE RAISING KIDS

"I never waxed or washed the kitchen floor in the winter. The skate blades chipped the wax away and the snow did the washing."

– Phyllis Gretzky, 1983.

When we first moved into the house on Varadi Ave. it had three bedrooms, living room, kitchen and bathroom and covered nine hundred square feet. Plenty of room for husband, wife and seven-month-old baby. Then, overnight it seemed, there were seven of us and the house wasn't big anymore.

One spring there was a sudden thaw. By this time we had box after box of scrapbooks, crests, medals, cups and trophies the kids were winning, and no place to put them but on the floor. When the snow melted it came through the window. We were looking at four inches of water and the boxes sitting in it. Well, we pumped the water out all right, but everything in the boxes had to be dried in a hurry. We went through the neighbourhood borrowing hair dryers. Burned out four of them, but managed to save most of the stuff.

Obviously, it was time to add a rec room. We did that in 1978 and in the fall of 1982 we extended the kitchen and dining room and added three bedrooms and bath upstairs, which gave us some breathing space. But when the kids were small the house was bursting. With all of them going in different directions winter and summer and the neighbourhood kids playing hockey or baseball in the back yard it wasn't exactly the kind of place you'd recommend for a restful weekend.

It was more than your life was worth to step through the front door without watching where you put your feet. You'd trip over bats, equipment bags, skates, shoes, hockey sticks – if they could carry it, they could drop it. And if they didn't have enough of their own to block the hall completely, their friends provided the rest.

You couldn't watch all of them all the time. There was always some project going on in the basement that required hammering. Once, when Wayne was thirteen, he and his friend, John Mowat, worked all day down there building a hockey net. They used two-by-fours for braces and potato sacks for the net, tacked on with what looked like the biggest nails they could find. When they finished they had to take the whole thing apart. They'd built it too big to go through the basement door.

Kids and sports. Life has sort of centred around the two for as long as I can remember. Maybe it's because Phyllis and I both come from large families and sport was always a part of both of them. She has four brothers and three sisters and in my family there are the six of us split three-three. Come to think of it maybe large families just come naturally to us. Wayne's girlfriend, Vickie Moss, is one of thirteen children. We could rent ourselves out as a mob scene.

Not that Phyllis Hockin liked hockey. When I started dating her, three years before we were married, she was fifteen and couldn't stand it. But with four brothers involved you know what was on TV Saturday nights. They'd want to watch the Leafs; she and her sister would want to watch some story. Those weren't two-TV-set days and the boys always won. Then she met me and everything changed. I was playing junior "B", and what better place to take a girl than a hockey game? "Big dates," she said. "Wally would pick me up and take me to his game so I could sit in the stands and watch. A real romantic."

The thing was, we were both used to noise and confusion and having all kinds of people around. And the way things worked out, it's a good thing. We never seemed to run short . . . .

And before we go any further, maybe you'd better meet the rest of the kids. Let's take them in chronological order. Phyllis likes to do it that way so she can tell people where I was while she was giving birth.

"With Kim, he dropped me off at the hospital. She was born an hour later and that night Walter was off to St. Catharines to do a job for Bell," she says. "With Keith and Glen he was at work. And when Brent was born, Wally was at a hockey tournament with Wayne. I remember saying, 'Walter, I'm going to the hospital,' and Walt saying, 'Nah! Come to the tournament! You're not due for six weeks yet!' 'Forget it,' I said. 'I'm going to the hospital.' So we compromised. They drove me to my father's place and *he* drove me to the hospital while they went to the tournament."

It must have been funny in there, all right. The nurses took one look at Phyllis's father and said, "Don't worry, Mr. Gretzky, your wife will be fine." By the time we got back Brent was born – February 20, 1972 – although for a while we didn't know it.

I'd been convinced when we left that Phyllis was rushing things. But when we got home about midnight she wasn't there. Her brother, Bob Hockin, Wayne's coach at the time, phoned his wife, Pat, to see what was going on. "Pat says Phyllis is in the hospital," he reported. "The baby's born, but I'm not sure what she said it was." So we packed Wayne, Kim, Keith and Glen off to Bob's house and I went to the hospital to see their new brother. Or possibly their new sister.

Phyllis says she heard me coming down the hall. She told me about Brent. I told her we'd won the tournament. Boy, was she excited.

Actually, Phyllis wasn't surprised that we'd gone with the baby that close. She'd had a hint just before Glen was born three years earlier. It was August, the baby was due soon, and we were all headed out for a lacrosse game. "You know," she said, "I shouldn't be going to any lacrosse game. What if we're on the way to the game and I need a lift to the hospital?" Wayne was eight years old. He looked up at his mother, grinned, and said, "Forget it. We're going to the lacrosse game."

From the time she was five years old Kim has lived with the benefits and burdens of being Wayne Gretzky's sister. At seven, people were already talking about what her nine-year-old brother could do with a hockey stick. He was travelling all over the province, playing in arenas in front of people who'd come out mainly to see the little kid from Brantford. She wasn't very old, but she was old enough to realize that a lot of people thought her big brother was something special.

At ten she was literally surrounded with brothers. Wayne was twelve, Keith was six, Glen was four, Brent was one. There was fuss over Wayne because of his hockey. There was fuss over Keith because by that time he was well into his skating and getting started in hockey. There was fuss over Glen because he was born with club feet, which meant doctors and hospitals and corrective surgery and the worry over it. And as for Brent – what year-old baby *doesn't* get fussed over?

And there was Kim, except for her mother and visitors, the only female in the house.

It got to be a problem. We knew something was wrong

but we weren't sure what. No matter what you'd do for her – buy her something, take her somewhere – she just wasn't a very happy girl. It boiled down to Kim being left out. When Keith was old enough to start hockey Wayne was still at home. That meant twice as many practices, twice as many games, and twice as many times that Phyllis, myself or both of us had to be taking the boys somewhere for sports. We dragged her to lacrosse or baseball all summer and hockey all winter. "Do I have to?" she'd ask. "Do I have to go to another one?"

From her point of view it must have looked as though it was never going to end. By the time Wayne left for Toronto at fourteen Keith was eight and Glen was six. Now it wasn't Wayne and Keith, it was Keith and Glen. And for a while there, until Kim went to school in Toronto, it was Keith and Glen and Brent.

Kim plays it down now. She's been to school in Toronto, and university in California. She's an adult secure in her own life and her own abilities. But it must have hurt back then. We could see it; we just couldn't figure a way around it. We tried everything. She figure-skated from the time she was seven until she was fifteen. We enrolled her in dancing classes. We even had her playing lacrosse one year, but when she put the ball in her own net we figured that wasn't the answer either.

We wanted to find something she liked that she could do well, something that would give her a sense of her own identity where she'd be just as important to herself as Wayne was to himself. Because she would *always* be just as important to us, but it was hard to make her understand that. She needed to get some recognition for being Kim.

So I said, "Let's try track." Kim was seven at the time, I think. She just shuddered. She wanted no part of it. But she was athletically inclined and she was a big girl for her age, so I talked her into going to the track club for a look, just to watch Wayne and the rest practice. And there we got a real break. Phil Hatcher, the track coach, was a nice, easy-going man, a schoolteacher. After a while he just came over very casually and said, "Okay, Kim, let's go for a run around the track."

They jogged around, just taking it easy. The next practice we went back and Phil came over again. It went on for a few times, and you could see Kim starting to get interested. Phil put her in a few Mite Division meets. In her first year she didn't do all that well, but Phil, being a really good coach, got it through to her that every time she went out she had to try to beat *her own* personal best, to compete against herself.

It was like someone had turned on a light. The longer she stayed with the track program the more self-confidence she got. It spilled over into her figure-skating and into her everyday life. She'd found something that was hers. She had a feeling of being part of something, a sense of belonging.

The second year she started to win, and before long they all knew who Kim Gretzky was around the track clubs, and she wasn't just Wayne Gretzky's sister. She was just a natural at the 100, 200 and 400 metre sprints. It was the nicest thing in the world to see her do the 400. She'd come around that far bend and she'd just be *leaning* into it, making it look like everyone else was standing still. She became an outstanding sprinter – and a different person.

At the Royal Canadian Legion age-class championships in Edmonton in 1976 she took bantam division silver medals in the 400 and the 4x100 relay, and was a member of the 4x400 metre relay team that won the gold. The following year at the same meet in Oromocto, N.B. she won the bantam 100 and 200, placed second in the 400 and was a member of the winning 4x400 relay team. I really believe if she'd kept progressing as she was then she'd have a chance eventually to make the Canadian Olympic Games team. I'd hoped that she could get an athletic scholarship. But she never got the chance. One slip, and it was all over.

She was fifteen years old when it happened. It was January, there'd been a sleet storm, and the ground was slick. Kim was on her way to visit a girlfriend up the street. Suddenly her feet slipped out from under her. When she got up, she couldn't put any weight on her left foot.

It wasn't a break. I wish it had been. Breaks repair.

When we took Kim to the hospital they strapped the foot and put her on crutches. She could walk, but it hurt. They immobilized the leg for a couple of months, cut away the cast, and it still hurt. Finally we took her to a specialist in Toronto and got the word. She'd torn all the tendons away from her ankle, absolutely demolished it.

The specialist who operated said the operation was more successful than he'd ever dared hope, but she'd have to be careful the rest of her life. If she ever twisted the ankle again she'd be right back where she started.

So there went track and there went basketball, which she'd been pretty good at, too. Suddenly, because she'd trained for so many years and couldn't anymore, she was into weight problems and diets instead of track meets and gyms. But it had been worth it. Track had helped Kim realize her own worth, which the rest of us had known all along.

She's in university now, taking business courses aimed at helping her realize a different dream – to own and operate her own day care centre. As for being Wayne Gretzky's sister, she's proud of it. Which is just as well, because no matter where she goes it keeps coming up.

In 1981, she was on the operating table about to have her appendix removed. The doctor looked down and said, "Don't I know you?" And as she was slipping under the anaesthetic she heard the nurse say, "Don't you recognize her? That's Wayne Gretzky's sister!"

She is that, but she's Kim Gretzky first. It just took a little while for her to prove it – not to us, but to herself.

Keith is probably doomed to be compared with Wayne for as long as he plays hockey. That can mean a lot of pressure. If he gets to the NHL he'll be the Second Gretzky. If he doesn't, he'll be the Gretzky Who Didn't Make It. The saving grace is that he knows it and knows how to live with it. He should – people have been making comparisons since he was six.

They're always asking me to make comparisons. Is Keith like Wayne? Is he going to be a superstar? The honest answer is "Who knows?" I've always thought he had the ability to play in the NHL, but there are all kinds of kids – kids who've set records as juniors – who didn't cut it as pros.

I'll say this: he's a smoother skater than Wayne, although Wayne isn't nearly as slow as people claim. And Keith handles the puck well. The things that set Wayne apart – the instincts, the ability to see so much of the ice, to see what's going to happen before it does – are things you can't assume are there. You have to wait and see.

Keith came up the same way Wayne did, although without as much splash. He was on skates at three and started with one small edge over Wayne. He was able to play with kids only one year older when he started, not four the way Wayne had to, because by 1972, when he was five, there were leagues for six-year-olds. They let him in early because he was born in February and was only a few months too young to be eligible. Wayne played against ten-year-olds when he was six, not because we wanted it that way, but because it was the youngest age group in organized hockey in the area.

Coming through minor hockey Keith got his share of hat tricks and all-star recognition. In 1982-83, he played his first year of junior "A" hockey at fifteen for the Brantford Alexanders. He wound up with 5 goals and 9 assists in 37 games and didn't play all that much. There was a lot of guessing as to where he'd be playing the following year, now that he was going into the junior "A" draft. The way it works, a boy can play junior "A" after he's finished his year of major bantam, but only in his home town. Then, at sixteen, when he'd normally be starting junior "A", he becomes draftable. Because Keith hadn't had a really big year, there was a chance he'd still be available when it came Brantford's turn to pick.

In a funny way, Wayne had a stake in this, too. He was part owner of the Belleville Bulls junior "A" team at that time. If Keith was still available when Belleville's turn came, Wayne would have picked him. But Windsor picked him in the first round, the fourth player selected. It was just as well Wayne didn't get him. A Gretzky playing for Wayne Gretzky's team? There'd be problems enough without saddling him with that.

Keith is built a little bit differently than Wayne. He's stockier. I don't think he'll be what you could call tall, but he'll be heavier and more solid. There's another difference, too. Keith has a temper. If you cross-check Wayne or knock him down he just gives you that funny little smile, then goes and tries to score the goal that will beat you. Knock Keith down and you're going to get it right back in spades.

It's always been that way. There was a playoff game when he was eleven years old playing for Magnetic Metal minor peewees. Keith was their big scorer. Stop him and you pretty much stopped the team. The whole family was there to see him play. With a minute to play and trailing 2-1, Magnetics pulled their goalie for one last shot. Naturally, Keith was on the ice. Suddenly there's this big pile-up, and everyone's sitting on Keith.

I can still see Keith, flat on his back and flailing away at everybody within reach. The referee gave him a penalty for roughing. Well, this was too much for Brent, who was seven at the time. The team was a goal down and his brother the scoring star had taken a penalty. He completely forgot himself.

"Well," he said, leaning over the boards in disgust, "it looks like we lost this damn hockey game!"

Everyone in the rink heard it. Phyllis pretended Brent didn't even belong to her. He was just this total stranger who happened to be standing beside her. Brent heard about it, of course. But I had trouble doing it with a straight face.

Keith has also been known to open his mouth and say the first thing that pops out. In fact, when he was five or six he gave me a family nickname that's stuck to this day.

We were watching television and a commercial came on for a liquid cleaner supposed to be especially good for walls. "Get Big Wally!" the announcer said. Keith picked it up like a shot. "Big Wally!" he yelled, pointing at me. "Big Wally!"

From that day on the kids called me Dad, Big Wally or just plain Wally. I don't mind. It's not intended to be disrespectful. And after all, I got the best of the deal. Once they gave me a nickname they figured they had to have one for their mother. For a while there, she was Silly Philly.

Keith played in Windsor this past season, living with Eddie Mio's parents. At first I wondered whether the hockey would work out. He just didn't seem happy. Then he settled in, the points started coming, and because he was with a re-building team he got his fair share of ice time. He finished with 15 goals and 38 assists, which isn't bad considering the slow start and a sixteen-year-old in his first season away from home.

Will Keith make it to the NHL some day? If he keeps working and progressing I think he's got a chance. Will he be another Wayne? Comparisons are silly. Wayne is Wayne, Kim is Kim and Keith is Keith. As for the advantages in being Wayne's brother, well, they barely see each other during the season so there's not much time for brother-to-brother tips. I do remember one he gave him, though.

We managed to be in Windsor for one of Keith's pre-season games. Afterwards we all went out for dinner and pretty soon there's Keith and Wayne huddled over a napkin on which Wayne is drawing diagrams. I heard Wayne give him one of those inside-the-NHL tips, those little bits of insight that can make all the difference.

"Don't crouch so low when you take face-offs," he said.

"They'll bring up a stick and you'll be spitting out teeth." So much for skill and science.

Keith will take all the help he can get, but he'll be his own person and go his own way. As to the pressures of being a Gretzky, I think he knows what might lie ahead. A reporter asked him about the NHL when he was about fourteen. "There's just two things I don't want," he said then. "I don't want to play in Edmonton – and I don't want to wear 99."

In the winter when the back yard is frozen over, late at night when the rest of the kids have gone home, Glen will be out there, skating in and out of those pylons, working to make himself that much better, struggling to overcome a handicap the others have never had to face. "Of all of them," Wayne said once in an interview in Vancouver, "I hope most that Glennie makes it to the NHL. Because Glennie wants it most."

Glen was born with two club feet. He had surgery on the right foot when he was eight months old and on the left when he was five. There's still a pin in the left one. You'd have to know in advance or look very carefully today to detect any difference in the way he walks. The surgery was successful – but for hockey it left a handicap that may be insurmountable for a boy who dreams of playing pro.

To get a good push-off in skating you have to move your skate in such a way that it's opposite to the body at a ninety-degree angle. It's a matter of turning your ankle to generate the push. But Glen hasn't got the flexibility in that right ankle. He's got to push *out*, and that cuts into his speed and manoeuvrability. He's also got ankles like sparrows', with hardly any strength in them at all. I think it's a characteristic of people who have club feet. When we put on his skates we'd put sponge under the tongue to fill them out enough so the sides didn't overlap when they were laced.

Glen has good hockey skills, very much so. He didn't start skating until he was six, but after two years of house league hockey he's played at the rep level ever since. He's not a big scorer, but he makes the club on his own ability, partially because he just won't quit. His determination is just incredible . . . try, try, try.

Glen knows it will be harder for him. He never talks about it, never says a word. His feet hurt him sometimes. At the start of a season being in skates for an hour is really tough on him. The soles and tops of the feet really hurt. But it doesn't keep him off the ice. If trying will do it, if heart means anything, Glen will get it done.

Not that he's totally wrapped up in hockey. None of the boys are. There's baseball and golf – and for Glen some day there might be an acting career if he wants it. He'd have a better shot, I think, than his eldest brother.

Last year, Wayne did a guest appearance on *The Young and the Restless*, one of the big American soap operas. He played a Mafia type visiting Hollywood from Edmonton. ("This is Wayne, from our Edmonton operation," this other hood says, introducing him to a girl.) The kindest review Wayne got suggested it was a good thing he hadn't given up his hockey career for acting. Well, Glen and Brent are soap opera buffs. They watched the telecast with Wayne and when it was over Glen went over to Wayne, punched him on the shoulder and said:

"Not bad for a beginner, son."

A couple of days later he went upstairs, borrowed one of the jackets Keith had left behind, put on a pair of dark glasses and came down the stairs hissing, "This is Wayne, from our Edmonton operation." Looked just like the guy in the program and did it better. Maybe we've got an actor in the family. So he doesn't win the Hart Trophy. What's wrong with an Emmy or an Oscar?

Brent was eleven years old when he attended the Progressive Conservative Party's leadership convention in Ottawa in 1983. He wasn't running. He had a much better reason than that. He was the only member of the family who'd never ridden in a private jet and this was his big chance.

Peter Pocklington, the Edmonton Oilers' owner, was gunning for party leadership. Having Wayne there with him with all the TV cameras around wouldn't hurt, even though Wayne was only there to show his support of the man and made it clear his appearance had nothing to do with politics. When Peter sent his private jet to pick Wayne up, Brent was hot to go.

Well, why not? The other kids had been on private planes. Brent hadn't. Mr. Pocklington said it was fine with him. Brent made the trip, sat on a bodyguard's shoulders staring around the convention hall and had the time of his life. And if nothing else it produced perhaps the strangest excuse for absenteeism ever received by his school.

The note Phyllis sent merely said that Brent hadn't been in school that Friday afternoon because he'd gone to Ottawa with Wayne. After the incident at Canadian Tire buying the sprinkler, she's become a little bit cautious. Imagine the reaction she'd have received if she'd written: "Brent couldn't come to school Friday. He was attending the Conservative convention."

Brent just floats along like a bubble, a little blond hustler who never quits. He'll play all day, never want to go to bed at night. Then his eyes will get big and he'll get quiet, and the next thing you know he's on the couch asleep.

He's a good baseball pitcher or catcher, and at hockey he's the one who most reminds me of Wayne at that age. He's a terrific scorer, although nowhere near Wayne as far as numbers are concerned. But he's got the dekes, the anticipation, all the stick-handling skills. Not that numbers mean anything. In 1982-83 Brent scored 41 goals as a defenceman in the major atom division. In Wayne's final year of major atom, when he was ten, he scored 378 goals. But there's a big difference. When Wayne played you might have two or three good kids on a rep team. Today you might have ten or eleven. They shoot better, pass better, and they make the competition that much better. I don't think you'll see a ten-year-old with 378 goals again.

None of that stuff bothers Brent anyway. Nothing does. Not for long. The business of being Wayne's brother is exciting and makes him proud, but it's not going to get him in a flap. One time someone, a reporter I think, asked Brent why he liked it so much when Wayne came home. He got all excited. "Wayne," he said, "takes us to Stan's for ice cream cones."

He's thought about his future, though. We were driving home from a baseball game in Kitchener where Brent had won and struck out seventeen. He hadn't said much for quite a while. Finally, very seriously, he said, "Dad, what am I gonna do when I grow up?"

"What do you mean, Brent?" I asked.

"Well," he said, "I think I'm gonna be pretty good at hockey *and* baseball. How am I gonna choose which one I'm gonna play?"

I tried to keep a straight face. "When the time comes, Brent," I said, "I think you'll know."

"Oh," he said, and we stopped at Stan's for ice cream cones.

So there they are, the Gretzky kids, each one different, each one special as every kid is to every parent. You know, a lot of fathers never get to live one lifetime with their kids and enjoy it. It's their own fault. They don't know how. But I tell you, I've lived a thousand lifetimes with Wayne and Kim and Keith and Glen and Brent. I've been on both sides of the fence. I know what it's like every whichway imaginable, the super-super and the not-quite-average. I just feel sorry for the fathers who've never been that lucky - the ones who've never given themselves the gift of enjoying their kids.

We're no different from any other family with two or three kids wrapped up in sport, except that our kids may be watched a little more because of what Wayne's done. But if their lives were changed by the publicity, the rules certainly weren't.

From Wayne through Brent we've made it clear that once

you started something, you finished it. School project, sport, hobby, it made no difference. You finished what you started, like it or not, because if you do it early in life you'll do it later, too. We wanted them to learn early: in everything you do, you follow through.

There was and is a curfew. Unless it was a special occasion – a hockey playoff, for instance, where the game ended late or there was a long drive home afterward – we made sure the kids were in bed by nine until they were fourteen or fifteen. Otherwise they'd be too tired to do a proper job in school.

Respect for others was and is essential, of course, especially towards adults, but for other kids, too. And you never laugh at anyone about what they are or what they do. Any time we saw one of ours do that, we'd stop it quickly and tell them why: "You're no better or no worse than anyone. Everyone is equal. Some are just more fortunate than others."

We taught them to share. We have a theory in our family: what's mine is yours, what's yours is mine. If one of us has something he or she doesn't need and another member of the family does, you automatically give it to them. They shouldn't even have to ask. And we taught them to be proud – proud of one another, and proud of being part of a family. That one sank in early, and took root. Nobody showed it better than Keith, on the day Glen first tried to skate in a rink.

There were other kids on the ice, of course, and even at eight years old Keith must have sensed there could be a problem. While Glen stumbled and fell and got up and fell and got up again, Keith walked around the ice surface just outside the boards, keeping pace with his little brother. And when two other kids leaning on the boards laughed at Glen, Keith grabbed one of them and yelled:

"Don't you *ever* laugh at my brother again!"

Keith was never shy about stepping in if the other kids had a problem. Once when he was about fourteen, Phyllis drove to Greenbriar school to pick up the kids because it was pouring rain. She packed them in quickly and had them all the way home before she noticed that Keith was among the missing. She recalled seeing a circle of boys in front of the school, but she'd thought Keith was in the car with the others.

"Where's Keith?" she demanded. Glen and Brent couldn't wait to tell her. He was in the middle of that circle. It seems two boys had been picking on Glen, and Keith jumped in to help. When the car came, Glen and Brent walked away and jumped in out of the rain.

"I guess he's still back there fighting, Mom," they said . . . .

Every large family has periods when life seems to be total confusion. For us, with the early fuss over Wayne's hockey and the others getting involved in sport so early, it became a juggling act that never seemed to stop.

When Wayne was playing junior "A" in Sault St. Marie, his road games were usually played on weekend evenings. On weekends, the younger boys' games were mostly during the day. So we'd watch Keith or Brent or Glen in the afternoon, then jump in the car and drive to wherever Wayne was playing that night. Unless, of course, Kim was figure-skating, in which case Phyllis would go in one direction and I'd go in another with the boys.

We developed a system early. Because we knew that eventually we'd have three kids playing and one skating and two parents to do the watching, we'd work it this way: if one boy had a practice and another had a game, we'd send the one practicing with a friend and go to the game. If one had an exhibition game and one had a playoff or a game that might end the season, we'd skip the exhibition. If the play-offs were just starting for the two kids I'd go to one and Phyllis to the other.

That took care of the games and practices. At home, the rink never closed. There were kids coming out of our ears. Phyllis would shovel it off in the afternoons and I'd come home and clean it again at night. As the other kids came along Wayne and Keith got old enough to shovel it themselves. When there wasn't anyone actually on the ice, we'd hear Kim and Wayne arguing over whether it was time for figure-skating or hockey. About the only thing it never was in our back yard was quiet.

Fortunately, Phyllis is sort of unflappable. When kids come to the front door with their skates on, walk through your living room and kitchen and tromp out the back door to skate, then tromp back in to line up at the one bathroom, while dropping a hint or two about being hungry, you sort of have to be. I do remember one time, though, when she got a little bit upset.

The front doorbell rang. She opened the door and there were two little neighbourhood kids, bundled up against the cold, skates clutched in their hands.

"Can we please skate, Mrs. Gretzky?" they asked.

"Sure," Phyllis said.

"Will you put our skates on?"

"Uh, why didn't your parents put them on for you?"

"They're too busy."

I guess Phyllis sort of exploded.

"Oh, sure," she said. "Come right in! Kim and I aren't doing a darned thing!"

But she and Kim put the skates on. It wasn't the kids she was mad at. If their parents had been there, they might have been wearing the skates somewhere a lot less comfortable.

It's always hectic, even with just Glen and Brent at home, because a lot of Keith's junior games are within driving range and a lot of Wayne's games are televised. But there was only one year when it was really bad. That was when Wayne was ten and playing, I was coaching a junior "B" team from Brantford that played out of Waterford, Ont., and Phyllis was at home with Kim, Keith and Glen and expecting Brent.

Once all the boys were playing, we'd let the oldest one go

by himself and we'd go to games or practices involving the younger two. And when it came time for out-of-town tournaments we depended on the billeting system and gave it a twist of our own. We prepared the young kids early. When Wayne would play in Brockville, for instance, we fixed it so whoever was billeting Wayne would also take Keith, even though he wasn't playing. It got him used to it. When Keith started travelling we insisted Glen go, too, and when Glen went, Brent went with him.

When you think about it, it makes a lot of sense. I've seen kids who can't stand to be away from home for a day. We've gone to tournaments where kids had to stay in the motel with their parents, because either the kids were crying and didn't want to stay with a strange family, or their parents wouldn't let them. With us, there was never a problem. In fact, with Brent the situation is reversed. At home after baseball or hockey games, he's always asking if he can stay overnight with a friend.

Mind you, Brent may have set the world record for early billeting. When he was six days old we had a tournament to go to. Obviously, Brent couldn't make the trip. We left him with neighbours and away we went. When you're a hockey family, you learn to be flexible.

Chapter 6

TALES OF
THE WHITE
TORNADO

"Numéro neuf! Numéro neuf! Vas-y! Vas-y!"

- Eight-year-old hockey fan, Quebec City,
  Feb., 1974.

There might never have been a White Tornado story if we hadn't been rushing to get to practice.

Wayne was twelve, just about to start his major pee wee season. He needed new gloves and naturally he'd left it until the last minute. So there we were in the sporting goods store run by our friend, Gerry Dallaway, shopping for gloves with practice due to start in half an hour and the rink twenty minutes away. We were not exactly prepared to browse around.

Wayne told Gerry he needed a pair of gloves. "Got just the thing for you," Gerry told him. He reached away up to a top shelf, rummaged around, and pulled out a pair of gloves – pure white gloves. He had them halfway down when I stopped him.

"Put those right back," I said. "I've got enough trouble now with people razzing Wayne. White gloves I don't need."

Gerry was determined. He knew me and the kind of

equipment I wanted. I always buy the boys the lightest equipment they can possible get and when it comes to gloves they had to be very flexible or they were good for the garbage can and nothing else. A boy should be able to feel the stick through the gloves, because then he can feel the puck on the end of the stick. If Gerry said they were good gloves I knew they were. But white? Wayne Gretzky in white gloves to give people another excuse to pick on him? Not a chance.

"Walter, just look at how flexible these things are," Gerry insisted. "Wayne, try them on. Don't say anything, just try them."

Wayne pulled the gloves on. "Nice, Dad," he said. "Really nice."

"You can have them for what they cost me," Gerry said. "Nobody will buy them because of the colour."

The price was pretty good. About six dollars, I think, and Wayne is wiggling his fingers around in the gloves and saying, "Look at this, Dad. I'll really be able to stickhandle with these!"

By this time we're late for practice. "Wally," Phyllis says, "take them. People are going to talk anyway. They might as well have something to talk about."

I looked at Gerry. "You know what you've just done?" I asked.

"Nah!" he said. "People will get used to them. Don't worry about that."

Six months later, when Wayne needed a police escort to get out of one rink and a police escort to get into another, and the Turkstra Lumber team was pulling in crowds of eleven thousand in Quebec City to see the kid they'd dubbed "Le Grand!" and "The White Tornado" I remembered that remark. "People will get used to them." Sure, they would.

Everywhere the team went we heard it: "Look at the little hotshot with white gloves!" Even Charlie Henry, who was coaching the Ottawa Voyageurs at the time and later became a good friend of ours, thought they were a bit much.

Charlie said they were so white they could be luminous. "He's gonna be great," he said, "but he doesn't have to play in the dark."

It would have been a lot easier to scrap the gloves and get something less noticeable, but Wayne liked them. And why should he get rid of them? They were good gloves. He kept them for a long time. He was learning a lesson he'd need through his career: do what you think is right and never mind what they think up in the stands.

He never forgot those white gloves, though. And neither did Gerry. A few years after we got them we took Keith into the store looking for gloves. Gerry didn't even blink. He just turned and reached up on the shelf.

"Got just the gloves for him, Walter," he said. They were pure white.

Maybe the simplest way to explain how quickly Wayne progressed is to trace his minor hockey career season by season. (Because his birthday is in January his age always changed in mid-season, so the ages mentioned here are at the start of a season.)

In his first year he had had that one goal. In his second, he scored 27, in his third, 104 plus 63 assists in 62 games. In 1970-71, as a nine-year-old he scored 196 in 76 games, plus 120 assists. People were shaking their heads and wondering how anyone could score that many. So the next year he played in 82 games and scored 378 goals.

In 1972-73, as an eleven-year-old competing against kids in major pee wee he scored 105 goals. A few people nodded knowingly: it was a lot of goals, sure, but not compared to the year before. The Gretzky kid was slowing up. But they had trouble explaining the 192 he got the next year. And in 1974-75, playing major bantam as a minor bantam in what turned out to be his final season of minor hockey, he scored 90 goals.

Now, a lot of kids have scored a lot of goals as minors and disappeared as the competition got tougher. So it wasn't as if people were looking at Wayne when he was eleven or twelve and saying, "There's the next Bobby Orr." But you can't rack up totals like that without getting noticed. Things began to happen that on numbers alone were incredible, and the wire services and out-of-town papers started to file stories about the little kid from Brantford.

For instance:

* In 1971, the Brantford *Expositor* ran a story asking the question: "What's the highest-scoring line in hockey?" and answering with "Gretzky, Halyk and Jamula." They were nine years old. Wayne had the league scoring title with 138 points (84 goals and 54 assists in league play only). Chris Halyk finished at 58-46-104 and Ron Jamula at 56-15-71. That's 198 goals, 115 assists for 313 points from one line. (Incidentally, Chris Halyk went through minor hockey, had a good junior career and played a while with Rochester in the American Hockey League, then went to University of Waterloo. Jamula did not play professionally. Two who did were Greg Stefan, now playing goal for the Detroit Red Wings, and Lennie Hachborn, called up last season by the Philadelphia Flyers. But it's the way I've told all the kids from the beginning: pro hockey isn't out there for everyone no matter how good you are as a kid. It's a lesson some boys, and a lot of parents, have a hard time learning.)

* Goal No. 1,000 in a career is a milestone for anyone. Wayne scored his, plus two others, on a slapshot from inside the blue line during Turkstra Lumber's 8-1 win over Waterford. It came on April 10, 1974. He was two months past his thirteenth birthday.

* You've heard of the 50-goal season? When he was eleven Wayne had a 50-goal weekend – 50 goals in 9 games at the Hespeler, Ont. Olympic Tournament.

It just went on and on – six goals here, four goals there, nine goals somewhere else. The more he scored the more the newspapers wanted to know about him. When they found out he was also starring in other sports, the publicity just took off. From their viewpoint he made a heck of a story,

79

this little blond kid. In the summer of 1971, coming off the 196-goal hockey season, Wayne scored 158 goals and added 66 assists in 31 games for Brantford PUC in the inter-city lacrosse league, pitched and played baseball in the house league and for Brantford Shanghai in the inter-county tyke baseball league. Was anyone else playing three sports that well? The media didn't know, but by the way they wrote and broadcast they obviously didn't think so.

For its April, 1972 issue, *Canadian Magazine* sent a writer named Paul Grescoe to our house to do a two-page spread on Wayne titled: "Wayne Gretzky has 300 Bubble Gum Cards and a Future You Wouldn't Believe." On one full page they laid out a bubble gum card on Wayne just as though he was a pro, his picture on the front, his "career" on the back:

> *Scoring is Wayne Gretzky's specialty. He picked up his first goal in league hockey at the age of five and once scored three goals in forty-five seconds. In the style of his hero, Gordie Howe, Wayne is good at quick shifts, dekes and has a terrific shot. He is shy, slight of build and no fighter. Bouncing back from his first major injury, which required caps for three front teeth, this Brantford-born eleven-year-old is a hot prospect for the peewee league next year.*
> *Ht: 4'10" Wt: 79 pounds*
> *Born: Jan. 26, 1961*
> *Brantford, Ont.*
> *First season: 1967-68*

Phyllis didn't like the piece much. It's one of the reasons she still tends to shy away from reporters. There were references to the "child-worn sofa in the Gretzkys' frugally furnished one-storey home" and "the Gretzkys sit down for dinner – meat loaf, canned corn and peas, salad – which Wayne picks at." We still kid her about that one. Actually, she makes a heck of a meat loaf. But the story did carry one quote from Phyllis' brother, Bob, who was coaching the

Nadrofsky Steelers at the time, that could have helped us a lot if people had paid attention.

"All the kids would like to be Wayne," he said. "But parents? There are a lot of parents who *despise* him. That's a rough word to use, but honest, too. A lot of Brantford people will go to see us play, pay their fifty cents and hope we lose. You wonder why *that* over an eleven-year-old kid."

As it turned out, not many of the people he was aiming at got the message.

Parents do tend to get a little excited, don't they, mother? Grandparents, too. Remember?

Wayne was nine or ten, playing against the Kitchener Krauts major atom team in a playoff game in Brantford. The Krauts had a defenceman named Paul Reinhart, who would go on to have a fine career in the NHL. Grandma Gretzky was at the game, sitting right down by the boards. When it came to Wayne or Frank Mahovlich, Grandma took her hockey seriously – and at that time there was no glass above the boards in the Brantford Arena.

So here came Paul Reinhart, checking Wayne into the boards and pinning him there, right in front of his Grandma. She didn't hesitate. "Leave him alone!" she yelled, and began beating Paul around the head with her purse.

I was embarrassed, but Paul was utterly flabbergasted. Years later at the 1982 world tournament in Finland, I was sitting next to him on a bus and asked him if he remembered. He started to laugh. "I keep telling people about it," he said, "but no one ever believes me."

Wayne took his hockey as seriously as only a small boy can. If there was a game he wanted to be in it. If there were two games in one day that was fine, too. He was nine, I think, when he did that: two games, one day, two places.

At the time you could play both minor novice and major novice in the same year if you were of age, and if you'd signed a card you could play tournament hockey in both divisions. Wayne had been commuting between tournaments, one in the major division in Hespeler for a team I coached and another for a minor division team coached by Phyllis' brother Bob in the Silver Stick Tournament in Welland. Hespeler is about fifteen miles from Brantford, Welland about sixty miles, and it's about seventy-five to eighty miles from Welland to Hespeler. It was a little hectic, but until the finals the only problem had been parents who objected to Wayne going back and forth.

We'd already decided that Wayne wouldn't be going to Welland. Up until then there'd been, say, a game in Hespeler at night and a game in Welland the next day. The finals were both scheduled on the Sunday – in the morning in Welland, in the afternoon in Hespeler. Two playoff games in one day seemed out of the question. Wayne was of minor novice age. His first obligation was to his team in Hespeler. We told Bob that Wayne wouldn't play the Welland final. Bob agreed. Wayne would play in Hespeler.

Game day arrived. Early in the morning a sound woke me up. It was Wayne, bawling his eyes out. He wanted to go to Welland.

Well, I thought it over. Wayne was upset. How much good would he be to his team in that frame of mind? If I timed it just right and had a little luck . . . .

I woke Phyllis. "Phone Bob in Welland," I said. "Tell him we're on our way, that we might be late, but to get Wayne's name on the scoresheet so he can play when we get there."

We hit the car on the dead run. Wayne dressed as I drove, skates and everything. Doug Whiting, the team manager, was standing at the arena door as we pulled up. He didn't even wait for me. He opened the car, picked Wayne up, carried him into the arena and sat him down on the bench. They were just going to start the second period. Bob said later that the game had already started when they'd got the call from Phyllis. "When the kids found out," he said, "it was like electricity running down the bench – and then through the stands, because somehow word got out. I could hear people, kids and fans, whispering, 'Gretzky's on his way! He's coming!' "

For a while it looked like the whole exercise was a waste of time. Brantford was down 2-0 when we got there and before long it was 5-0. The other coach had set up a defence designed specifically to stop Wayne. He had three boys in a triangle, one at the blue line and two just inside it. Body-checking was allowed for kids at that time and they were taking Wayne out. He just couldn't break through. In the third period, frustrated and upset at things he was hearing from the stands, he was almost reduced to tears. Bob just looked at him and said, very calmly, "Get one at a time, Wayne. We're not out of this yet."

And sure enough, Wayne started whittling away at them. He began to find holes in that triangle, and when he found one he scored. He finished with four goals and Brantford won 6-5.

But we couldn't stick around to celebrate. The game in Hespeler started at 1 p.m.

I got the car started and the door open. Bob carried Wayne out again so he wouldn't have to waste time taking off his skates. It was all too much for some guy who'd been standing at the door when we came in.

"Jeez!" he said, "I've never seen anything like it! They carry the kid in and they carry him out!"

We made it, though. We rocketed off to Brantford, stopped at the house long enough for me to pick up my team's sweaters and for Wayne to get a glass of milk, and headed for Hespeler. Wayne was there from the beginning that time, and helped Brantford win his second game in a matter of hours. That one was routine, a bit of an anti-climax, actually. All in all, we'd had a pretty full day.

There was a game a lot like the one in Welland a year later in a tournament in Peterborough. Teams were playing in arenas all over the city. The Kitchener Krauts were waiting to start their game when word came down that Brantford was about to be eliminated. "Losing 5-0 going into the third period," they said excitedly. "They're out!"

"Don't be too sure," warned Murray Freid, their coach. "There's a period left and Gretzky hasn't started yet." It might have sounded silly, because periods at that age level were only fifteen minutes long, straight time. But Murray called it.

With a minute gone in the third period, Bob took Wayne off the ice, put his arm around his shoulders and said, "Look, Wayne, there's a whole period left. You can score enough to beat them yourself." Then he sent him back out. For the next ten minutes, Wayne was a magician. He scored five straight goals to tie it. Then, with a minute left, he took a long shot. The puck went over the net, bounced, came back over the net, hit the goalie in the back and rolled into the net for the winner.

Puck luck? Sure. But first he had to score five.

Stories like these got around. It wasn't long before teams in other towns wanted to book the Steelers into their rink. Wayne's picture started appearing in ads for tournaments. "See Wayne Gretzky"; "Ten-Year-Old Scoring Ace Here Saturday." There was a great public curiosity about this little kid who was playing against the big boys and scoring all those goals. That curiosity could be turned into full houses, which meant more money to sink into the local minor hockey programs. In the 1972 Golden Horseshoe Tournament in Burlington, Ont., for instance, they drew thirty thousand people in six days. Wayne wasn't the only attraction – there were sixty-four teams from across Canada and New York State – but there's no doubt he was the *major* attraction.

Toward the end of Wayne's final atom season with the Steelers they had an exhibition lined up in Milton, Ont. Because we had a sister living nearby in Brampton we went there the night before and arranged to meet the team in Milton. But there was a parade in Brampton, we got caught up in the traffic, and didn't get to the game on time. The Milton people had advertised that Wayne would be there. By the time we actually made it they were accusing Bob of putting them on, of saying that Wayne would be there when he wasn't going to be. I'm glad we didn't have car trouble. I don't know what would have happened if we hadn't made it at all.

Sometimes it just got unbelievable. Here was this kid who quite obviously was just a normal, everyday boy doing all the crazy things kids do and who happened to have a lot of athletic skills. But when this ordinary boy with ordinary boys' likes and dislikes laced on skates, it was as though people suddenly considered him an adult.

You ever hear of a nine-year-old who needed a police escort to get out of a hockey rink? Wayne did. He was in zone playoffs in Welland and word got around that some bigger kids, teenagers with little brothers on the other team, were going to beat him up. The Welland minor hockey people took no chances. They arranged to have Wayne wait until the rest of the team left, then had a policeman escort him out. The only thing they forgot to do was to tell me. When he didn't come out with the team, I was scared to death. And when he came out with a policeman . . . . Oh, well, another day in the life of the Gretzky family.

Wayne was performing so many incredible scoring feats even his supporters started to take them as a matter of course. One night I missed a game and the next day after practice I asked assistant coach Bryan Wilson, a family friend and as big a Wayne Gretzky booster as ever lived, how it had gone.

"Boy, Wayne played like a dog last night," he said. "He just wasn't Wayne."

"Wait a minute," I protested. "Didn't they win 7-6?"

"Yes," he admitted.

"And didn't Wayne get all seven goals?"

"Well, yes," Bryan conceded. "But I've never seen him play that badly. He played like a dog."

Wayne got his own back, though. Nobody tells the story better than Bryan. "I was helping with the coaching when he was twelve," he recalls, "and I was new to coaching kids. I didn't realize that with kids sometimes the rules have to be a little different. I always thought being a team man meant passing the puck, and Wayne held on to it a lot. He'd play defence and take it from one end of the ice to the other. Six kids, ten kids, it made no difference, he could do it.

"We have this practice and I'm supposed to be coaching the defence. Wayne gets the puck, goes end to end, takes a shot, the goalie makes the save, and Wayne goes into the corner to get the puck. He's quite capable of getting the puck in the corner or anywhere else and going in for another shot, but he's a defenceman, so I'm yelling, 'Get back! Get back!'

"Wayne goes back, but I can tell he's mad at me. Well, later that night I'm back on the ice playing defence for a team in an amateur league. Half way through the game I get the puck behind the net, I go end to end, I take a shot, the rebound goes into the corner and I take off into the corner after it. And I'm a defenceman.

"I'm in the corner fighting for the puck. There's no glass, just a screen. And there, staring me right in the face, is Wayne. And he screams, 'You're a defenceman! What are you doing in the corner?'

"I know what he's talking about. Everybody's looking at me, or so it seems. Maybe they don't know what he means, but I do. And there's only one thought going through my mind: 'I'm gonna kill that damned kid. So help me, I'm gonna kill him.' "

And there was another good example of people who, with the best intentions in the world, sometimes forgot that the person they were dealing with was just a little kid – an incident that was also an example of the class of a man named Gordie Howe.

Gordie was a guest at the 1972 Kiwanis Great Men of Sport Dinner in Brantford. The head table guest list was impressive, to say the least. Quarterback Joe Theismann of the Toronto Argonauts was there, former Chicago Black Hawk coach Rudy Pilous, baseball great Sal Maglie, Tom Matte, running back for the Baltimore Colts, tackle Angelo Mosca of the Hamilton Tiger-Cats – and eleven-year-old, 4'9", eighty-pound Wayne Gretzky, just coming off a 378-goal season.

Wayne was nervous, of course. But at least he knew he wouldn't have to make a speech the way the others did. That had been arranged from the start. We thought it was clearly understood. But there was a foul-up, and Wayne was called to the microphone.

Well, Wayne didn't know what to do. He just stood there, tongue-tied and blushing. Then Gordie Howe stood up, walked to the microphone, put his arm around Wayne and said, "When someone has done what this kid has done in this rink, he doesn't have to say anything." It was the perfect touch. The crowd applauded and Wayne sat down, totally off the hook. Gordie always did have the great moves.

Gordie influenced Wayne's career in a lot of ways. The day of the banquet, for instance, they were riding in a limousine to a reception and Gordie asked him if he still practiced the backhand shot. "Always work on that," he told him, and Wayne always did. His first goal in junior "B", his first goal in junior "A", his first goal in the WHA and his first goal in the NHL were all on backhands. When Gordie Howe speaks, smart players listen. That applies no matter what league they're in. Because Gordie can help you in ways you'd never dream. Take, for instance, the case of Wayne's All-Star sweater.

Take a look at Wayne's sweater the next time you see him play. He tucks the right side into his hockey pants, the pad sticking out over it. He's done it almost as long as he's played and I doubt he'll ever stop. People have called it a superstition, but that's not it at all. It's a habit.

When he was six years old and playing against ten-year-old kids, the uniform sweaters were always miles too big.

They'd come right down to his knees. Because he was usually two or three years ahead of his age group and uniforms are handed down year to year, the situation never changed. I'd tuck one corner in for him to keep the thing under control. By the time he was big enough for the sweaters to fit him, the habit was so deeply ingrained it became automatic.

Then came the 1978-79 WHA All-Star game in Edmonton. Suddenly the eleven-year-old was almost eighteen and playing on the same team with his hero. And the All-Star sweater was too wide. As usual, Wayne started to tuck in a corner. That wasn't good enough for Gordie.

"Gimme that thing," he said. And Gordie Howe, perhaps the greatest legend in the history of the game, took a needle and thread and sewed a tuck in each side of the sweater so it would fit.

Wayne still tucks in the sweater. But then, Gordie doesn't play for the Oilers.

There are all kinds of memories from Wayne's years in minor hockey – the goals, the records, the tournaments, the pressures, the fun. But one stands out more than any other. It has to. There was never anything like the 1974 peewee tournament in Quebec City.

The 15th annual Quebec International Pee Wee Hockey Tournament was billed as the largest of its kind in the world, and I can't imagine one any bigger. There were sixty-five teams entered in four divisions brought in from across Canada and the U.S., when Brantford Turkstra Lumber got there in 1974. It wasn't just an invitational tournament, although some teams got there through invitation. Basically you had to be one of the top teams in your division at Christmas. In theory there are no weak teams. They play the entire tournament in the Colisée in Quebec City, home of the Quebec Nordiques, and for a week it's as though the pee wees had jumped to the NHL. They draw good crowds early in the week and by the time they get down to the semi-finals the place is filled to near capacity.

The newspapers go crazy. The day Brantford got there the *Québec à Propos* carried a big story headlined "The Gretzky Tornado Is In Town!" There were ten thousand people watching their opening game that night. When Brantford beat Richardson, Texas, 25-0, and Wayne scored seven goals and assisted on four to tie Guy Lafleur's single-game tournament point record, it was as though Wayne was the only story in town. *Québec à Propos* ran a front-page picture of Wayne with two team jerseys and a caption reading ". . . With Traces of Bobby Orr." *Le Journal de Québec* ran two front-page pictures and a splashy headline in red ink, the size you usually see when someone declares war: "At Eleven, 950 Goals, 140 This Year – and 7 Last Night!" They had the age wrong, but they sure jumped on the story.

It was a bit deceptive, really. The Richardson team was virtually brand new, the first crop of a start-up hockey program there just for the experience, and they ran head-first into one of the good teams in an old, established program. They'd been skating for only two years, had no hockey background and had never played before crowds larger than a hundred. They'd also never seen slapshots. When they hit the Colisée ice and saw that crowd and watched Brantford warm up, they naturally panicked a little bit. "The goaltender we used had never played goal before," the coach explained later. "We had to put him in because our regular goalie was so scared."

For Brantford and for Wayne it was hardly a fair test. But seven goals is seven goals and the papers had been filling people for days in advance with stories about this little guy from Brantford who'd scored 378 goals in one season. Everybody wanted to see him. Reporters were in from Montreal and Toronto. Little girls wanted autographs. Wayne would walk by and people would nudge each other and whisper, "C'est le grand Gretzky!"

Remember, now, this was a boy just one month past his thirteenth birthday, a boy small for his age and shy with people, who blushed easily and would rather just have played hockey. (Keith would have handled it. Keith would have *loved* it. He was only seven at the time and already telling people how good he was.) It was a big tournament, and exciting for Wayne. He wanted to wander around the building and look things over. But he couldn't because everywhere he went people stopped him for an autograph. Finally, he figured a way around it.

Greg Stefan, playing goal for Brantford, was blond like Wayne and roughly the same size. The Brantford team jackets had the boys' names on the sleeves. So when Wayne wanted to go for a look around he'd switch jackets with Greg. "For a while I'd be Greg and Greg would be me," he says. "I wonder sometimes how many kids are out there today with Greg's version of my signature in their autograph books."

In their second tournament game Brantford beat Beaconsfield, Que., 9-1. Wayne had a touch of flu, but, except for two minutes in the penalty box, he played the entire third period until he took himself off in the final seconds. He finished with two goals and three assists. By now just finding tickets to get into the arena was becoming a problem, whether you had a boy on a team or not. That always bothered me a little. It had been the same way back at the Golden Horseshoe Tournament in Burlington, and at that time it led to kind of an embarrassing situation: I'd stood in line for tickets for the family. When I got to the wicket and bought them, I asked the girl for tickets to the next game, too. She told me I'd have to come back the next day and line up all over again. I decided to kid her a bit.

"Well, if I'm in line out here tomorrow," I said, "my son, Wayne Gretzky, will be out here with me." She didn't laugh. She panicked. Before I could stop her she was out of the booth – just left it empty with the line-up waiting – and came back with the manager, who was all apologies and gave us a family pass. I was never so embarrassed in my life.

Now Brantford was in the quarter-finals against the Verdun Maple Leafs, a team that included a young man named Denis Savard who now stars with the Chicago Black Hawks. For Wayne it was getting a bit scary. So many people stopped him on game night he was afraid he couldn't get to the dressing room in time. Finally, he stopped a policeman, asked for help, and was escorted the rest of the way.

Brantford won 7-3 with Wayne scoring three goals, two of them unassisted. The next day in the Montreal *Star*, Verdun coach Aldo Giampolo asked a question about Wayne. "How do you stop a pee wee who thinks like a professional? Having talent is one thing, but when you have the brains to go along with it the job of stopping him is much more difficult." *Montréal-Matin* carried two full pages of pictures the same day, plus a shot on the front page. I guess that front page kind of showed where Quebec City's priorities lay during tournament week. It carried only two items: a huge headline on a scandal surrounding Montreal's Mirabel Airport, which was big news all over the country – and a picture of Wayne.

It was pretty heady stuff. But Brantford and Wayne were riding for a fall.

What no one on the outside had noticed or bothered to mention was that the Brantford team had no depth. It had good goaltending and could produce a lot of goals, but it had only thirteen players. Oshawa always seemed to beat us by a goal, often in overtime. All through minor hockey Oshawa was Brantford's stumbling block. And the tournament semi-final was Brantford vs Oshawa.

It was the same story. Oshawa won again. Wayne was playing defence as usual, but with the score tied at 4-4 coach Ron St. Amand moved him to forward. It was a gamble, a calculated risk. Wayne finished with a goal and three assists (for a total of 13 goals and 13 assists in 4 games) and Brantford lost, 9-4.

We were all bitterly disappointed. I remember saying, "I'll be back in this arena some day." I was, too, for Wayne's first WHA game there. But along with the loss came a couple of valuable lessons about minor hockey and, in a way, about life.

The first was for Wayne, delivered at the post-game press conference by a kind and understanding tournament director. He spotted Wayne slumped in a chair, tears in his eyes, looking as though the world had come to an end. He went over to him and said: "Wayne, you have to understand that this is a sport and one team has to win and one has to lose. The team that won was the best one, I'm sure you'll agree. I know you wanted to win but that's the way it is in sport. But there's one thing you can be really proud about: a lot of people came to see you play. We packed the arena for four games." (Tournament attendance totalled 140,166, about twenty-five thousand more than in the previous year.) "There are a lot of kids who aren't fortunate enough to be able to play hockey. All the money we raised at this tournament is used to help those kids, and you played a big part."

The second lesson was how deceptive the whole minor hockey picture can be when kids start dreaming of professional hockey careers.

Oshawa had a fine young player named Grove Sutton who scored five goals in the Brantford game and finished with seventeen as his team went on to win the class A final over Peterborough. When the Brantford game ended, Oshawa coach Bill White told reporters: "All the talk has been about Gretzky. But I wouldn't trade Grove Sutton for him anytime."

Grove Sutton never made it to the WHA or the NHL. It's a long, long road from kids' hockey to the pros. Taking the first steps, no matter how easily you do it, doesn't necessarily mean you're going to take the last.

Chapter 7

LADY, YOUR SON IS A PUCK HOG

"At ten they were saying I'd be washed up at twelve. At twelve they were saying I'd be nothing at fifteen. We got used to it – but it was never nice to hear."

– Wayne Gretzky, 1983.

There are times, you know, when parents are a lot smaller than their kids.

I don't know why it has to be that way. Jealousy, maybe, or frustration. Perhaps they were good athletes themselves and expected their kids to be just as good; or they wanted to be good athletes and never made it, and were trying to relive their own childhood through their kids. When it doesn't work out, when their kids can't live up to their expectations, no matter how hard they try, that adult frustration can turn to resentment – and what better target than some kid who's doing all the things their own kids can't?

I'm not saying that's why some of the parents on teams Wayne played for started needling him. Maybe there was some other reason we never figured out. All I know is that, for whatever reason, the resentment was there. Wayne was attracting all this attention, particularly after the Quebec tournament. Newspaper and magazine articles were being written, there were radio and TV reporters around. Maybe it was natural that there'd be bad feelings, that other parents would get their noses out of joint. Personally, I couldn't understand it. There was never a problem with the kids themselves who, after all, were the ones playing with and against Wayne – the people minor hockey is supposed to be for. There was just this small minority of parents trying to chop Wayne down to their size. They razzed him, they insulted him, they complained to coaches that he was getting too much ice time. Some of them would sit there at games with pencil and paper, marking the times Wayne came on and off the ice and when their own kids did, and taking the lists over to the coaches as soon as the game ended.

Once in Wayne's ten-eleven-year-old year after the Nadrofsky Steelers lost a tournament in Brampton, two fathers – with Phyllis obviously within earshot – said they weren't going to the tournament the next weekend in Brockville just to watch one kid on the ice all the time. They called a meeting of the other parents and informed the Brantford Minor Hockey League representative that they wanted a new coach because Bob Hockin was playing Wayne too much – and they weren't sending their kids to Brockville. Fortunately all the parents didn't feel that way. When the rep phoned to hear Bob's side of the story and found out we had eight boys ready to play, he just said, "Go ahead." And when some of the other parents found out we were going anyway they didn't want their kids left out, so we wound up with twelve.

Understand, now, these were *nice people* – people we knew in Brantford. Their kids played with Wayne. Some of the ones doing the yelling were our friends. Or at least, so we thought. But as Phyllis says, "You learn quickly. At the rink, you don't have friends." You wind up building little defences. Phyllis stays away from groups of parents now, except at tournaments. She'll sit with one or two. It doesn't take long to figure out who you can sit with and who to stay clear of. She went through it with Wayne and then with Keith and Glen, and now it's Brent's turn.

It's funny, the differences in the boys. I don't think Wayne ever heard the razzing when he was little. He's probably more aware of it now in the pros, because the more success he has the more boos he's going to generate when the Oilers go on the road. At this point it's a form of flattery. Keith hears it and sometimes answers back. He's likely hearing it a lot more now that he's in Windsor playing junior "A". He's a Gretzky. That makes him a target. With Glen there's been no problem. He doesn't score a lot of goals and no one can say he's getting extra ice time. He's out there enjoying himself. Brent, now, he hears it all. He's a real rabbit ears. He just turns to the stands and gives them this great big smile. Probably hopes it will drive them crazy.

It used to bother me. When they'd razz Wayne or shout things, I'd get bitter about it, but after a while I just felt sorry for them. What they didn't realize was that by being so busy resenting Wayne, they never really got to appreciate and enjoy their own children. There weren't that many of them. They definitely were a minority. It was just that we could never seem to get away from them. With Wayne playing so many sports and playing them all so well, we found them in baseball, lacrosse, and any sport you'd care to name. Mostly, Wayne was able to ignore them. Sometimes, though, they got through to him and it hurt. Ed O'Leary, a sports writer with the Brantford *Expositor*, still remembers the day he stuck his head in the dressing room and saw Wayne slumped in a corner, crying his eyes out. "It was what he'd been hearing all game," he says. "There was no other reason."

As I mentioned earlier, Wayne was a heck of a lacrosse player until the other sports got in the way and he had to drop the game. He had a great touch with the stick. He could shoot, he could pass, he could roll off a check – a skill learned in lacrosse that he took with him into hockey. One day when he was ten, he had a game in which he scored two goals and assisted on the other nine, including seven by one boy. The boy's mother was delighted. She rushed to congratulate him, then turned to Wayne and said, "Great game, Wayne!" He felt pretty good about that.

The very next game, Wayne scored nine goals and drew two assists. He'd skipped a baseball game that night to play lacrosse, because the lacrosse game was a playoff. He'd had a big night. The *same woman* who'd praised him the previous game came over and said, "Oh, you missed a baseball game tonight, eh?"

"Yes, I did," Wayne said.

"Well," she snapped, "Let's hope there's a ball game next time!"

Phyllis and I have different philosophies about how to handle those people now, the ones who gave Wayne such a bad time. I tend to say, "Forget it; it's over." Phyllis doesn't forget. Wayne has a theory on that: "I think Dad can walk by those people who were so critical and not let it bother him, because really he's had the last laugh. I'm in the National Hockey League and I've made a success of it. My mother can't be that way. I can walk into an arena with her, meet people I've known and grown up with, and if she walks on by I know they've said something bad about me over the years. She's not being snarly or backhanded about it. She'll tell them to their face: 'How can I talk to you when ten years ago you were calling my son a (BLEEP)?' And it's true. That's what they were doing, and she has no time for that. There are a lot of people in minor hockey she's come to know and like. There have been a lot of good associations. But would you be happy if someone was critizing your son and then coming up the next day and saying, 'Hi! Let's have lunch'? I wouldn't be. And neither is my Mom."

That's Phyllis, all right. She's got a good memory and she's too honest to be hypocritical about it. There was one man, one of those real holler types with a voice you could hear all over the rink, who just cut Wayne up something terrible. One day he came over to Phyllis and apologized for

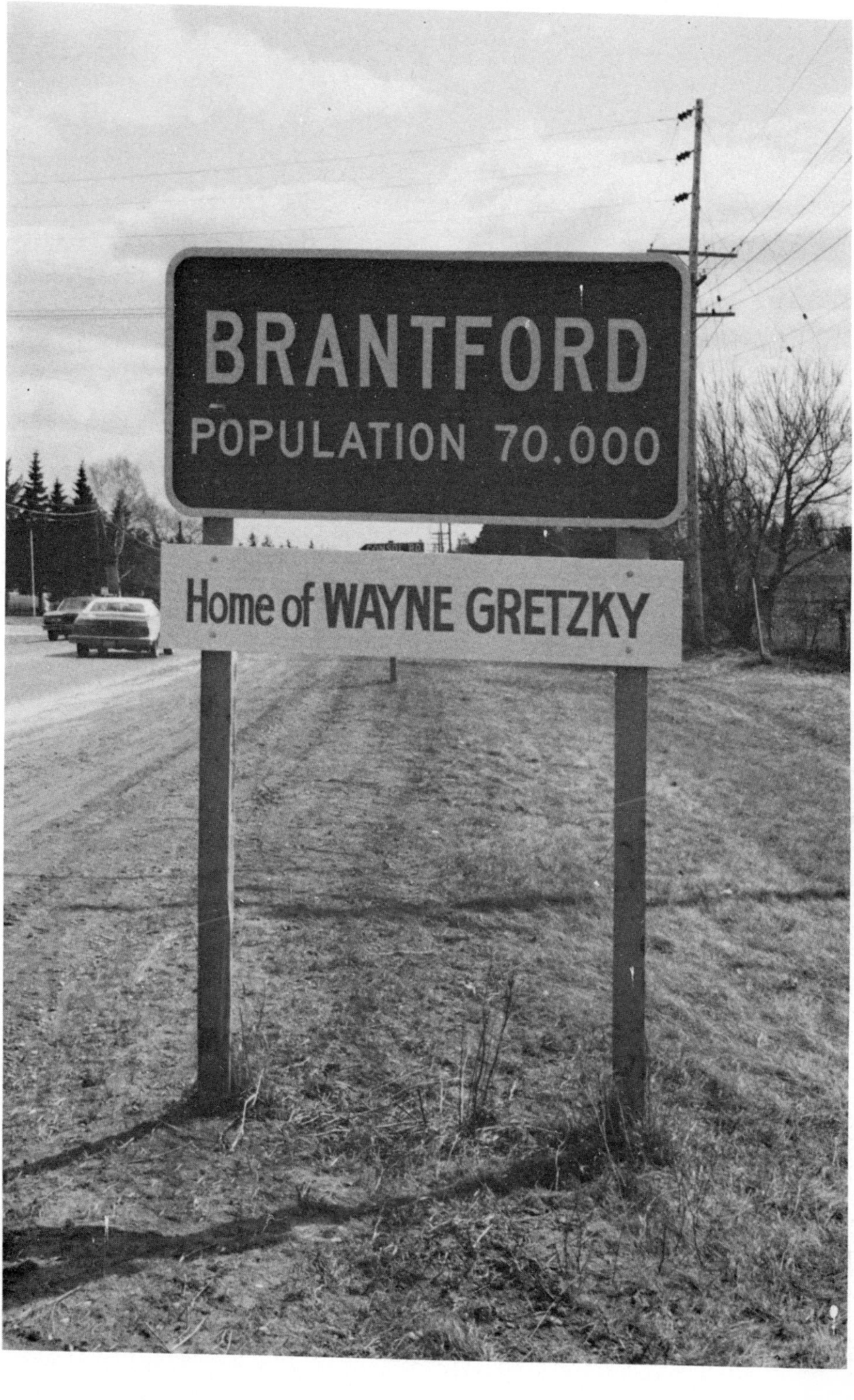

WALTER GRETZKY

Grandma Mary Gretzky on her farm in Canning.

Mary Gretzky sitting outside the farmhouse.

Grandpa Tony Gretzky on the farm.

Tony Gretzky in the farmhouse living room.

WALTER GRETZKY

WALTER GRETZKY

Wayne Gretzky and Gordie Howe move to the attack during the 1979 WHA All-Star game.

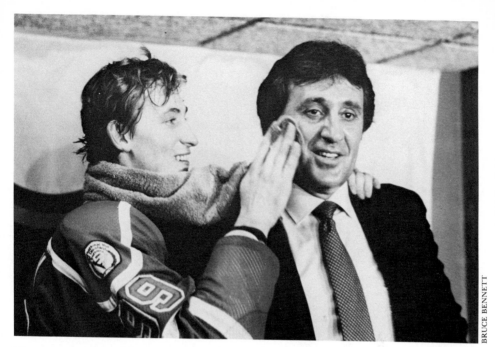

Wayne consoles Phil Esposito after breaking Espo's single-season record with goal number 77 in Buffalo on February 24, 1982.

Gretzky beats Buffalo Sabre goalie Don Edwards for his record-breaking goal number 77.

Wayne exults after scoring his 50th goal in 39 games – breaking Maurice Richard's "impossible" 50 in 50 – against the Philadelphia Flyers in Edmonton during the '81-'82 season.

Wayne scores the winning goal in a game against the Soviet Union in Edmonton.

The Edmonton Oilers'
record three 50-goal
scorers in 1983-84: left
to right – Jari Kurri,
Wayne, Glenn
Anderson.

Wayne and Michael
Barnett, Director of
Marketing of
CorpSport
International.

Wayne lets loose a hard drive against the Calgary Flames during a 1981-82 pre-season game.

Brent Gretzky, age 8, on the Varadi Ave. back-yard rink.

Glen Gretzky, age 11, on the famous Gretzky back-yard rink.

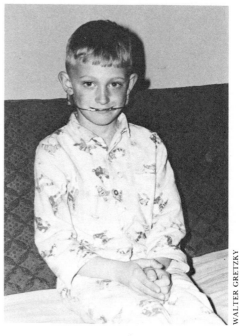

An unidentified Gretzky fan in one of the many popular Gretzky T-shirts.

Nine-year-old Wayne with the orthodontic mouthband he wore for two years.

From left to right: Glen, Brent and Keith Gretzky at work on their Grandma's farm.

Two stars at centre ice: Wayne with Sally "All in the Family" Struthers.

Wayne at age 16 playing for Team Canada at the world junior champion-ships in Montreal, January 1978.

Eleven-year-old Wayne gets ready for a game with the Brantford Nadrofsky Steelers, March 1972.

Wayne during a practice in Brantford at age 10.

The first Gretzky goal: Wayne (11) scores his only goal of his first hockey season in 1967 for the Nadrofsky Steelers in Stratford, Ont.

The making of a champion: Wayne's early days on the Nith River at the farm in Canning, Ont.

Baseball started early for young Wayne.

Wayne practises his high-jumping over the chicken fence after feeding time at the farm.

Wayne leaps over the home-made high jump at the farm.

Chicken-feeding time at the farm for Wayne.

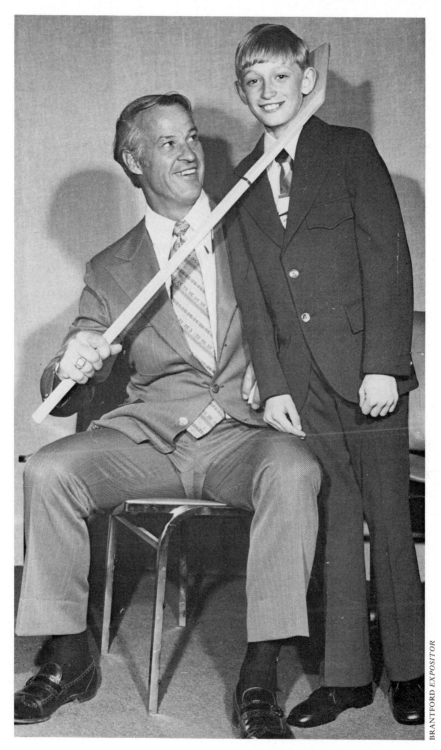

Wayne and life-long friend Gordie Howe at an awards banquet, May 1972.

Fans mob Wayne during his record 1981-82 season.

Super pie for super-scorer Gretzky at a junior golf tournament in Chicoutimi, Que.

Wayne plays floor hockey with the kids at Oakridge School in Vancouver, 1980.

Wayne and girlfriend Vickie Moss.

Brent, age 8, fishing on the
Nith River at the farm.

Brent gets his equipment
together before heading out for
hockey practice.

Kim Gretzky with her track trophies at a provincial track and field championship meet in Toronto.

Kim at the height of her track career.

They start 'em young at the Gretzkys: Keith wields a lacrosse stick in the back yard at Varadi Ave.

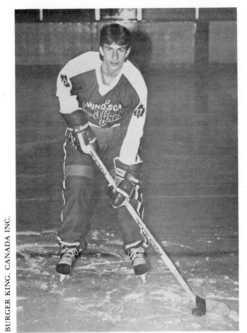

Keith as a Windsor Bulldog (1983-84), his first year away from home.

Keith takes a sip of water during a break between periods.

The back yard in summer: Glen defends the net during a ball hockey game.

Glen cleans off the back-yard rink while Brent practises.

Young Wayne and his little brother Keith out in the yard. Wayne has already started tucking in his sweater on one side.

Glen stands on the back-yard rink in front of the net attached with target hoops.

Famed Soviet goaltender Vladislav
Tretiak and Wayne switch uniforms
during a film session in Moscow. From
left to right: Tretiak, Gretzky family
friend and hockey associate Charlie
Henry, Wayne.

Phyllis Gretzky and Soviet goalie
Vladislav Tretiak in Moscow.

Wayne and his good friend Vladislav tour the streets of Moscow.

Mission to Moscow 1982: from left to right - Glen, Wayne, Tretiak, Keith and Brent.

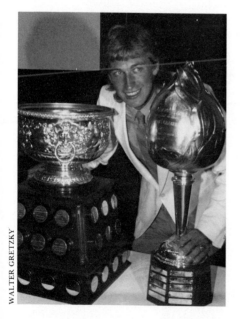

WALTER GRETZKY

A proud Wayne Gretzky with the Art Ross (left) and Hart trophies as the NHL scoring champion and outstanding player respectively, 1982-83.

BOB MUMMERY

Wayne receives the Grecian urn at centre ice as winner of the *Sports Illustrated* Sportsman of the Year award for 1982.

Wayne dressed to the nines, complete with 99 cufflinks, as the Man of Distinction award winner.

Wayne takes a break on the court during his annual Wayne Gretzky Celebrity Tennis Tournament in Brantford in 1981.

Champagne and strawberries: Wayne with Edmonton Oilers' owner Peter Pocklington.

A touch of glamour at Wayne's 1983 Tennis Classic: from left to right – Detroit Red Wings' goalie Eddie Mio and winger Ron Dugay with model Cheryl Tiegs.

Wayne and M*A*S*H star Jamie Farr swap uniforms during a trip to the
M*A*S*H set.

Friends and celebrities: Goldie Hawn, Wayne, Burt Reynolds.

Three all-time hockey
greats: Wayne Gretzky,
Gordie Howe and Guy
Lafleur.

Wayne and Anne
Murray at the Tennis
Classic in Brantford.

Brantford meets the Bunnies: Hugh Hefner, Wayne and some of the Playboy Bunnies.

Walter Gretzky.

Father and son: Walter and Wayne during the early days with the Oilers.

Sixteen-year-old Wayne at home with, left to right, Keith, Glen, Brent and Kim.

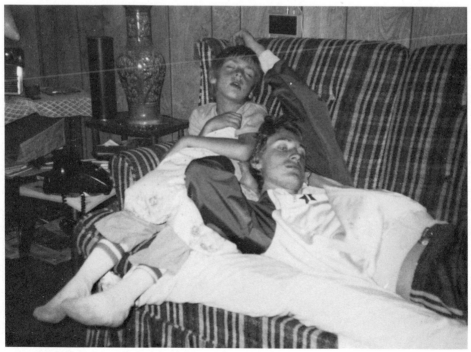

Down home takin' it easy: Wayne and Brent enjoying a snooze.

Wayne and Kim.

Wayne has breakfast with Nelson Skalbania, owner of the Indianapolis Racers, after signing his first contract.

Phyllis and Walter add another trophy to the basement collection.

Happy Mother's Day, 1981.

Wayne and Gordie Howe at the 1979 WHA All-Star game.

what he'd been doing, and he quit. But that didn't happen often, and it's not likely to as Brent grows up, if he keeps progressing as he has. I really think Phyllis would be just as happy if the stands were empty. It would make things a lot easier.

They're funny, though, some of those people. They come knocking at the door now asking for autographed pictures like nothing happened. Or they drop off books that have been written about Wayne (when we started this one there were about a dozen on the market, all written without any authorization from Wayne or the family, by people trying to jump on the bandwagon to make a few bucks) and say, "Will you get Wayne to sign these and mail them to this address?" It's amazing.

The neighbourhood kids make up for a lot of it. They find out when Wayne's home, and they come knocking at the door for autographs. Sometimes when Wayne's in for a fast hello between games he'll be dead tired, and the temptation is to tell them he's sleeping. But you look at their big eyes and they're kind of half scared, knocking on the door like that, and there's no way you can say no. The little guys are still what minor hockey's all about. It's too bad some of the big people keep forgetting.

The really strange thing was that while Wayne was playing a lot those parents couldn't see that no one was losing ice time because of him. The team had three lines and two sets of defencemen, which meant that the defencemen went out every second shift and a line went out every third. Because Wayne played defence he was out every second shift. And when Bob left him out there he rotated the other three defencemen. So at the very worst a defenceman might be going out every third shift – which is exactly what the forwards were doing.

What seemed to bother people most was the attention Wayne was getting. But given the fact that he had this talent and that he played on good teams (from the time he was six until he left for Toronto the teams he was on either won the Ontario championship or lost in the final), I don't see how we could have avoided it.

The calls from parents kept coming, though. Bob would get them the night before almost every game during the Steelers' big year. "Is Wayne going to play the whole game?" "Is Wayne going to play a lot?" "Is your nephew ever coming off the ice?" That last one really burned him. At the rink, whether it was practice or game, he was always "Coach" to Wayne just as he was to all the other kids – so much so, in fact, that a lot of people didn't know there was any family tie.

As for the other kids' ice time, no one could say the boys weren't getting a lot. We played too many games for that. If there was a tournament or a game available, we went for it. If there wasn't, we looked until we found one. We had two telephones in our kitchen and it was nothing for Bob and I to sit there until 2 a.m. setting up a game for the next night, or returning calls from some coach who wanted one. We always got a game. Wouldn't leave the phones until we did.

Ice time was no problem. We booked it ahead, and if we couldn't get a game, we gave up the ice to someone else. What with practices and games, Bob figures the Steelers were on the ice five out of seven nights. Teams were more than willing to come to Brantford to play us, because that meant they'd get a return game in their rink. And that meant money, because the Steelers and the little Gretzky kid who scored all the goals were becoming a drawing card. They played 82 games that season and went 76-2-4. The irony of it was that minor hockey groups outside of Brantford made more money off Steelers games than Brantford did, because in Brantford the people just wouldn't come out.

I don't want to give the impression that every parent was thinking about nothing besides Wayne and his ice time. The hecklers were a tiny minority. As Wayne says,

"Twenty-six parents out of thirty were super to me. The other four I'd as soon forget." But it doesn't take many adults to spoil a kids' game.

The ones I don't understand are the ones who should know better. Sometimes – again, only a few out of many – you'll get a coach or an executive member who forgets why he's there. They're not just in hockey. Ron Birkett, Wayne's bantam baseball coach, often mentions the time at a tournament when the coach of the Brampton team walked up to Wayne and casually said: "You won't live to see Christmas, Gretzky!"

That wasn't an enjoyable year for any of us. Wayne was eleven, coming off that final season of atom hockey when he'd scored the 378 goals, eligible to play minor pee wee, but planning to skip that group and go directly to major pee wee, which is for twelve-year-olds. He didn't have to, but as he said: if he didn't, they'd be calling him a baby and saying that he was staying with the minors just so he could score a lot of goals. No matter what he did he always seemed to be caught in the middle. He was playing well, the team was doing well, but nothing he did seemed to please anyone.

After two games as a pee wee, he'd scored five goals when he tried something different in a practice. He huddled with his wingers and said, "When I bring the puck in over the blue line I'll stop, you go around the defencemen and I'll dump it in." They tried it, it worked, and the coach blew the whistle and told Wayne not to do it again.

A few minutes later they huddled again. This time as Wayne brought the puck in he coasted and the wingers went around the defencemen. The plan was that he'd take a shot and try to nip in for the rebound. The defence didn't know what to do. The coach did. He blew the whistle and there was a bit of a confrontation.

"You know," he told Wayne, "you're a pretty good little hockey player, but we don't want any hotdogs on this team. You remind me too much of that hotdog Gilbert Perreault."

Gilbert Perreault, a hotdog? Wayne was mystified. He asked the coach what he meant.

"You haven't got time to do that in hockey," the coach replied.

"All I'm trying to be is a good hockey player," Wayne protested. "That play, Perreault uses it all the time and . . . ."

"He's a hotdog," the coach snapped, and that ended that. He was the coach. When the coach says something you do as you're told. But Gilbert Perreault, a hotdog? Wayne was baffled. How could anyone that good be called a hotdog? These adults sure were tough to figure out.

The coach is the coach. I'm not disputing that. Once Wayne had one who wanted him to go behind the opposing net when his wingers went into the corners after the puck. Wayne thought it was a silly move when his team didn't have possession. "I might as well sit in the stands," he said.

"Wayne," I said, "if he tells you to stand on your *head*, you do it. He's the coach. You do it his way, and at the end of the year just forget everything he told you, because the next season when you move up you'll have another coach."

Over the next couple of years it didn't get any easier. The capper, I guess, came in 1975 – February 2, 1975, to be exact.

Wayne was a week past his fourteenth birthday, finishing his first season of bantam hockey with the Brantford Charcon Chargers. It was Brantford Day at Maple Leaf Gardens in Toronto with Brantford teams at various age levels playing each other. It should have been a thrilling kind of afternoon – Brantford kids playing in the home of the Maple Leafs. The Chargers were playing Bryan Wilson's minor bantam Whites. The boys all knew each other. All the ingredients were there for a really good time for everyone. What we wound up with was something that, even now, Bryan calls "the saddest thing I've ever seen in hockey."

When Wayne skated out onto the ice, the Brantford people booed. He was from Brantford, it was Brantford

Day, and some Brantford people booed a fourteen-year-old kid.

They didn't know it, and neither did we, but it was one of the last shots at him they were going to get. The booing and the pressure had been building up. Something had to give. When the explosion came, it rocked all of hockey.

Chapter 8

I'M NOT COMING HOME, DAD, REGARDLESS....

"Let him play Junior "B"? Against twenty-year-olds? Are you crazy?"

– Walter Gretzky, 1975.

Hockey has taken Wayne all over the world. He's been to the Soviet Union, he's played in Europe, he's hopped back and forth across North America, and sometimes he's made the planes with seconds to spare and the door starting to close because, except for game trips, that's the way he is. But the longest, toughest trip he ever took covered only sixty miles, from Brantford to Toronto. It took four months, counting a detour to the Ontario Supreme Court, and before it was over I was starting to wonder whether the whole world had gone nuts. To me it became a classic example of what can happen when adults get so deeply involved in kids' games they forget who those games are for.

It was 1975, Wayne was fourteen, and by that time we knew we couldn't let things go on the way they had been. The pressures of being Wayne Gretzky in his home town, and a small town at that, were too much. It got to the point where we were afraid that he was losing his childhood.

To really understand you'd have had to have known Wayne then. When you see him now being interviewed on

TV or making a public appearance, he's outgoing. He's relaxed, he's confident. All the exposure has given him that poise. But back then he was just the opposite. If someone said something to him he'd blush and turn away. He was all right in interviews because he'd been doing them since he was six, but in normal situations he was backward and shy. He never let anything out. We thought it was affecting him mentally, that he was getting all locked up inside. It should have been the best time of his life, but he was obviously unhappy.

We wanted him in a situation where he could live a normal life. As Wayne Gretzky in Brantford that could never happen.

But there was a solution: we could send Wayne away. We could move him to another city, some place where he would have a chance to be just another one of the kids. He'd play hockey, of course, but in a place the size of Toronto, where there were a lot of good players, we thought we could hide him in the numbers. That was our intention, anyway. As it turned out, everything backfired.

A lot of people have said a lot of things and jumped to a lot of conclusions about what happened and why we did it. According to some of them all we could think of was Wayne's hockey, and we were just trying to get him into a better league. We were giving up our son just to push his career. Talk about your pushy parents: those Gretzkys – who do they think they are?

But at first we didn't want to do it. And for the record, it wasn't our idea – it was Wayne's. For a long time we said no. The way he changed our mind was a lesson in how mature he'd become – more mature in a lot of ways than some of the adults who tried to stop him.

Over a couple of years at hockey and baseball tournaments, we'd come to know a man named Sam McMaster, who was in charge of the Young Nationals, an organization that operates teams in all divisions of the Metropolitan Toronto Hockey League, a league which had about ten thousand registered players in the various age groups. The Young Nats were a good organization and at tournament time they always seemed to be winning or coming close. Wayne knew the team and had a lot of respect for it and for Sam; so when Sam phoned the house to arrange a baseball game and asked Wayne how his hockey season had gone, Wayne had no hesitation in telling him.

Not too good, he said. He told Sam that he'd played with the same kids for the last few years, that he'd be with them again, and while the kids were fine, there was some animosity and resentment from the parents.

"Well," Sam said, "if it's that bad, how'd you like to come to Toronto and play with us?"

It was just that casual. Sam was not recruiting. He was not trying to stack a team or build an empire. When Wayne said he'd like to come, Sam just told him to talk it over with his parents and to let him know. Then he let it lay. There was absolutely no pressure on us. Except from Wayne.

He wanted to go. He was excited about it. And that only confirmed our suspicions of how tough things had gotten for him in Brantford. He'd found an escape hatch and he wanted to take it right now.

We said no. He was our son. We wanted him at home. We'd find another way around the problem. There had to be one somewhere. We weren't sending our boy to Toronto. Things happened to kids in big cities. There was booze and dope and a million ways to get into trouble, no matter how good your intentions. He wasn't going, and that was that.

He wouldn't let up. He'd ask, we'd say no, he'd ask, we'd say no, and we'd go around again. Finally one day he asked us to give him a reason why he couldn't go.

"Drop it, Wayne," I said. "You're not going. Now don't ask again, I'm tired of arguing about it."

"Just tell me why," he insisted. "Just give me a *reason*."

He was turning our own gun on us. Phyllis and I have always taught the kids that for everything we do there is a reason. Now he was asking us to prove it. He had us cornered.

"All right," I said. "In a big city it's easy to get involved with the wrong crowd and wind up doing what they're doing, even though you know it's wrong, because there's peer pressure to go along with the group in order to be accepted."

I'll never forget the look he gave me.

"You mean drugs and things like that?" he asked. "Is that it?"

That was about it, I admitted.

"And that's the *only* reason?" he repeated.

"Yes!"

"Okay, give me some money, tell me what kind of drugs you want and I'll be back in half an hour with anything you want."

I couldn't believe it. It hit me like a ton of bricks. I even remember feeling a little bit faint, I was so shaken up. Our fourteen-year-old son was telling us that drugs were everywhere, that even in Brantford there were places where he could just go out and get them – and could have been using them if he'd wanted to.

I looked at Phyllis. She just shook her head.

"Now," Wayne asked. "Can I go?"

I looked at Phyllis again. "Might as well," she said. All of a sudden we knew he *was* mature enough to handle it. We checked with his principal, his teachers, the president of his minor hockey, and they all agreed.

Then we called Wayne in.

"Yes, you can go," I said. And I never worried about it again.

As it turned out, saying yes was the easy part.

Wayne phoned Sam to say he could come. That weekend Sam came to Brantford to go over the details.

"Are you sure it's legal?" I asked him. "Are you sure it's okay?"

"A piece of cake," he said positively. And that's when Phyllis piped up. "It better be," she said, "because we're not going to court."

105

"A piece of cake," Sam repeated. Oh, sure.

It all seemed to be going smoothly enough. The MTHL said it was perfectly legal for Wayne to play in Toronto, providing he had his release from the Brantford association and was residing in Toronto. No problem. Ron Sevier, president of the Brantford Minor Hockey Association, gave us that release and wished us well. Bill Cornish, manager of the Nats' major bantam team for which Wayne would be playing, had a boy who'd played on it two years earlier. Bill and his wife, Rita, offered to take Wayne into their home. He could live there, go to school, be in a good family situation, mix with new kids, even get a trip to Europe with the Nats for a couple of exhibition games. His horizons would broaden, the pressure would be off – it couldn't be better.

And it wasn't as though he was leaving home. As I kept telling people when all the fuss started: "This is the modern age. We have *telephones*. He calls home every night. He's home on weekends. We see him at his games. Brantford is only sixty miles away! We can be together in ninety minutes! Why is everybody getting so upset?"

It was the strangest thing. If we'd sent him off to boarding school twice as far away no one would have thought anything about it. People do that all the time, mainly because they want to give their children a better education. And that's all we were doing: trying to give Wayne a better chance. Not to play better hockey. It's always baffled me that people thought that. We have one of the best minor hockey leagues in the country in the Brantford area. There were more players and maybe a level just as high in Toronto, but it wasn't better. Anybody who followed hockey had to know that. But you'd think we were selling Wayne into slavery or something.

Part of the reason, I guess, was that in moving Wayne to Toronto we had signed papers making Bill Cornish his legal guardian. There is a residency rule in minor hockey, and it's a good rule. If I live in Brantford, my children should play in Brantford. If it had been strictly a hockey move then people would have had a right to be upset. But it *wasn't* totally

106

a hockey move; it was a move for Wayne as a *boy*. With Bill Cornish as his legal guardian, Wayne was living at home. The Ontario government accepted that. When we enrolled him in West Humber Collegiate Institute in the summer there was no problem. He was just another Toronto boy going to school.

But to hockey people, that was different. We were the Gretzkys, and we were pushing our kid. And come September when it was time for Wayne to register, the Ontario Minor Hockey Association was waiting for us.

We'd made no secret of what we were doing. The OMHA knew back in July and no one had said anything. (If the OMHA had ever informed us officially that it wouldn't honour the transfer if Wayne made the move to Toronto, we'd never have done it.) Wayne had the MTHL's blessing. He'd signed their card. Now suddenly, in September, with Wayne living in Toronto and established in school, we began to hear things.

First Sam got word from the MTHL that there might be trouble: the OMHA was claiming that clearance from the Brantford association wasn't enough, that for Wayne to play in Toronto he also had to have OMHA permission, and that that might not be easy to get. Then, on September 15, I was sitting at home listening to Arnold Anderson, sports director of CKPC radio in Brantford. All at once he was saying that Vern McCallum, secretary-manager of the OMHA, had announced that Wayne Gretzky would not be allowed to play hockey in Toronto unless both his parents lived there. It was strictly a hockey move, he said. I remember some time later when he was even a little bit of a smart Alec about it. "If it's not a hockey move then he can play high school hockey," he said. "No one would stop him there."

Wayne wasn't the only one in trouble. The parents of a thirteen-year-old named Brian Rorabeck of Brighton, Ont., had also arranged to have their boy live in Toronto under legal guardianship so that he could play for the Young Nats' minor bantam team. So in fact there were two similar cases, not one. But because Wayne was Wayne and had received so much recognition in his career, most of the publicity centred around him.

We launched an appeal. Sam had written to Alan Eagleson, lawyer, and one of the most influential men in hockey, outlining the situation and requesting help. Eagleson's firm, Blaney, Pasternak, Smela, Eagleson and Watson, assigned us a lawyer named William Pearce and off we went, the Gretzkys and the Rorabecks, to a meeting at the Royal York Hotel in Toronto, to ask a bunch of grown men to let two kids play hockey. The boys were there, too, but they needn't have been. It was as though they weren't part of it. The fight now was between the adults.

They turned us down.

I'll remember that meeting as long as I live. There were about sixty OMHA people there, I think, all dressed in their dark pants and their red blazers.

We went round and round. They asked us why he was moving and we told them. One man said he understood what Wayne was going through in Brantford, that he had seen him play and seen it happen. We told them it was for Wayne's well-being more than for his hockey. The Rorabecks said they wanted Brian in a different school system, and in an area where he could play hockey at his own age level rather than with boys a year or two older as he'd been doing in Brighton. In Wayne's case the reasons seemed obvious. We thought we'd win on sheer logic.

It wasn't even close.

Jim Kinkley, president of the OMHA, said he could sympathize with us, but they couldn't concern themselves with one person, they had to think of the precedent: if one boy did it, everybody would do it.

That one really got to me. "Everybody?" I said. "I wouldn't even let one of my other kids do it. This is an unusual situation. He's an unusual boy. Even people here will admit that."

We couldn't change their minds. "In our judgment," Mr.

Kinkley said, "it is in the best interests of the boys that they stay home with their parents."

After the meeting he issued an official statement: "The decision upholds our original decision, based on rules formulated over a long period of time and supported by the Canadian Amateur Hockey Association." Earlier in the week he'd said that CAHA rules make it clear that players under eighteen may move from one area to another only with their families or guardians. The guardian's relationship was to be established by January 1 of the year in which the player moved. Bill Pearce disputed that. He said there were several circumstances under which a boy could switch teams, and that the fact that both boys had releases signed by the president and secretary of their previous clubs was enough to allow them to play in Toronto.

It did no good. The OMHA ruled against us. When we left the meeting both boys were crying. Outside, the TV cameras were waiting. All we were trying to do was let our boys play hockey where they wanted to, while we put them through school where we wanted to. The whole thing had turned into big news. Everybody wanted a statement.

Well, I gave them one.

"My Dad came from Russia," I said. "He came to the U.S., then came up and joined the Canadian Army and went overseas. When they came back he settled in the Brantford area and stayed. He was always so proud of being a Canadian. 'In Canada,' he said, 'you can do what you want, go where you want, say what you want within the law of the land.' Well, my father would roll over in his grave if he knew that Wayne's parents couldn't send their own child to the city of their choice, have him live with the people he wanted to and do what they all wanted as a group. It's not right."

The meeting was over. The fight wasn't.

Going back over all this, it's hard to believe now how it all snowballed. We appealed the OMHA decision to the parent

Ontario Hockey Association, which bounced it right back to the OMHA and left it up to them. We went before the Ontario Supreme Court to seek an injunction allowing the boys to play bantam hockey in Toronto, while we were filing our appeals with the CAHA. Mr. Justice Southey denied it on two counts: he believed that because the boys were under eighteen they did not have the legal right to take the OMHA to court; and in his opinion we had not exhausted all the appeal avenues available in hockey.

There was one avenue left, a sort of court-of-last-resort. We could go before a three-man OHA tribunal, an independent body that rules on such things when the parties can't get together. But that could take months. We were into October by then. Wayne could miss half a season. They'd beaten us. Wayne had three options left: go back to court and appeal Mr. Justice Southey's decision, go back to Brantford and play bantam or play junior "B" hockey in Toronto. None of them made any sense. We were whipped. But Wayne wasn't. He didn't know how it could be done or if it could be done. He only knew what the result had to be as far as he was concerned.

I'd about given up. "Wayne," I said, "why don't we just go home and you play wherever you can in Brantford?"

"Dad," he said – and there wasn't a shred of doubt in his voice – "I'm not going home. Regardless."

That left junior "B" or nothing. Why could he play junior "B" in Toronto when he couldn't play bantam? Because junior "B" comes under the jurisdiction of the Ontario Hockey Association, not the Ontario Minor Hockey Association. (Fortunately the OMHA had never suspended Wayne; it had only refused to let him transfer. If he'd been *suspended* the OHA would have honoured the suspension and he'd really have been up the creek.)

"He's living in Toronto and going to school here," Sam McMaster said. "Why not let him play for our junior "B" team?"

"Are you *crazy*?" I exploded. "There are twenty-year-olds

in that league. They're men! He's fourteen years old and weighs 135 pounds! He'll get *killed!*"

"Walter, he'll be all right," Sam said.

"Dad, I'll be all right," Wayne said.

So off we went to the Vaughan Arena in the township of Vaughan, home of the Vaughan Nationals, to meet the head coach, Gene Popiel. He was really something. In fact, after a while he started to irritate me.

For all his talk, Wayne was very hesitant. Remember, now, we are still talking about a fourteen-year-old boy. He didn't want to go back home, but if he stayed in Toronto and signed with the Nationals maybe he'd practice and practice and never get to play. Maybe they'd keep him on the bench and never let him on the ice in a game.

He needed encouragement. But after a "Hello, Wayne," Popiel isn't saying anything. He's taping a hockey stick, winding the tape around the handle. Just winding, and winding . . . .

Sam is looking at Wayne, trying to get an answer.

"Well, Wayne, are you going to sign this card or not? Gene doesn't have all day."

Wayne isn't moving. It's not that he doesn't want to sign; he's just nervous. And Popiel isn't saying anything. He isn't even looking up. He's just winding . . . and winding . . . and winding. He was driving me crazy.

"Sam," I said, "you have to understand what Wayne is thinking. He doesn't really know what he's getting into, or whether he might be jumping from the frying pan into the fire."

Gene looked up then. "Wayne," he said, "I've heard a lot about you. You come highly recommended, but I've never seen you play. If you go out and give a hundred and ten per cent, I owe you the right to play yourself off this hockey team. Until you do that, you're there."

Wayne picked up the pen and signed without any hesitation. He'd get a chance. That's all he wanted.

Gene kept his word. He worked the team hard in practice. Wayne thrived on it. For the first time in months, he had a place to play. And in his first game as a junior "B" he scored two goals.

Phyllis and I were there, of course. We were scared stiff. He looked so *small* out there. When he first joined the team, Wayne had tried to compensate by wearing defencemen's shinpads so that at least his legs would *look* bigger. He had to ditch them, though. He couldn't do a crossover step to save his life. The pads would catch and he'd fall down. Now here he was, a calf in a herd of buffalo. If Popiel had any doubts, Wayne must have ended them when he scored, because later on the Nats were two men short and Gene had him out killing the penalties. "Is he *crazy or something?*" I asked Bill Cornish. "Two men short, he's fourteen years old in his first game and he's got him killing *penalties?*"

"Shhh!" Bill said. "He'll be all right."

He was. With the score 3-2 the other team pulled their goalie and Wayne put one in the empty net. He had survived a game against the big kids and scored two goals. Phyllis and I quit worrying – about the on-ice stuff, anyway. Off the ice, it seemed we never got the chance.

Wayne played seven games with the Nationals and had five goals and five assists. He had a lot of things to learn – he couldn't make those soft passes he'd made in minor hockey. The league was too fast for that. And he was having trouble getting face-offs. But generally he was doing pretty well. More important, he was happy. He was smiling again. We thought we were over the hump.

And then came the telegram. It was from Mr. Kinkley and the OMHA. They still hadn't given up. The wire was to the Brantford Minor Hockey Association: "Be advised that Wayne Gretzky of your association has been indefinitely suspended by OMHA from all competition until junior eligibility clarified. Please advise player soonest." Isn't that something? They knew Wayne was doing well in junior "B", that he wasn't going to play bantam again so therefore he was out of their jurisdiction. But they were still trying to get him. The way they must have had it figured was that, although they couldn't touch Wayne themselves, the OHA and the OMHA honour one another's suspensions. If they could get the OHA to honour this one, then Wayne couldn't play junior "B".

What good would that do them? Well, Mr. Kinkley did admit that if the OHA did honour the suspension to keep him out of junior "B", then the OMHA might allow Wayne to come to Brantford to play minor hockey. "Every option would be looked into to see that he could play hockey," he told reporters.

Newspapers all over the country were having a field day with the story. Most of them were taking Wayne's side and saying that given the unusual circumstances he should be allowed to play where he wished. And here was this man offering to see if Wayne could be allowed to come back to play in Brantford. Wasn't that nice of him? They'd driven him out of bantam hockey in Toronto, now they were trying to drive him out of junior "B" – but they'd consider the possibility of taking back the biggest drawing card they'd ever had and let him play minor in Brantford. I wonder if they thought Wayne should be grateful?

In fact, that was the second time the business of Wayne going back to Brantford and forgetting the whole Toronto thing had come up. Shortly after we had failed to get the injunction, I had gotten a call from the coach of the major midget team at home. He had said he'd like to have Wayne on his team.

"Oh," I said. "And what would your plans be for him?"

"Well, I can use another body," he said. "There'll be sickness, and maybe injury. I might even want him for penalty killing."

I had thanked him for his generosity and hung up. The following week we went to see Sam McMaster and Popiel.

Fortunately, the OHA took a sensible attitude toward the whole mess. OHA president Cliff Phillips announced that while OMHA suspensions were as a rule recognized by his organization, it was a matter for the full executive to decide. Since there wasn't a full executive meeting scheduled until December 5, which was a month away, Wayne would be allowed to keep playing until then at least. Finally, somebody was thinking about Wayne playing, instead of hockey politics.

And in the end, the OHA backed us up completely. The executive met December 5 and refused to support the suspension. "The OMHA thinks he was improperly transferred to Toronto and we don't agree," Mr. Phillips said. "We feel that the transfer was proper and he remains eligible to play junior."

So, after a court case, six months worth of bickering and enough turmoil to give us all ulcers, the simple little move to Toronto was accomplished. There was, however, a final installment.

Five years later Sam McMaster was getting married and we were looking for an appropriate present. We thought and thought, and naturally our thoughts went back to the days when the whole mess had started, when Sam kept assuring us that there'd be no trouble and we'd never go to court. "A piece of cake," he had kept saying, "a piece of cake." We knew there could be only one present.

Inside a box, carefully wrapped, we placed a piece of cake.

Wayne stayed with the Nationals, playing three age groups above his years. (The age difference made for some funny situations. "Look at that guy, Dad," Wayne said once pointing to a teammate. "He's married, he's got a family – and I can't even get a driver's licence!") Although he hadn't started until the season was almost two months old, he scored 27 goals and got 33 assists for 60 points and was named the league's rookie-of-the-year. In one sense, though, we'd failed: we certainly hadn't taken the spotlight off him. If anything it was brighter than ever.

There were all kinds of stories and rumours about the money we'd received from the Nats for moving Wayne to them, and the gifts we were supposed to have been given. None of them were true. The only gift we got was the gift of friendship from the Cornishes, and we'll treasure that always.

They wouldn't accept anything for Wayne's board and room. During the summer after the first season, I tried to give Bill an envelope with some money in it for board and he got all upset. "We took Wayne here because we wanted him here," he said. "Put your money in your pocket." The second year the Nats helped Wayne with his board, which made Wayne feel better – but later on the Cornishes were at it again. Kim stayed with them for two years while she went to school and they wouldn't take anything then, either. Later on, after he'd turned pro, Wayne sent them to Hawaii for a holiday. It was the only payment they ever accepted.

So the master plan to take the pressures off Wayne hadn't quite worked out the way we'd hoped. But he'd grown in a lot of ways through that year, and had proved a lot of things. Most of all, he was happy. You know, it's ironic how it all worked out. If the OMHA had left him alone he'd have played bantam hockey in Toronto and never got the chance to play junior "B" that early. And the final irony was that in the end the OMHA was proved wrong.

Remember the Brian Rorabeck case? We hadn't gone to that last court of appeal, the OHA tribunal, because it might have taken months. Well, Brian Rorabeck went all the way. Sam McMaster took his case before the tribunal, which ruled 2-1 that he had complied with the MTHL residence rules, and that no rules existed that required him to obtain OMHA permission before transferring. So Wayne was never guilty of any rule-breaking and had we wanted to, once the Rorabeck case was cleared, we could have gone before that tribunal ourselves and been given the same clearance. He could have gone back and played bantam in Toronto if he had wanted.

He never bothered. By that time he was having too much fun in junior "B". And that's all the three of us ever wanted.

Chapter 9

WAKE UP, WAYNE, THE GAME'S ON

"I was in jail. Behind bars! And all I could think of was 'What will Big Wally say?' "

– Wayne Gretzky, 1983.

It was supposed to be the year we could relax. After all the arguing and bickering and fighting with the OMHA, after the court case and the hearings and all the publicity that had come with them, Wayne was firmly settled into junior "B" hockey. He'd been rookie-of-the-year despite missing almost two months of the season. Most of all he was *legal*. The only people running at him now would be wearing skates, and he'd always been able to handle that. It was going to be a fun season, a no-problem season when we could just sit back and watch. We could hardly wait.

I went to see his first game, and he looked terrible.

Well, that was all right. There were adjustments to make. Gene Popiel wasn't there. He'd had a disagreement with the organization. Wayne had a new coach, a man named Bruce Wallace. The Nats had moved their headquarters to Seneca College and were now the Seneca Nationals. After that rookie season Wayne was bound to be a marked man. He'd get straightened out.

I went to his second game. He was still terrible. He had no zip, no drive, he just wasn't Wayne. And every time I asked him what was wrong he'd say, "Nothing. Nothing's wrong." It went on game after game. Finally, after an exhibition game in Oshawa, I stood at the bottom of the stairs waiting for him (I never go into the dressing room. I always figure parents have got no business in there.) and asked him one last time. What was wrong?

"Nothing," he said, and tried to brush past me to go up the stairs.

Well, that was about enough. "Wayne," I said, "you either tell me what the trouble is right now or you're coming home tonight. That's all there is to it, I'm not going to argue with you anymore. You're not yourself. Something's the matter. You tell me now, or we go home."

It was like all the air went out of him. He looked a little bit scared – not of me, but of something else. "I fell asleep on the bench tonight," he blurted. "*I fell asleep*. I can barely get up and down the ice, I'm so tired! I didn't want to say anything because I didn't want to get benched, and I thought it would go away. I don't know what it is."

Naturally, the first thing we thought of was mononucleosis. It hits kids sometimes, and when it does the only cure is a complete rest. That would be too bad, but no real disaster. At least we'd know what it was. So we took him to a doctor in Toronto. He ran all the tests. It wasn't mono. Now we were really worried.

We took him home to our own doctor in Brantford. He couldn't find anything, either. Meanwhile Wayne was staying at home doing nothing but sleep – and no matter how much he slept, he was still tired. He'd get home from school at 3:30 and go to bed. He'd get up at 5:30 long enough to have something to eat, then go back to bed. By 11 p.m. he'd be up because he was hungry, but then he'd fall back into bed and sleep until it was time to go to school. It went on like that, day after day.

We didn't know what to do. Finally, Popiel suggested we take him to Dr. Charles Bull, who'd been with the Team Canada program since 1972. Dr. Bull checked Wayne out. He described what he had as "an atypical type of mono," prescribed a lot of rest and gave him a tonic crammed full of vitamins he said Wayne was lacking. Wayne started taking the medicine, and I'll be darned if he didn't start to recover, just like that. We never did find out exactly what the problem was – a virus of some kind, I guess – but whatever it was it went away and never came back. Now, finally, Wayne could concentrate on hockey and start playing the way people expected him to, the way I knew he could.

Checking him out with the various doctors took about two weeks, all during the pre-season. Wayne didn't miss a league game, although he probably should have. In the meantime, he was finishing his Grade Ten at West Humber Collegiate, playing for the school basketball team and running cross-country. It was Christmas before he felt totally right, at which point he was so far down in the scoring race you'd have had to tunnel to find him. In the end he did have a pretty good season. The Senecas won the league title and Wayne finished fourth in scoring with 36 goals and 36 assists for 72 points, plus 75 points in 23 playoff games.

By that time he was starting to fill out, too. When Wayne was twelve he'd gone to Jim's Gym in Brantford because he was a little guy. It didn't look like he was ever going to be very big, and he wanted to do something about it. Jim put him on a weight-training program – but not to put bulk on him; his bones were still growing and at that age heavy lifting can do damage. Wayne stuck with it and in a fifteen-month stretch he'd gone from 5'1" and 89 pounds to 5'8" and 130. "When he first got here," general-manager Colin MacKenzie told reporters during the playoffs, "he was so small we were embarrassed to put him on the ice – until he scored a couple of goals."

By now he was starting to attract further outside attention. Under major junior "A" rules, a boy is eligible to be drafted by a junior "A" club once he is one year into the midget age group. Although Wayne had played two years in junior "B", from an age standpoint he was just completing his first year of midget. Naturally, the "A" teams were keeping a close eye on the eligible kids. That was why he'd insisted on playing right away: he had this bug in his head that if he missed any games he might get overlooked in the draft.

Although each junior "A" club has its own scouts, the league has a central scouting organization to provide information to all clubs in the form of a list of players rated in numerical order according to playing potential. At first Wayne wasn't rated too highly. I think he was something like a hundred and eighty-sixth on the early list. As the season went on his name kept moving up on the list. At mid-season he was seventy-ninth, then somewhere in the thirties and, finally, second behind Steve Peters of the Peterborough Petes.

Not everyone believed. During the playoffs that second year, I was standing in the corner in the Seneca Arena behind the general-manager of one of the junior "A" clubs. Wayne had gone into the corner after the puck and been knocked down. As the other team started down the ice, the GM leaned over to one of his scouts and said, "See, I told you! There's no way that kid can play major junior "A" hockey. Forget about him."

So much for scouting. But we knew he'd be drafted and we knew he'd go early. Our concern was which club would do it.

We wanted Wayne close to home. Toronto was one thing, but there's a heck of a difference between driving sixty miles and driving five hundred. We even discussed Niagara Falls, which is also about sixty miles from Brantford. But word was that they "had seen these sixteen-year-old wonders before," and Wayne had heard something else.

"You know what they're saying, Dad?" he asked. "They're saying that if they draft me they get two for one."

"Two for one?" I asked. "What do you mean, two for one?"

"Dad," he said patiently, "They're saying that if they get me, they get you, too."

"Oh," I said.

I guess they had me figured as one of those interfering parents. We suspected Niagara Falls wouldn't draft Wayne.

Oh, well, Toronto had worked out fine in junior "B". Why not in junior "A"? So I sat down and wrote letters to teams in places like Niagara Falls, Sudbury and Sault Ste. Marie. "Please don't waste your draft choice if you have any plans for drafting Wayne; he will not report."

I thought that was fair. Junior "A" hockey is a competitive business and the top draft picks coming out of midget can make a lot of difference in success and dollars over the next four years. There was no sense letting one of those teams pick Wayne when we knew he wouldn't go.

Angelo Bumbacco paid no attention. He phoned me from the Soo and told me he was going to draft Wayne. "Forget it," I said. "He doesn't want to go and we don't want him to. You're wasting your time and your pick. He won't show up."

Angelo was determined, I'll give him that. He told me the Soo was a nice place, that the team travelled by plane, that the organization was first-rate. "Good," I said. "He's not coming."

"Mr. Gretzky," he said, "I'm a pretty good judge of character, and you're not the type of father who'd do anything to harm your son's career. And I know Wayne wants to play "Junior "A". That's why I know I won't be wasting our pick."

The draft was held in Toronto. Wayne was there and called us as soon as he was selected. "Better buy a plane, Dad," he said. "It's the Soo."

Angelo had drafted him anyway. He had third pick after Oshawa Generals, who took Tom McCarthy of the North York Rangers, and Niagara Falls, who took Peters. (In 1979, they were both second-round NHL draft picks: McCarthy by the Minnesota North Stars, Peters by the Colorado Rockies.) I couldn't believe it. I'd told him again and again that if he drafted Wayne he wouldn't report. Every time he'd phoned I'd told him. When you're told by mail and by telephone that something's not going to happen, shouldn't you perhaps get the message? I work for a phone company. I know about telephones. You talk into one end and the message comes out the other end down the line. It's wonderful. But no one was listening.

Even Reg Quinn, the owner of the Senecas, thought we were making a mistake. He had no axe to grind. He just liked Wayne. So one night he invited Phyllis and me out for dinner. "You have to think of Wayne's welfare," he said. "You could risk ruining his career by doing this. Let him go to the Soo."

I couldn't get over the irony of it. Two years before we'd wanted him to play in Toronto, sixty miles from home, and hockey said no. Now hockey was telling us that if he wanted to play junior "A", he'd have to play five hundred miles from home. We were still talking about a young boy, sixteen instead of fourteen, but now it wasn't a case of what *we* wanted, it was a case of what *hockey* wanted.

Finally, Bumbacco phoned Gus Badali. "Just get them up for a look," he pleaded. "Just a look around, that's all I ask."

We flew up for a look. Wayne hated the place.

He was angry and hard to get along with all day. Angelo and Jim McAuley, one of the team owners, took us everywhere and showed us everything. They couldn't have been nicer. They were wasting their time. There was no way.

Finally, they took us to the Bodnars, a family that used to live in Brantford. Wayne had played minor hockey and lacrosse with Jim and Sylvia's boy, Steve. I'm sure it was a last resort on Angelo's part. By now even he was beginning to understand we were serious. Then an incredible thing happened: they said Wayne could live with them, and he did a complete about-face. He'd sign with the Greyhounds. He'd stay in the Soo. No problem. Is there anyone out there who really understands kids?

For us, of course, it still wasn't the ideal situation. The Soo was still five hundred miles from Brantford. This time there'd be no hopping down to see his home games the way there'd been with the Nats. But with the Bodnars looking after him it was the Cornish situation all over again. We knew he'd be well cared for in a good home. And there was something else: it wasn't our hockey season, it was Wayne's. By now he knew he had a good chance to play professionally. None of us needed another mess like the one we'd gone through getting him moved to Toronto. And Wayne was happy. What else was there?

We flew back to Brantford. We all had work to do. Wayne had to get into the best shape of his life for the jump to junior "A". And me? I had to start fooling around with a tuner and a bunch of copper wire to build an antenna. By the time the season started I wanted a radio that would pick up the Greyhound games, home and away. Maybe we couldn't see Wayne play, but there was no way we weren't going to listen. And Wayne did get off to an exciting start. It was so exciting he wound up in jail.

One of the first things Wayne found out when he joined the Greyhounds was that the club had an initiation rite for rookies. They had to "streak" naked through the park. But the rookies weren't worried. It had to be a joke.

Then one night the word came: "Rookies outside. Wear T-shirts, shorts and shoes. Nothing else." The six rooks and one veteran "supervisor" were piled into a van and driven to the park. They were standing there feeling kind of silly and a little bit nervous. Then the vet took their T-shirts, collected them in a sack, tossed the sack into the van, and started to eye their shorts as the van pulled away.

They have now gone from nervous to scared. They were still staring at one another when the sirens started. Engines roared, brakes squealed, and suddenly they were surrounded by police cars and a paddy wagon. "All right," a policeman snaps, "get in the wagon!"

Well, Wayne's taking a law course in school. He's not going to stand for this. "Officer," he protests, "what's wrong with standing around in our shorts? What law are we breaking?"

They don't seem impressed.

"Gretzky," the policeman snarls, "Get in the *wagon!*"

They got in the wagon. Before they knew it they were in the station house behind bars. Wayne's whole life is flashing before his eyes. What would his Dad say? If he got a criminal record he couldn't cross the border into the U.S., so there would go the whole pro career. He was one scared kid.

But he's a competitor, Wayne is. "I'm entitled to one phone call!" he fumed. "Why haven't I been given my one phone call?"

He is *hot* - so hot that he almost doesn't notice the veterans on the team come around the corner with Muzz MacPherson, the coach. They're laughing so hard they're almost crying.

He looks around, and the police are laughing, too. And all of a sudden six rookies know they've been had.

It turns out that after the streaking session the year earlier the police had come to the Greyhounds with a proposition. How about forgetting that joke, which could get the kids in trouble and force the police into actions they didn't want to take? Instead, fake it, and the police would co-operate to make it realistic. It would be a better initiation, and no one would get hurt.

The Greyhounds agreed. The police co-operated beautifully. Even the six kids admitted it had been a heck of a good joke - once they stopped shaking.

The morning after Wayne's first league game as a Greyhound the Soo *Star* carried the following, overheard in the dressing room as the boys were dressing to leave the rink:

Wayne Gretzky: "What's this Brut stuff?"

Doug Kimball: "It's aftershave lotion."

Wayne Gretzky: "Aftershave lotion? What am I supposed to do with aftershave lotion?"

It was a pretty good way of summing things up. Here was

this kid who'd just scored 3 goals and had 3 assists in a 6-1 win over the Oshawa Generals in his first game of junior "A", and he was still too young to shave. (I guess Wayne was a little self-conscious about it, too. He asked Kimball if it was all right if he put the Brut on even if he hadn't shaved.) Because by that time people were beginning to shake their heads a little bit.

When the Greyhounds drafted him, even MacPherson wasn't all that sure of what they were getting. "I'd never seen him play and I asked our scouts if they were sure," Muzz told reporters just after the regular season started. "They said he was exciting and would fill the building." Then he kind of giggled and said, "I heard that line about how we'd have to be patient, too."

Right there he burst out laughing. In pre-season Wayne had 31 points (9 goals and 22 assists) including 6 in his first game as a junior "A". He was sixteen playing against eighteen- and nineteen-year-olds, and it was reaching the point where teams were getting excited if they held him without a point. During one game in Windsor he took a stiff check early – a bit of a cheap shot – and didn't get a point. The next day in the Windsor paper it was big stuff – they'd stopped him and maybe intimidated him.

When the league schedule opened, he started with the 6 points against Oshawa. In his fourth game he had another 6 points and in the seventh he set up the first 6 goals and scored the last one into an empty net in a 7-5 win over the Ottawa 67s. After seven games he led the league in scoring with 10 goals and 16 assists. He had at least one point per game, and twice he'd had a point on every Greyhound goal. I don't think he was intimidated.

It more or less went on that way all year, with Wayne battling Bobby Smith of Ottawa for the scoring title, and Dino Ciccarelli of the London Knights hanging in third place in points, but making his own run for the goal-scoring championship. It ended up with Smith on top with 69 goals and 123 assists for 192 points, Wayne second at 70-112-182, and

Ciccarelli third at 72-70-142. To show you the kind of year it was in the OMJHA, Wayne would have set the all-time league scoring record in any other year. As it was he broke the old record of 170 points set by Mike Kaszycki of the Soo the season before. His problem was that Smith broke it better.

Wayne settled for the rookie scoring record, which had been held by John Tavella of the Soo at 137 points. He also broke Tavella's goal-scoring record of 67 for a rookie by getting a pair in his second-last game to tie, and a hat trick in the final game to set it at 70. He was named both the league's most-gentlemanly player (fourteen penalty minutes on the season), and was runner-up to Smith as most-valuable player. Only one thing kept it from being a perfect year. As a team, the Greyhounds weren't doing well.

Oh, the Greyhounds were bringing in the people. Attendance the year before in the Soo had averaged 1,750 per game. Now they were filling the 3,400-seat Memorial Gardens, and when they went on the road the fans were filling other rinks. Because by then the publicity surrounding Wayne was getting fantastic.

And from that October on, he was No. 99.

Say that fast enough and it sounds easy. Believe me, it wasn't. It was Muzz MacPherson who suggested it. Wayne had worn No. 9 all through his career, but when he got to the Greyhounds it was already in use by a returning vet, Brian Gualazzi. In training camp and pre-season he wore 14 and 19, but he'd never liked numbers starting with 1. Mac-Pherson said: "Well, if you can't have one 9, how about two? Wear 99."

Wayne looked at him kind of funny. "Guys see that, and they'll be running at me," he said.

"Wayne," Muzz said patiently, "they're going to be running at you anyway."

"Okay," Wayne answered. "Why not?"

And that was how it started. The Greyhounds phoned Phil Esposito of the New York Rangers, who'd started the big number craze when he was traded from the Boston Bruins to the New York Rangers, had found his No. 7 taken and jumped to 77. Neither Wayne nor the Hounds wanted Phil to think it was some kind of snide shot at him. Phil just laughed and said "Go ahead," so away they went.

The fans picked up on it right away, particularly on the road. "Hey, Gretzky! This isn't football!" "What are you try-ing to prove, you hot dog?" But Wayne had expected it, especially the hot dog part. He'd been living with that one almost from the day he started scoring – and to be honest, there was one time he deserved it.

Because it started when he was so young, he's learned to live with the razzing, or ignore it. Oh, occasionally when it gets really bad he'll point to the scoreboard – not looking at the fans, just pointing as if to say, "Who's winning, you turkeys?" Generally, though, he lets his performance speak for itself. But there was one time when he couldn't resist.

It happened during his first season with the Nationals, in the fifth and deciding game of a best-of-five quarter-final playoff series against the Bramalea Blues. With just under fifteen minutes left in the third period, the Blues led 6-3. For the Nats it was all over but the crying, and the Blues were giving it to them pretty good from the bench. It turned out to be a mistake.

As Wayne skated past, one of them shouted, "Let's see you get four in a row now, hotshot!"

Wayne looked over at him for a second, then lined up for the faceoff. He won it, carried the puck into the slot and fired it over the goalkeeper's shoulder. Now it was 6-4.

At 9:25 he scored again on a power play to make it 6-5. Brian Wood, another Brantford minor hockey product, tied it at 10:39, and fifty-seven seconds later Wayne cut loose with a thirty-foot slapshot the goalie barely saw to put the Nats up 7-6.

The opportunity was too good to pass up. He skated in front of the Bramalea bench and stood there, holding up four fingers and waving them at the Blues, who sat stunned by the turnaround. Then he went back and drew the assist on the Nats' fifth straight goal, which turned out to be the winner as they won 8-7. Was he a hot dog that night? You bet.

It was the only time I saw him act that way, though, and considering the attention he was getting it's a wonder it didn't happen more often. It wasn't just on the ice. When he got to the Soo, his minor hockey reputation, combined with his fast start as a junior, brought the media people in droves.

In a way it was kind of funny. All those reporters and TV and radio people coming at him from all directions, and one of the first questions they all asked was how he was managing to cope with all the publicity.

"I'm not trying to hide from it," he told them. "I think it's fine. I don't want to get older and wonder what it would have been like. This way when I'm thirty or thirty-five I can look back and say, 'Gee, that was nice!' "

It just built and built. His teammates started calling him Ink because of the publicity (when they weren't calling him Pretzel because they thought they could break him about that easily). One day in November, a man phoned from *Weekend Magazine* and asked for an interview. Wayne said, "Sure, as long as it's over breakfast and you buy." That same day he had to do an interview with the Toronto *Star*, one with the Toronto *Sun*, do some filming with CBLT-TV, and finally a film with the *Hockey Night in Canada* crew. I guess he figured breakfast wasn't too much to ask.

But the team wasn't winning. For quite a while it was in last place, even though Wayne's line with Dan Lucas and Paul Mancini was really flying. And the criticism started to come, the same kind Wayne had faced so often before: he was a good scorer, sure, but his checking was suspect. MacPherson had an answer for that. He was using Wayne every second he could get him onto the ice. When Wayne was out there, there was that much better chance that the Greyhounds would score.

"Two years ago Reggie Leach scored 63 goals for Philadelphia," he snorted, "but Fred Shero said he couldn't backcheck. So last year Leach scored 32. Any time you've got a guy who can score 63 goals, let him, and find someone else to backcheck. Hell, Bobby Clarke did it for Leach all the way through junior in Flin Flon."

There are a lot of different theories in hockey and there's no saying for sure which ones are right and which are wrong. In any season the one that's right is the one that wins, and Muzz wasn't winning. On February 22, 1978, he resigned, Paul Theriault was hired, and for Wayne it was a drastic change.

Theriault did turn things around a little bit. In their last eleven league games they went 9-1-1 and just missed finishing fourth. Wayne was happy about that, but personally he felt like he was in chains. Reporters covering the OHA final series against Ottawa questioned the fact that Theriault had Wayne down to one regular shift instead of using him as much as he was used to. They couldn't believe it. Theriault didn't budge. "I happen to think he's more effective that way," he told them. Well, maybe. But the Greyhounds lost the eight-point series in eight games and Wayne got only two goals. Slump or system? We'll never know.

I do know one thing, though. It all worked out for the best – because while Wayne was trying to settle his problems, the pros up above were back into a shooting war and Wayne was ticketed to be one of the bullets.

Since 1963, the National Hockey League had had an agreement with the Canadian Amateur Hockey Association that it would not sign juniors under twenty years of age. That way the junior clubs wouldn't lose their star attractions early, and it gave them a better chance to make money and (from the NHL standpoint) kept what amounted to an almost-free farm system pushing that talent along. But the WHA changed all that. It needed star players right away if it was to survive. So it went after the kids.

When Bassett signed Dillon in 1973 and took Napier two

years later, while at the same time the Houston Aeroes grabbed another under-age Marlie, John Tonelli, the NHL started screaming. They demanded that the federal government put a stop to the practice by refusing funding in WHA cities like Winnipeg and Edmonton, where they were trying to build new arenas. The NHL also asked the International Ice Hockey Federation to refuse to sanction the WHA's exhibition games with European teams.

Finally, in 1977, the WHA agreed to cut it out. But Bassett ignored the ruling and signed Linseman. League president Howard Baldwin promptly suspended him for six months. The war was supposed to be over – and now Skalbania and the WHA wanted to start it up again.

Really, they had no choice. Except for some cities, the league was dying. Skalbania's average attendance in Indianapolis was under five thousand. The cream of the established players, except for the ones signed early on in the WHA's existence, was under NHL contract. To survive, the WHA had to merge with the NHL or bring in a bunch of fresh young talent by going back to the under-age draft. The only way they could possibly achieve a merger was to force the old league to let them in – by stealing juniors before they were old enough for the NHL to sign them.

That was where Wayne came in. If there was an under-age junior to sign, he was the logical choice: he was already a star in junior and his age would get him a lot of media attention what with all the arguing and speculation over whether a seventeen-year-old should or could play pro. Wayne was unhappy where he was. If he waited for the NHL, he faced three more years of junior. For the WHA, he was perfect.

There is a point here that people have missed. Skalbania's offer wasn't the only one we had, or even the first. Actually, it was the third. Bassett made the first – to sign Wayne with Birmingham. Next came the New England Whalers, with an offer of a $250,000 signing bonus and a five-year contract with a three-year option. It was funny, really, because Gus and I were saying, "No, we don't want to tie you down that long!" and Wayne was saying, "We can't throw that kind of money away! I don't care whether I play NHL or WHA, I just want to play!" The fact that the Whalers had Gordie Howe didn't hurt, either.

It wound up being settled without us, because the Whalers withdrew the offer. They figured a merger with the NHL was coming and that they'd be one of the teams accepted; but signing an under-age junior, despite the NHL policy against it, might hurt their chances of being included in the merger. (The thing Wayne remembers most about that offer was that the salary for the first three years would have been $50,000 each year. Jack Kelly, who was general manager then, had said Wayne shouldn't get big money for the first three years because "without the WHA he'd only be playing junior anyway for $25 a week.") So New England was out of the running for Wayne – but the WHA still wanted to sign him in order to keep the pressure on for a merger with the NHL. The logical team was Indianapolis, because with attendance as bad as it was the Racers didn't figure to be one of the teams taken in by the NHL anyway. Colleen Howe, Gordie's wife, phoned Skalbania and suggested he sign Wayne.

You'd almost think fate had a hand in it. If Theriault hadn't changed the system with the Greyhounds, Wayne might have been content to stay another couple of years in junior shooting for the Memorial Cup. He wouldn't have gone to the Racers, which means he wouldn't have wound up in Edmonton. If he'd stayed in junior until the draft, he could have been shipped off to the last-place team in the NHL, and a lot of great things might not have happened.

And Phyllis and I wouldn't have been flying out of Indianapolis on a private jet, leaving a seventeen-year-old down there to make his mark in a game where everyone was older, almost everyone was bigger, and everyone would be looking for a piece of the superkid.

"He'll be all right," Phyllis said.

"Sure," I said. "He'll be fine."

Chapter 10

THE INCREDIBLE SHRINKING FRANCHISE

WAYNE GRETZKY . . . PHENOM OR PHONY?

– Action Sports Hockey magazine headline, Nov., 1978.

Training camp for the Indianapolis Racers opened September 11, 1978. Fifty-three days and eight games later, Wayne was an Edmonton Oiler.

It seems sort of silly now, when you look back on it: all the fuss over whether he'd turn pro, all the secrecy in sneaking off to Vancouver to meet Nelson Skalbania, all the excitement about the signing. His entire pro career in Indianapolis is contained in one line in the NHL record book:

1978-79 Indianapolis . . . WHA   8   3   3   6   0

Eight games as a Racer: 3 goals, 3 assists, 6 points and no penalty minutes. Somehow, when signing that contract on the plane, we'd thought it would last a little longer.

The thing was, Mr. Skalbania's plans to make hockey go in Indianapolis had hit a slight flaw: Indianapolis didn't want it. At least, not in sufficient numbers to make it anything close to a break-even proposition. He'd bought fifty-one per cent of the franchise for one dollar, plus agreeing to assume all existing debts. Before the season was over he wound up folding the team, saying he'd spent $1 million plus $200,000 in personal expenses. "To break even in Indianapolis I have to gross $60,000 per game," he said. "We grossed $30,000. Once we played New England, the first-place team, and drew 4,372 people. The gross was $29,000. It cost me $33,000. When I'm paying more to watch the game than the entire crowd combined, that tells me something."

Back in November, though, he thought the franchise might be saved if he could lower the payroll and get a cash transfusion to help him over the bad spots. Selling Wayne seemed an obvious answer. He'd tried to give the Indianapolis fans a budding superstar and it hadn't made any difference. So why not sell him, use the money to get two or three young kids, and start over? (Ironically, one of the young players he did sign was Mark Messier, who played five games in Indianapolis, moved to Cincinnati, and became an Oiler when Edmonton joined the NHL.)

Mr. Skalbania flew to Indianapolis, broke the news to Wayne, and gave him a choice: did he want to go to Edmonton or Winnipeg? The way we decided on Edmonton is a real indication of how much of what happens in hockey is based on rumour.

There was a rumour that John Ferguson, the former Montreal Canadien star, was going to coach in Winnipeg. That scared Wayne a little bit because we'd heard Fergie was kind of a rough, tough guy who liked his hockey and his players just that way. I thought he wouldn't like a player of Wayne's style. On that basis we thought he'd be better off in Edmonton. We also heard another rumour that Rudy Pilous, the Jets' general-manager, had advised the team owners not to buy Wayne because there was no way he was worth the money Mr. Skalbania was asking, and there was no way he'd be that big in the NHL, where the Jets figured they'd be once the leagues merged, which now seemed inevitable.

As it turned out, Fergie did go to Winnipeg on November

28 – but as vice-president and general-manager, not as coach – and the rumour had been wrong, anyway. He actually thought Wayne was a great player, even comparing him to Jean Beliveau. And during the playoffs, the majority owner of the Jets, Michael Gotuby, came up to me and said he was really sorry it hadn't worked out, that he'd been given the wrong advice.

But he was wrong. It *had* worked out, for Wayne, anyway. Things ended on a disappointing note because the Oilers lost the league championship series, four games to two, to the Winnipeg Jets. But from a personal standpoint, his first pro season couldn't have been much better.

In shifting from Indianapolis to Edmonton Wayne hadn't missed a game. He'd played the full 80, and in this first season as a pro – a year he'd entered with a target of 20 goals and 40 assists – he'd wound up with 46 goals, 64 assists and 110 points. He'd finished third in WHA scoring and been chosen rookie-of-the-year as well as second-team All-Star centre behind Cincinnati's Robbie Ftorek. He'd played on a line with fifty-one-year-old Gordie Howe on right wing and Mark Howe on left as the WHA All-Stars swept three games from a touring Soviet Union side. ("Ain't it somethin'?" Gordie chortled. "One kid is seventeen, the other is twenty-three and the line is still the oldest in hockey because of the old goat on right wing.")

Considering the short time Wayne was there, a lot happened in Indianapolis. He scored his first two goals as a pro in the fifth game of the season – against the Edmonton Oilers. The Ayres young men's wear store in Indianapolis set up the Ayres Great Gretzky Fan Club. (For $2.50 you got a glossy membership card, autographed picture and the Racers' pennant and patch. Among the first of the fifteen hundred to sign up: Keith, Glen and Brent Gretzky.) He boarded with the Dr. Terry Fredrick family, bought a sports car, enrolled for twice-weekly four-hour night classes at the Broad Ripple High School, (where his fellow students had no idea he was a hockey player) and went about the business of proving he belonged in pro hockey at seventeen.

As usual, there were doubters. Shirley Fischler, writing in *Action Sports Hockey* magazine, put it this way:

". . . There are those who suggest that Wayne Gretzky is the best young prospect since Bobby Orr arrived in the NHL twelve years ago. Others are not so certain; they suspect that rather than being a phenom, the abundantly-paid, 5'11", 164-pounder could be as phony as a three-dollar bill. As a big leaguer, that is . . . the question persists: will Wayne fold up under the pressure? He says he will not; that he *is* for real . . . Now we will see if Wayne is a young man of his word."

There was also some question as to whether he'd even be playing pro hockey that season. All summer there had been reports that the merger was at hand; and that if it did come, the NHL would stick to its guns and refuse to sign or use under-age players. Mr. Skalbania admitted to the possibility. His options, he said, were to rent Wayne out to the highest bidder elsewhere in hockey until he reached signing age (several teams in the Western Canada Hockey League were interested), or to let him out of his contract and take his losses on what the signing had cost him to date (which, although it wasn't public knowledge, would have been the $50,000 he'd given me the day we had talked in Vancouver in the event of just that kind of hitch).

Wayne tried his best to ignore it all. He took power skating lessons, taught at a hockey school for a couple of weeks in New Brunswick, did some promotional appearances for the team in Indianapolis and for the league in New York, and played baseball for two teams, the Polonaise Vets midgets and a few games with the Brantford Red Sox of the Inter-County major men's league. Naturally, reporters followed him and talked to the guys he played with so they could do more "What's Wayne Gretzky Really Like?" stories. Garry Stockdale, the Polonaise manager, gave them one scoop. "I asked Wayne for his registration fees," he said. "I told him you have to pay to play minor baseball. 'See my Dad,' he said. I tell you, money hasn't changed the kid a bit."

He pitched five games in a midget tournament in Oshawa, won the first four and lost 3-2 in the final. There are still people who'll tell you that hockey might not have been Wayne's best game, that he could have been a great pitcher had he chosen baseball, which is really his first love. But this was just for enjoyment and for getting himself into shape. He knew the pressure would be on once he got to Indianapolis. What he didn't know was the direction from which most of it would come.

The Racers' coach was Whitey Stapleton, who'd spent ten years on defence with the Boston Bruins and the Chicago Black Hawks and had played a big part in Team Canada's victory over the Soviet Union in the eight-game series in 1972. He was a good coach and a considerate man – too considerate for Wayne in his situation. He was so conscious of Wayne's welfare that he was determined not to put him in a pressure situation where people would expect wonders of him right away. "He's got years to do that," he said. What he didn't realize was that Wayne had been under pressure all his life, and that by trying to bring him along slowly he was actually making it worse. I really believe that if Whitey hadn't been concerned – for all the best reasons – and had just turned Wayne loose from the start, he'd have blossomed right away.

And then, suddenly, Wayne was an Oiler.

Peter Pocklington paid Mr. Skalbania $850,000 and agreed to assume the personal services contracts with Wayne and Indianapolis forward Peter Driscoll. The Oilers also got Eddie Mio. Mr. Pocklington was released from a key condition of sale in his original purchase of the Oilers from Mr. Skalbania, a clause under which he agreed to sell the team back to Mr. Skalbania should it ever join the NHL. Now he had Wayne and a team almost certainly bound for the NHL. And Nelson Skalbania, who'd started it all, was a few weeks away from being out of hockey entirely.

For his first five days in Edmonton, Wayne moved in with Glen Sather's family ("I've never seen a kid who eats like that one," Sather told reporters. "He eats more at meals than my whole family, and he's always up for snacks.") Then he moved in with Ray Bodnar and his wife. Ray was the brother of Jim Bodnar, with whom Wayne had lived in the Soo, so he was comfortable right away. In his second season he shared an apartment with Kevin Lowe, who happens to be a great cook. Of all Wayne's great moves, one of his smoothest is to the nearest fridge.

Incidentally, the move to Edmonton brought one last brush with the Canadian Amateur Hockey Association. Under the original WHA-CAHA agreement, a team signing a WHA player would pay $20,000 to the Canadian Major Junior Hockey Association – plus a bonus of $20,000 if he was under age. The three CMJHA leagues – Ontario, Quebec and Western Canada – would deduct administrative expenses, etc., and pay the remainder to the club. But now the WHA wasn't paying development money. To my knowledge, Wayne was the only one who did. Mr. Pocklington paid $20,000 on behalf of the club and another $20,000 on behalf of Wayne, which came off his signing bonus.

That really made me mad. Phyllis and I spent half a day with a lawyer. He said he didn't think Wayne should pay anything because, after all, he'd only been in the OHA for a year and was such an attraction he brought money in for everybody. "I'd pay them nothing," he said. But we did. Wayne felt grateful to Angelo and knew that his departure would cost the Greyhounds in attendance. I couldn't see it that way. The CAHA had stopped Wayne from playing bantam in Toronto, they'd tried to stop him from playing junior "B", and we'd had to go to court – and now we were paying them $40,000. I'll never understand that.

Money. Sometimes it seemed there were more Gretzky money stories than Gretzky hockey stories – stories about how much Wayne was getting under the table as a junior, stories about how much his contract with the Racers was worth, stories speculating on how much he was spending now that he was a seventeen-year-old rich kid. They had two things in common, those stories. Everybody was guessing, and everybody exaggerated.

Actually, Wayne has never been too concerned about money. When we flew to Vancouver to meet Mr. Skalbania to sign a deal we knew would be for more money than any of us had ever seen, this kid, who supposedly was getting so much under the table from his junior team, reached into his jeans, pulled out every cent he had on him for the trip, and began to count it. It didn't take long. It came to $1.50. Even now, when he's home in the summer, he'll be bumming five or ten dollars from Phyllis or me. He goes through dough. He's generous, sometimes too generous. He doesn't buy stupid things, but he's always buying things for someone else. There's nothing he wouldn't do or buy for the family. He just never carries any money for himself. He never did, and he certainly hasn't done anything to show he'll change.

In 1982, the people of Brantford honoured Wayne by renaming the North Park Arena Complex the Wayne Gretzky Sports Centre. At the official dinner, Wayne stood up and thanked everyone, including all his former coaches. But first he called Bob Hockin to the front and made a special presentation. "Here's the quarter I owe you, Uncle Bob," he said.

Well, that one went back a few years. When Wayne was ten he was constantly borrowing a quarter from Bob after games so he could get a Coke out of the machine. Every game, the same story: "Uncle Bob, can I borrow a quarter? Pay you back at practice." He paid back that quarter faithfully – and after every game he'd borrow it again. Somehow, he just never managed to have his own quarter on him when he needed it. And now, years later, he was making a point of paying off that twenty-five-cent debt once and for all.

"Isn't that nice?" I asked Phyllis.

"Oh, I don't know," she said. "Just before he did it he sent Brent over to me with a message: 'Mom, Wayne says will you please lend him a quarter.' "

When the money came, it came so quickly and Wayne was so young, it was more funny than a problem. The way it was set up all the cheques were deposited to an account with Wayne's accountant in Toronto, and he set up an account for Wayne in Edmonton. When Wayne needed some spending money, he wrote a cheque on that account. One day the teller, who'd seen Wayne depositing cheques for thousands of dollars, asked him why he didn't get a credit card.

"I can't have one," he said.

"Of course you can," she insisted. "Everyone can."

"Not me," Wayne said. "You have to be eighteen."

He was becoming such a name, you see, it was easy to forget how young he was. Sometimes even Wayne forgot. Once, he was sitting in the bar in the Edmonton Coliseum with some of the players shortly after being traded, just sipping on a soft drink, when the bartender came over and asked him to leave. It didn't matter what he was drinking. The rules were quite clear: no children allowed in the bar. And for a few weeks more, pro hockey player or not, Wayne Gretzky was a child.

The day he ceased to be one is a day we'll never forget.

He'd been in Edmonton about two weeks, when Mr. Pocklington phoned Gus and told him he wanted to sign Wayne to a twenty-one-year contract – nine years plus two six-year options, at $180,000 per year for nine, plus a $100,000 bonus. In a nice little promotional touch, that would make No. 99 an Oiler until 1999.

"No way," Gus said.

Peter called back and offered the same deal, only at $280,000 for each of the first nine years, plus the $100,000 bonus. The first contract, the one he'd purchased from Mr. Skalbania, was four years with a three-year option. In effect he was tearing up the option and adding five years to the deal to make nine, then adding the two six-year options. He wanted to have the official signing at centre ice the night of Wayne's eighteenth birthday, just before a game against Cincinnati.

He had his reasons. The merger with the NHL was still in the works. There was speculation that part of the NHL's price would be that all under-age players signed by the WHA would go into the NHL draft when they hit draft age. For Wayne that would have been 1981. All kinds of teams were manoeuvering to see if they could get the No. 1 pick and have a shot at him. If Peter could sign Wayne to a long-term deal, he'd be telling the NHL that the merger would have to be accomplished without stripping the WHA teams of their under-age talent. He'd also be keeping Wayne out of their clutches no matter what happened.

So there was Wayne with the decision: take the security and the raise, or stick to the original contract and gamble that he'd do really well and be in a strong position to renegotiate when the four-year option came into effect in 1982-83, or else negotiate with whatever NHL team got his draft rights should the merger situation work out that way.

Security won. Wayne kept thinking, "How could I live with myself if I hurt my leg tomorrow, knowing I'd thrown away $280,000 a year for nine years? I couldn't." Gus phoned Peter, and the party was on.

But first there was another party, far more informal. Word was out that the signing would take place. It was a big story and the Oilers wanted to get as much mileage out of it as possible. To the players it made no difference. They had party plans of their own.

Wayne's birthday fell on a Friday. The previous Tuesday, in a game against New England, he'd been knocked down by Gordie Roberts. As he fell, Wayne got mad and threw his stick and gloves in disgust. The next morning at practice, Steve Carlson, who'd had a role in the comedy hockey movie *Slap Shot* and naturally was nicknamed Hollywood, did a slapstick impression of Wayne's performance, even pretending to take off one skate so he could throw that, too. Wayne stood there, red-faced. He'd been had, and he knew it.

Already the guys were calling him Brinks. Now this. What next?

Well, next came a birthday cake: a soft, gooey Black Forest cake because, they explained, his fall during the New England game had looked so fake they all wanted to yell "Timber!" They gave it to him at the Thursday morning practice – right in the face.

It was all in good fun. Wayne was the youngest guy on the team. He was being razzed all the time. But he never hesitated to go to some of the older players for advice, particularly in the matter of the new contract. Because, although he'd agreed to sign the new deal, we had no idea what he was going through – or how close he came to making hockey history of a different sort.

Let Wayne tell it:

"I'd been thinking, and thinking, and thinking. I really didn't know what to do. Even when I went to the rink for morning practice the day I was supposed to sign, I wasn't sure. Some of the players were saying sign, some were saying don't. I had to call Dad – and I couldn't find him.

"I checked everywhere in Brantford. I phoned neighbours. They didn't know where he was, either. Finally, about 5:30, I got a call. He was in Edmonton. Peter had flown the whole family out so they could be there for the signing. And I really didn't know if I was going to sign.

"At the rink I was still thinking about it, still asking the older players. The best advice I got was from Ace Bailey. 'Sign it,' he said. 'Play to the best of your ability and you'll get a new contract two years from now anyway.' It was the same thing my Dad had told me – but I had other advice, too.

" 'Don't sign,' one of the older guys told me.

" 'But I've got to,' I said. 'They're having a *ceremony*! At *centre ice*!'

" 'Well, sign *Bob Smith*,' he said. 'They'll never know, and the contract won't be any good. You can renegotiate it or wait until you're really sure.'

"Does that sound silly? Maybe – but I was this close to doing it. When I signed, I actually started to make the B. On the contract the W isn't straight, it's kind of on a slant. That's because it started out to be a B. But I thought, 'I can't!'

"And to this day I wish I'd done it. I wish I hadn't signed that contract. I don't live in the past – but I'd like to see where I'd be today if I hadn't signed it. I'm happy and I'm grateful, but sometimes I lie awake thinking about it.

"Ace was right. Two years later Peter did rip up that contract and we signed a new one. He just came to me and said we'd readjust. He wanted to add five more years. I said no. We just worked out a new deal on the money. And it's *not* $1 million a year as everyone seems to think. Basically they just rubbed out the $280,000 per year for five and readjusted it.

"As it stands now I'll be twenty-seven when it's time to negotiate the first six-year option. I've got the security. I'm with a great team in a great hockey town. But sometimes I can see myself back there at centre ice with my Mom and Dad and the boys looking on and the fans cheering. There's this big birthday cake and the bottle of Baby Champagne from the players. I've got the pen in my hand and I'm signing: *Bob Smith.*

"I wonder if anyone would have noticed right away? I wonder what would have happened when they did? I wonder . . . ."

Kids. Here I was thinking everything was just fine, and here was Wayne wondering if he should sign as Bob Smith. Do you ever really know what they're thinking?

Anyway, Cincinnati spoiled the party. On December 12, Wayne had scored his first hat trick as a pro against them – after being benched by Sather the entire first period "for not helping out enough on defence." This time Cincinnati won 5-2 and held Wayne to one assist.

But he was legal now. No. 99 was eighteen. He could go into the pub with the boys and he could afford to buy a round. If he remembered to bring any money.

141

Chapter 11

WAIT 'TIL HE SEES NHL CHECKING

"They cost our league $6 million. You don't usually go to bed with people who cause you a lot of trouble."

– Harold Ballard, Toronto Maple Leafs, March, 1979.

The Oilers were in the National Hockey League. For only $6 million apiece, plus agreement to share equally the $6.35 million "closedown costs" of folding the Cincinnati Stingers and the Birmingham Bulls, plus agreement to give back all former NHL players signed by WHA teams and pay $125,000 for every player they bought back in an "expansion draft," the Oilers, the Winnipeg Jets, the Quebec Nordiques and the New England Whalers were grudgingly granted membership in the lodge.

Seven years, twenty-three franchises and thirty-five ownership groups earlier, franchises in the new World Hockey Association had sold for $25,000 apiece. Now the war was over, but generosity toward the POWs was not in the NHL's plans. The vote to expand had been 14-3, with Toronto, Boston and Los Angeles saying no. The war was over, but the casualties had been high. Bill Jennings of the New York Rangers estimated that from 1972-73 when the

WHA opened, to the day of the "expansion" – so called because other names like "merger" have a nasty sound to government people who investigate possible monopolies or anti-trust violations – the total cost to both leagues was around $100 million. It was a war the WHA had triggered by forming in the first place. As we found out in a hurry, the NHL was not about to forgive and forget.

Edmonton fans couldn't have cared less. The Oilers put season tickets on sale and sold all 15,242 in eleven days. Wayne was going into the NHL. We could hardly wait. We'd been hearing for a year that he'd never do in the big league what he was doing in the WHA. "They check in the NHL," people said. "He'll get bounced all over the rink." Now we were going to find out. The answer affected different people in different ways. For a Brantford man named Chuck Savory, it meant a few hundred dollars down the drain, midnight phones calls, and a razzing that didn't die down for months . . . .

Phyllis met Chuck on the street during the summer. He's a good guy and a Wayne Gretzky booster, but he's also a hockey fanatic not above placing a bet or two. Now he was doing his pre-season scouting.

"How do you think Wayne will do this year?" he asked her.

"Oh, he'll do all right," she said, not really giving it that much thought. "You know Wayne."

"No, no," Chuck insisted. "How many *goals* do you think he'll get? How many points?" Phyllis wasn't about to be drawn into that one. Later she made a bet with someone else that he'd get at least 42 goals, but for now she was playing it cool. "He'll do all right," she repeated.

Chuck thinks about it for a couple of days. He sits down, looks over the rosters, then heads for the rink where he and a few buddies have ice each Sunday for a pick-up game and bull session. They've done it for years. It's not unusual for the odd bet to come out of the afternoon's discussions. Chuck has thought it over. "I'll bet anybody whatever they want," he says, "that Wayne will not finish in the top twenty NHL scorers this season."

He got razzed, of course, but he hung in there. "I'm as big a Wayne fan as anyone here," he said. "But this is a hockey bet. Are you taking, or not?"

Oh, he had takers, that day and for days after as word got around. Brantford isn't that big a city. Stories like that spread quickly. People started looking him up. Chuck took them all. He hadn't rushed into this thing. He'd done his homework. Wayne was Wayne, but this was for money.

The season began. Wayne got his first NHL point opening night, an assist on a goal by Kevin Lowe at 9:49 of the first period in a 4-2 loss to Chicago. His first goal came four nights later with sixty-nine seconds to play to give the Oilers a 4-4 tie with the Vancouver Canucks. It wasn't your classic shot – he admitted later he half fanned on it – but he was on the board in the NHL. Slowly, he started creeping up through the pack. The more points he got, the more Chuck got ribbed. Finally, around Christmas time, it made Ted Beare's column in the Brantford *Expositor*.

"A local sportsman who should have known better bet a number of his friends that Wayne Gretzky wouldn't be among the top twenty scorers in the NHL this season. A few hundred dollars were involved. But that's the story of Wayne Gretzky's life. He's had to keep proving himself over and over with each step up the hockey ladder."

Now the razzing really started. People wouldn't let up. One midnight, Chuck's phone rang and someone said, "Is that the turkey who bet against Gretzky?" There was a wild gobbling sound, hoots of laughter, and the connection was broken.

Chuck was crushed. He even telephoned me to explain how he'd reasoned it out and it made sense in a way.

"You know I've always been a Wayne booster," he said. "But there are twenty other teams in the league. I looked at each roster and found at least one guy I thought had to beat out Wayne in his first year. Like, I looked at Montreal and saw Guy Lafleur. Could Wayne be expected to beat Lafleur? I looked at Toronto. Was he going to get more points than Darryl Sittler? Every team had at least one guy. So: twenty teams means he wouldn't finish in the top twenty. It was a logical bet!"

The next day he phoned the *Expositor* and asked for Beare. Ed O'Leary answered the phone. He recognized the voice immediately. He should have. He was one of the guys who'd bet. "Ted!" he whispered, putting his hand over the mouthpiece, "It's *Savory!*"

Ted takes the call. "Hello," he says, all innocence.

"Ted? Chuck Savory. Listen, you wrote a column that made me look like a damned fool. I think you should give me the privilege of responding."

Well, an item is an item. "Certainly," Ted responded. "What would you like to say?"

"I want you to say," Chuck answered, "that I'll pay 50 cents on the dollar if they take their money right now."

A lot of people did, because there was always the chance that Wayne could slump or get injured or something. And Chuck was happy to pay off. Paperwork, rosters and logic be damned. He knew when he was whipped.

Speaking of bets . . . .

There are a lot of hockey pucks in our rumpus room among the trophies and sticks and awards and ribbons the kids have collected over the years. Pucks for Wayne's first goal as a pro, his first goal in the NHL – milestone pucks, all of them, to give us a special sort of record of the high points in his career. And there's one that has special significance only for Phyllis.

During all the speculation about how Wayne would do in the NHL, Phyllis had quietly made one bet. I'd forgotten about it. I wasn't even aware that Wayne knew about it. So it caught everyone by surprise when he scored his 42nd goal, in a game March 15 in Edmonton against the Montreal Canadiens – and dove into the net to retrieve the puck. No. 42? What was the big deal about No. 42? At the rink, reporters went through the *NHL Guide* and the Oilers' fact book. Nothing. But Wayne knew. He had remembered his mother's bet – a forty-ounce bottle of rye that he'd score at least 42 goals on the season. It was no milestone in the NHL, but it was a big, big goal in Brantford. The least he could do, he figured, was present her with the puck.

Isn't it nice when the children don't forget?

Wayne doesn't say much about what people say or write about him, but he files it away. I think it helps him to establish personal goals. When he hears or sees that he can't do something, or won't be able to hit a certain level, he's got a new target. Early in his rookie season, he found one in an article written in the hockey program at Maple Leaf Gardens. Gretzky, it said, had had a great year in the WHA, finishing third in league scoring. But there was no way in the world he'd finish third in the NHL.

That did it. "Third," he told Oilers' PR man John Short. "I want to finish at least third."

And he took out after the leaders.

At the half-way point of the season, he was sitting in fifth place in the scoring race with 22 goals, 35 assists and 57 points, 26 points behind Marcel Dionne of the Los Angeles Kings – and the Oilers were dead last in the standings. Nowadays, with the team a success, people forget that: Edmonton wasn't always in love with the Oilers. There were times in that first year when they were considered kind of a joke. "Memo to Edmonton moneybags P. Pocklington," the Edmonton *Journal* reported the day after the team hit the basement. "Your employees have come down with that common business sickness known as the Peter Principle. After being promoted from the WHA where they won the '78-'79 league pennant they have reached their level of incompetence in the NHL."

"It's getting closer," Sather insisted.

"So's football season," sniffed the *Journal*.

The team was struggling, but Wayne was pecking away. After 52 games he had reached third – a distant third, but

146

still third – with 84 points, trailing Dionne by 15 and Guy Lafleur by 10. The three of them were to fight it out the rest of the way.

He was attracting a lot of attention now. "Amazing," people said. And they only shook their heads when I kept saying, "Wait till he gets healthy."

Because he wasn't healthy, and hadn't been most of the year. He'd picked the early part of his first NHL season to come down with tonsilitis. As the games went by it got steadily worse. On October 25, he played two periods in a game in Atlanta. Two days later he managed only one period at home against Washington. Glen Sather wanted him to get into hospital and have the tonsils taken out right then. Wayne said no. Two nights later Sather sat him out, the only game he'd missed as a pro.

He'd lost eleven pounds. He hadn't eaten in three days. But three nights later at home, he played against the Islanders. He knew then something he was to tell Keith three years later when Keith got sick playing junior "A" in Windsor. "You've got to be prepared to play 80 games half dead if you have to," he said. "If you're not, give it up. Because that's what you get paid for."

He finally had the tonsils removed after the season ended. We tried to keep it a secret. We registered him in the hospital in Paris under the name of Smith. That part of it worked, but word about the operation did get out. It must have. The hospital in Brantford, the logical place to expect him to be, was flooded with flowers and cards.

On March 21, Wayne scored three third-period goals in a 9-2 win over Pittsburgh to reach 121 points. Now he was in second place, only five back. And with three games left for each team, he tied Dionne for the lead at 133 points after two goals and four assists in an 8-5 win at Maple Leaf Gardens, in what Sather called "the greatest game he's ever played."

Wayne was pumped up for that one. The night before there'd been a big dinner in Brantford honouring him as Athlete of the Year. Growing up watching the Leafs on TV, he'd always dreamed of playing as a pro in the Gardens some day, and there he was, not just playing, but starring. This one was for the folks at home.

It was a great night, but it could have been even greater. In the dying seconds of the game Wayne burst in alone on the Leaf net for what should have been his third goal and eighth point. He had the goalie beaten. It was like shooting at an empty net. He backhanded from a few feet out – and put the puck so high it didn't just miss the net, it missed the boards. The darn thing went right over the glass into the stands.

Naturally, the reporters flocked around him after the game. "My dad always told me to put the puck upstairs," Wayne told them. "Well, I *really* put that one upstairs."

Everyone had a good laugh and the quote made all the papers. But later that night when Wayne and I finally got together, he made one to me that turned out to be even more significant, although we didn't know it at the time.

"Wouldn't it be something," he said, "if I lose the scoring title by one point?"

Down at *Maclean's* magazine things were getting a little tense. Dionne was already on their cover in anticipation of his winning his first scoring crown. It had seemed safe enough. He'd been so far ahead. But now Wayne was on a roll – and so were the Oilers, locked in a scrap with the Canucks and Washington for the sixteenth and final playoff spot.

The Canucks were to play a big part in both the playoff and scoring picture. They, too, were struggling. ("Last year we couldn't win on the road," moaned coach Harry Neale. "This year we can't win at home. My only failing as a coach is that I can't think of anywhere else to play.") They played the Kings twice and the Oilers once in their last three games, and they had a guy named Jerry Butler who had become one of the league's best checkers. Butler would be assigned to both Wayne and Dionne.

On the Tuesday of the final week of the schedule, the Oilers went into Vancouver and lost 5-0. Butler held Wayne to only one shot on goal. On Wednesday, Wayne scored his 50th goal of the season in a 1-1 tie with Minnesota. On Thursday, Butler shut out Dionne as the Canucks beat the Kings 5-2. On Friday, Wayne took a two-point lead with a goal and two assists in a 6-2 win over Colorado in the Oilers' final league game. Now the scoring race was up to two men – Dionne and Butler, the man the Canucks called The Shadow. Wayne could only sit and wait.

Dionne, great player that he is, came through. The Kings lost, but Marcel shook Butler enough to collect two assists in a 5-3 loss to the Canucks. So now Wayne and Marcel had finished in a tie for the scoring title with 137 points. They'd share the Art Ross Trophy, right?

Wrong. The trophy, the title and the $1,000 went to Dionne because he'd scored 53 goals, two more than Wayne. I didn't agree with that. The trophy is for the player with the most points, not the most goals, and two players had tied on points.

The player with the most goals had the trophy for the point-scoring title. The player who had just as many points didn't get to share it. That's contrary to everything we teach. How do you tell a minor player now – how do I tell Brent – that an assist is as good as a goal? And don't think the kids aren't aware of what's going on.

The following summer Wayne was speaking at a banquet in Thamesford, Ont. One of the young players had a question: "Do you still think an assist is as good as a goal?" he asked.

Wayne thought it over.

"Well, " he said quietly, "I won the Hart Trophy."

Let me introduce you to the *NHL Guide*, a book just crammed full of facts and figures about professional hockey and the people in it.

You can find out almost anything about anyone in major professional hockey in the *NHL Guide* – but in all the years of the WHA's existence the *Guide* carried not a single word about it. It was as though the league did not exist. Players who'd jumped NHL teams to go to the new league were treated as though they'd died or were missing in action. Gordie Howe – *Gordie Howe* who set so many records with the Detroit Red Wings, retired for two years, then joined Houston and spent six seasons in the WHA – was listed in the *NHL Guide* among "Players Out of Pro Hockey Since 1950-51 Season." (Meaning any player who'd retired from the NHL since the '50-'51 season.) When Gordie scored his historic 1,000th professional goal, Harold Ballard wouldn't allow the news to be announced at Maple Leaf Gardens because he said goals in the WHA couldn't be considered big league. Johnny McKenzie played for seven years in the WHA – but as far as the *NHL Guide* was concerned his last season in hockey was his last one with the Boston Bruins, in 1971-72.

There was a section on the American Hockey League. There was a section on the Central Hockey League. They were considered the top minor professional leagues, and at least they were listed. But there was no section on the WHA. That left only one conclusion: in the eyes of the NHL, the WHA wasn't even a top-notch *minor* league.

Wrong again.

Before the first season of the merged – pardon me, expanded – league, the NHL made a couple of announcements.

* *Statistics compiled by players in the WHA who were now on NHL rosters would not count in NHL totals.*

Well, all right. The excuse that the WHA played overtime and so their records couldn't count, seemed sort of silly when you remember that up until 1942 – when the trains were full of troops during the war and couldn't be held at the station waiting for the teams if the games ran late – the NHL had *played overtime*. Records of those players are in the *NHL Guide*. But what the heck, if the NHL considered the WHA a minor league, that was that.

* *First-year NHL players coming in after playing the WHA would not be eligible for the Calder Trophy as rookie-of-the-year because "they have already played a full*

150

season with a MAJOR PROFESSIONAL LEAGUE."

Excuse me? The WHA's statistics and player records didn't count because it wasn't a major league, but its players, who'd never been in the NHL, weren't eligible for the rookie-of-the-year award because it *was* a major league? Will you run that one by me again?

Actually, the NHL had been pretty cute about it. In preparing the 1979-80 edition of the *NHL Guide,* heading into that first one-league season, it had listed the individual WHA season records of players now on NHL teams, with separate totals for each league (dark type for the NHL years, light type for the WHA). And it had added a few key words to the eligibility rules for the Calder Trophy.

Prior to that season, the award went to "the player selected as the most proficient in his first season of competition in the NHL." The rule added that "the player cannot have played in more than twenty-five games in any single preceding season, nor in six or more games in each of any two preceding seasons." The rule was now amended by adding to that section these words ". . . *in any major professional leagues."*

It wasn't a rule aimed at Wayne. With all the under-age players on the rosters of the four teams coming in, there were all kinds of good young players who'd gone directly from junior to the WHA. And despite the fact that most of the major media people across the country started demanding that Wayne be named the Calder winner, as he clearly was having the best season by far of any player in his first NHL season, the fact that he couldn't win it came as no surprise. The rule had been in place, and publicized, before the season opened. We knew from the start he had no chance.

But it cost him more than the Calder Trophy.

On February 15, in an 8-2 win over the Washington Capitols, Wayne collected seven assists, tying the NHL record set by Billy Taylor of the Detroit Red Wings in 1947. They also had to give him a share of Taylor's record for the most assists in a single game by "a player in his first NHL season," because the word rookie didn't appear in the definition. But if you look in the *NHL Guide* today, you'll see that Peter Stastny of the Quebec Nordiques holds the records for most assists (70) and most points (109) by a rookie in a single season, set in 1980-81. Stastny had played for the Czechoslovakian national team before defecting to Canada, and by any definition the Czechs are professionals. A year earlier Wayne had had 86 assists and 137 points in his first NHL year. But he wasn't a rookie. You figure it out.

You know the sad part about it? In his first season in the NHL, where he was supposed to struggle under the superior competition and the heavy checking, he finished with 24 more points than he'd got the season before in the WHA; he made the second All-Star team (behind Dionne at centre); he won the Lady Byng Trophy as "the player adjudged to have exhibited the best type of sportsmanship and gentlemanly conduct combined with a high standard of playing ability"; and he won the Hart Trophy as "the player adjudged to be the most valuable to his team" – in other words, the NHL's MVP award. Had the league seen fit to share the Art Ross Trophy for the scoring championship – which seems fair, since two players did accumulate an identical number of points – and had it not fiddled the wording on qualifications for the Calder Trophy in what seems to have been nothing more than a final shot at the WHA, Wayne could have swept every major award available to him – in his first NHL year.

But for the second straight year there was a major disappointment. The Oilers had put up a tremendous fight in their first round of NHL playoffs, taking the Philadelphia Flyers into overtime in the first game and double overtime in the third. But they'd bowed out in three straight games. Still, a couple of steps had been taken. The NHL and the fans knew now that the Oilers were for real, and Wayne had answered the people who doubted he could star in the NHL. Like it or not, the *NHL Guide* was about to get an overhaul. It was only a matter of time.

Chapter 12

A YEAR LIKE YOU WOULDN'T BELIEVE

"He's worse than Bobby Orr. At least Orr started in his own end and you could brace yourself. Gretzky just materializes out of nowhere."

– Bobby Clarke, Dec. 30, 1982.

It was probably the silliest prescription anybody ever got, and the guy who gave it wasn't even licenced: "Tape two aspirin tablets to your knee and you'll be fine." He didn't even add, "Call me in the morning."

It was December 30, 1981. Wayne was sitting in the Oiler dressing room getting ready to play the Philadelphia Flyers in Edmonton. He was five goals short of Maurice Richard's record of 50 in 50 games, the one scoring record set in 1944-45 that had survived expansion and the changing style of hockey, until Mike Bossy of the Islanders had tied it the year before. Wayne would beat it, there seemed no doubt about that. This was only Game 39 and lately he'd really been on a tear with 10 goals in 4 games, including four the last time out against Los Angeles, two of them shorthanded. Five goals in 12 games? No problem. In fact, on the way to the rink he'd even told Kevin Lowe he thought he might do it that night.

But he felt lousy. He'd banged up his right knee in LA. It ached. The pressure was starting to get to him, not on the ice but off it. The knee wouldn't stop aching. Then Glen

Sather came over with two aspirins and a piece of tape. "Put these on your knee," he said.

Wayne cracked up. But he taped them carefully to his knee, inside the kneepad. Then he went out and made history – two goals in the first period, one on a breakaway in the second, one after five minutes of the third. One more would do it. The crowd was going nuts. Up in the radio booth, play-by-play man Rod Phillips was screaming so loudly that people in the booth worried that Wayne would get No. 50 and Rod wouldn't have a voice left to describe it. The thing was, there was a game going on. The Flyers had been down 4-1 and had climbed to within one at 6-5. Now there was 1:14 left and they pulled goalie Pete Peeters.

The net was empty. The puck came to Wayne at centre. He wheeled, fired – and shot wide. The Oilers were called for icing. Then, with seven seconds left, Glenn Anderson grabbed a rebound and he and Wayne had a two-on-one break on Bill Barber. Glenn never hesitated. He flipped the puck to Wayne, who shot from the blue line. The puck hit the back of the net with two seconds to play, and Wayne had the fastest 50 goals in the history of professional hockey.

What people didn't know was that Barber had tried to make history on the play himself. He told Wayne later that when he saw he was beaten, he was going to throw his stick along the ice and block the puck. Under NHL rules it would have counted as a goal anyway. "That way," Barber said, "you'd be the first player in history to get credit for his 50th goal without the puck ever going into the net, and I'd have a kind of an assist on the goal that broke The Rocket's record."

"Why didn't you do it?" Wayne wondered."Change your mind at the last second?"

Nah!" Barber said disgustedly. "I tried, but the tape at the end of the stick caught in my glove and I couldn't let the damn thing go!"

None of us ever thought the 1981-82 season would turn out

the way it did – but then, how could we? There'd never been a season like it for anyone.

Wayne's third season as a pro and second in the NHL (1980-1981) had been a triumph. He'd scored 55 goals, set NHL records for most assists (109) and points (164) in a season, while winning his second Art Ross and Hart Trophies and making the first All-Star team at centre. The Oilers had swept past the Montreal Canadiens in three straight games in the first round of the playoffs. They were so young that Wayne, Jari Kurri, Mark Messier, Glenn Anderson, Kevin Lowe and Paul Coffey could still have been playing junior hockey. ("Their Trac IIs are still at 0," huffed the Vancouver *Province*. "They worry about over-time games because Dad warned them to have the car home by eleven. The Canadiens, sent home in three by Richie Cunningham and the gang at Arnold's? Don't be ridiculous.") They were so loose that in the Oilers' media guide under Boyhood Idol, Anderson had written "Wayne Gretzky." He's older than Wayne by a whole three and a half months.

They'd followed the upset of the Canadiens by losing the quarter-finals 4-2 to the New York Islanders, but they were obviously a team to watch. Over the summer people wondered what they'd do for an encore. They'd given themselves a tough act to follow. This time they wouldn't catch anyone by surprise.

But they did – first by what they did do, and then by what they didn't.

Wayne remembers the 1981-1982 season as starting off innocently enough. He was going along on points at roughly the pace of the last season. After 34 games he had 35 goals, so obviously he had a chance at 50 in 50 – but Bossy had done that the year before. Then he got three goals and four assists against Minnesota, two goals and an assist against Calgary, a goal and three assists against Vancouver and four plus an assist against Los Angeles. Now it was starting to occur to people that the Richard-Bossy record might just be the beginning. Wayne might even have a shot at Phil Esposito's season record of 76.

Wayne tried to play it down. The night after he hit 50, he'd been held without a point in Game 40 in Vancouver. "To hit 76, I'd have to get 26 goals in 40 games," he said. "Never mind what's happened up till now, that's a lot of goals."

No one was listening. He was going to break Espo's record. He might even score 200 points – which, if they'd thought about it, was ridiculous in that they were assuming he could break his own league record by 36.

As it turned out, they were right. But along the way things got a little bit crazy.

If you asked me what I remember most about that season, I'd have to say two telephone calls.

The first was from Edmonton the night he hit 50. I was sitting at home glued to the radio, picking up every sports-cast. With the two-hour time difference it was getting pretty late. At 11:30, word came that he had four goals after two periods. A bit later they broke in with a bulletin that he'd hit 50. It couldn't have been more than forty minutes later that the phone rang. It was Wayne, calling from the dressing room.

"Did you hear?" he asked.

"Yeah," I said. "How come it took you so long?"

"Aw, I didn't want to do it *too* quickly," he said, trying to sound nonchalant.

"You excited?"

"Yeah, but I have to go now. The place is full of reporters. I just wanted to make sure you knew. Bye."

And he was gone.

You know, people are always asking what it's like to have Wayne in the family. I could have answered them so easily that night. There he was, surrounded by TV cameras, microphones, magazine and newspaper men, and he'd ex-cused himself for a minute so he could phone home. It might sound corny, but the record seemed small compared to that call.

The other call came with five games left in the schedule. The Oilers were playing in Calgary the next night and here was Wayne saying, "Why don't you and Mom come on out for the game?"

Well, Phyllis was in Kingston, where she'd driven Keith and some of the boys for a tournament. Keith would be looked after and there'd be a ride back, but it was a lot of trouble and a lot of money to fly out for one Saturday game when I'd have to leave the next day to get home in time for work Monday.

"No, I don't think so," I said. "It's not worth it."

Wayne was insistent. "C'mon," he said. "Get Mom to drive in to Toronto, you meet her at the airport and come out. I'd like you to be here."

"But why?"

"Dad," he said patiently, "it's not every day a guy hits 200 points. No one's ever done it. I'd really like you here to see me do it."

He'd broken Esposito's goal record twelve games earlier in Buffalo. He had 199 points with five games left. He knew he'd break 200. But he wanted us there to share it when he did. There was only one answer for that. We made the plane, got to Calgary two hours before the game, watched him hit 200 with an assist on a goal by Pat Hughes, get another assist and score two shorthanded goals on the same Calgary penalty. The next morning we were back on the plane for home.

Maybe it was foolish. Points are only points, and records are only records. But a moment like that stays with you forever. Not the moment he got the point; the moment I got the call.

The Oilers were flying. In any other year the media would have been raving over Mark Messier, who scored 50 goals, or Paul Coffey, who got 89 points and made second-team All-Star on defence, or Glenn Anderson, who had a wonderful year with 105 points. These were kids, all of them, and they were ripping up the league. Jari Kurri, in his second NHL season after coming over from Finland, was only a year older and had 32 goals and 86 points. Just looking at him you knew he was going to be a superstar. They got some attention, but probably not as much as they deserved. The media were too busy watching No. 99.

Wayne calls it the year he lost the last of his privacy. There'd been media attention since he was six or seven, but it was mostly with hockey people. Now every time he passed a magazine stand, he saw his picture on a cover; not just on sports magazines, on all kinds. He was recognized on the street now. Sitting down in a restaurant meant signing between bites. In chasing Richard and Esposito he'd caught the imagination of the whole country.

The media were going crazy. Heading into Toronto for Game 47, there were so many requests for interviews that Sather finally ordered one special, mass press conference at the Westin Hotel. When the requests hit a hundred and thirty-two they moved into the governor-general's suite. "Everyone asks the same questions," Wayne says, "and everyone wants to do it privately."

It was wearing him down. We could see it that night when he slipped home to spend the night with the family. The next night, with Maple Leaf Gardens jammed and scalpers outside getting $300 for a pair of seats, the Oilers got thumped 7-1. Wayne got a goal, but he missed an open net and Bunny Larocque stopped him on a penalty shot.

It was almost as bad during the next game in Detroit, and that was only a taste. About three weeks later they were there again, this time with Wayne needing one goal to tie Esposito at 76. The game drew 20,270, and afterwards it looked as though there were at least that many media people. They couldn't let them into the dressing room, there were so many. Wayne scored the record-tying goal, grabbed two precious days off at home in Brantford doing absolutely nothing, then drove to Buffalo, where someone started a rough count of radio, TV, magazine and newspaper people there from across North America – and stopped when it hit three hundred.

Among the crowd were Esposito and NHL president John Ziegler, who'd been following him for a few games as he got closer to the record. Wayne kidded about it. "Having two guys following me, just waiting for it, is more pressure than trying for it," he said. But he was particularly pleased that Esposito had come. Mr. Ziegler was there on behalf of the league. Esposito was there because he wanted to be. He'd come on his own. He was in Detroit to see the record tied and he was in Buffalo to see it broken. He knew better than anyone the feeling Wayne would have when it fell. He'd had it himself.

For a long time it seemed he and Mr. Ziegler would have at least another game to go. Don Edwards robbed Wayne three or four times. With less than seven minutes remaining the score was tied 3-3. Then Wayne stole the puck at the Buffalo blue line, walked in and beat Edwards with a wrist shot.

The Oilers poured out onto the ice and mobbed him. The crowd gave him a standing ovation, and the game was stopped while Esposito came to the timekeeper's box and presented the puck to Wayne, whom he called "the most talented and one of the nicest guys in hockey." Wayne had beaten his record, but Esposito was happy for him. "Thank you, Wayne," he said, "for letting me be a part of this."

I don't know if Wayne realized how much strain he'd been under. But now he could relax. Less than two minutes after they resumed the game he got No. 78, and with seventeen seconds left he made it 79, as the Oilers won 6-3. It was the perfect end to a great night. What none of us knew then was that it was also the last high point of the season for the Oilers. From then on it was to be all downhill.

Only the Islanders finished the regular season with a better record than the Oilers, 118 points to 111. Edmonton set

NHL records for most goals (417), most assists (706) and most points (1,123). They hadn't played too well since the Buffalo game, but the playoffs were a new season. In the first round they were up against the Los Angeles Kings, a team they'd beaten by 48 points in the standings and whipped 6-2 and 7-3 the last two times they'd met, in Games 78 and 79. What could go wrong?

To this day no one knows what it was, but something sure did. The Kings won the best-of-five series. It went the full five games, and when the Kings won the last one 7-4 in Edmonton, it was as if the whole season had meant nothing. The Edmonton *Journal*, which had run an Oiler fight song on its front page the day of the game and trimmed that page in Oiler colours, used the same page the morning after to turn on them.

"THEY CHOKED!" the headline screamed. "Weak-kneed wimps," the story called them.

Personally, I think they were worn down. They were a young team with no knowledge of how to pace themselves over a long season. Blood tests showed that Wayne, Kevin Lowe, Dave Semenko and Mark Messier were suffering from iron deficiency. The season before they'd been the young team nobody expected to do much. This time people had figured them for a shot at the Cup. When people think you've let them down, they sometimes turn on you. In Edmonton, the media turned on the Oilers.

Wayne didn't have time to think about it then. The day after the last game, he was on the way to Europe to join Team Canada. But it was the beginning of something that would haunt the club and spill over onto Wayne personally: the accusation that they couldn't win the big one.

In 1981-82, Wayne had broken his own NHL records for assists (120) and points (212). Islander Mike Bossy's total of 147 had been the third highest in league history – and he had finished second, 65 points behind Wayne. It had been the widest winning margin in league history. Wayne had shattered Esposito's goal record with 92. He'd won the Hart

Trophy for the third straight time. But the Oilers hadn't made it past the first round of the playoffs.

The following season in 1982-83 he led the league in goals (71), assists (a league record 125) and points (196). He had one more assist than Peter Stastny of the Quebec Nordiques, who finished second in the scoring race, had total points. He set playoff records for assists (26) and points (38) in 16 games. They had made it all the way to the Stanley Cup final that time – but lost in four straight to the Islanders.

The Oilers set records, they filled rinks wherever they went, they were young and fast and exciting – but that season they still had that black cloud over their heads: Can't Win the Big One. It was a disease for which there was only one cure, and it wasn't aspirin tablets taped to the knee. It was the Stanley Cup. In Edmonton, they wouldn't settle for anything less.

Chapter 13

KEN, BARBIE – AND WAYNE

"If you could put a tail on a Cheerio . . . ."

– Michael Barnett, 1983.

The man was standing at Michael Barnett's table in a posh Edmonton restaurant. He was wearing these huge gumboots and carrying a brown paper bag. He'd barged past the maitre d', who was not impressed. Neither was Michael's date, especially when the guy started talking in a voice that rattled knives and forks tables away.

"You're Barnett – Gretzky's guy – ain't ya'?" he asked.

"Uh, right," Michael said.

"Well, I've got something here the people who make hockey gear should know about," the guy said. "If you and Wayne could take it to some of those companies Wayne works for . . . ."

People were staring. Michael thought it over for a second. "Why don't you sit down?" he asked. Now his date was *really* unimpressed.

The guy sits, reaches into the bag and pulls out something that looks like rubberized foam. It was a type of padding he'd developed. Now he's looking for a company that would use it in manufacturing protective gear. What he wants to do now is to demonstrate it.

First he clears everything on the table off to one side. Then he takes Michael's hand, lays it flat on the table, puts the padding over it and begins pounding. "See? (*Pound! Pound!*) That doesn't hurt, does it?"

162

Michael agreed that it didn't hurt much at all and that they really ought to get together some time and talk about it. "Okay," the guy said, and gumbooted past the maitre d' and into the night.

Things like that happen a lot these days. Wayne has become a hot item in the market place. His name on a product, his appearance on a commercial, his presence at an opening, all generate big dollars for the company and for Wayne. Financial and advertising magazines are always pointing out that he actually makes more money from activities outside hockey than he does from playing the game – which is fine as long as they also remember that it's the hockey that generates it.

They run these great lists of items Wayne endorses and licences: athletic footwear and clothing, breakfast cereal, chocolate bars, hockey sticks and equipment, life insurance, children's bedspreads, pillows and wallpaper, wrist watches, table hockey games, lunch kits, even a Wayne Gretzky doll – and they play games trying to estimate what it's worth to him. *Advertising Age* magazine obviously figured it was an awful lot. "This simple, down-home boy could endorse Coke and Pepsi at the same time and get away with it," a 1983 article said. Obviously a lot of people have the same idea. They phone or write by the hundreds every year, all with just the product for Wayne to endorse.

Most of them phone or write to Michael at CorpSport International in Edmonton. Because he makes a point of responding in one way or another to all inquiries, it can lead to some strange situations. Take the man who wanted Wayne to endorse his sizzling down-home chili.

The call had come in a day or so earlier. Sometimes, with sixty to seventy calls per day they tend to get backed up. But now Michael was on the phone listening to this pitch about the chili. Why not? Chili is popular. It's available in all the supermarkets. If this was a big enough company with a good distribution system . . . .

"Where do you manufacture your chili?" he asked.

There was a brief silence. Then: "Manu . . . manu . . . .

Oh! You mean like where do I *cook* it! Well, on my stove! Where in hell do you think I'd cook it?"

The company wasn't that big. It wasn't a company at all. It was just this man, his kitchen stove, and a recipe his family had used for years. Michael had to tell him, with regret, that chili wasn't in Wayne's plans right now.

The Marketing of Wayne Gretzky. That's how people refer to it. Makes it sound like a movie title or some sort of merchandizing plan for moving cereal or sausage. But thinking back, I don't think there was ever a conscious plan that Wayne would be "marketed." We weren't thinking in terms of commercials or endorsements when we flew out to see Nelson Skalbania about Wayne turning pro. When he went to Indianapolis with all that fuss and when he was traded to Edmonton eight games later, no one was figuring out how much he could make lending his name to something. We were thinking hockey and what was best for Wayne. And those are still the two things that matter. Hockey is Wayne's business, not modelling or acting or doing commercials. No one realizes that better than Wayne himself. As long as he's playing the game that will never change.

But the way the signing came about, the dollars involved, the NHL-WHA war, and Wayne's amateur career, it all added up to someone who was Big News. People who are Big News are people in demand – and people who are marketable. Wayne was on the treadmill almost before he knew it.

Initially, all his affairs were handled by Gus Badali out of the Toronto office. But by 1981, those affairs had become so complex that having Wayne in Edmonton and the office in Toronto was too awkward. That was when Michael came into the picture. He owned the SportsPage restaurant in Calgary, and later another in Edmonton. He'd played hockey, had a lot of friends among the players, and had always been interested in business and marketing. In six years his SportsPage Celebrity Classic charity softball tournament, involving NHL players, grew from a game played before three hundred people, with nine players to a team and sides chosen when they got there, to a game televised nationally from Edmonton's sixty-thousand-seat Commonwealth Stadium. It was the forerunner of the current NHL Slo Pitch Classic. In fact, Michael was negotiating with the NHL for a marketing position in the league's New York offices when Wayne intercepted.

Wayne had met him through the Oilers. Michael says he must have known instinctively that he'd be doing something with Wayne some day. "He was seventeen, old enough to be in the restaurant in Northlands Coliseum," he says, "but not old enough to have a beer. Well, any seventeen-year-old has the occasional beer. Whenever I saw a player slip him one, I'd order a coffee cup and pour the beer in it so no one would notice."

He and Wayne became pretty good friends. So when things began to pile up, Wayne suggested that Michael get together with Gus and me to see if something could be worked out. That led to formation of Sierra Sports Group. Gus had Sierra Sports Representatives in Toronto and handled Wayne's and other hockey contracts as he'd always done; Michael was president of Sierra Sports Marketing in Edmonton handling the licencing, promotional and endorsement work. To avoid conflict in handling similar assignments for other players – there'd been approaches from some who weren't handled by Gus – Michael's firm went independent in January, 1983 and became CorpSport International. The way it's set up now, Gus handles the hockey contract through Sierra in Toronto: CorpSport looks after endorsements and marketing; and, as of January, 1984, R.I. Barrigan Management in Edmonton handles all his investments. All of this leaves Michael free to take on other clients, but in a way that became a bit of a laugh.

The other clients are there, all right, but other people in the firm are handling a lot of the work. For Michael, Wayne had become a full-time assignment.

Logically, you'd think that people wanting hockey players to endorse their products would be people who sell hockey equipment. Well, that's correct up to a point, but that point is only the tip of the iceberg. One of the first products Wayne endorsed had no connection with hockey whatever: a frisbee.

Not an ordinary frisbee, mind you. This one had little lights around the outer rim and, when you flicked a switch on the inside, they glowed. Throw it and you had a flying saucer. It was called a Star Flyer, and the manufacturing company wanted a star's name on it. Wayne was young, just about the same age as the kids you see fooling with them on the beach. "Get Gretzky," they thought.

They got Gretzky. For a long-term, guaranteed contract in six figures. I mention this for two reasons: first to show the craziness of the world of marketing, and second to show the guidelines we've had to set up to meet it.

Marketing breaks down into two categories: endorsements, in which Wayne actually serves as spokesman for a product, doing television appearances, photo sessions, guesting at company functions, things like that; and licencing, in which he is paid a fee for allowing his name to be placed on a product the way Roy Rogers did. Things like lunch kits, pencil boxes – or frisbees.

Wayne licences a lot of items. There's even been some criticism that he does too many. What people don't understand is that a lot of them are done in self-defence. Because there are pirates out there in the market place.

You can't copyright a number or a colour. As 99 became as synonymous with Wayne as the black mask is to the Lone Ranger, people started slapping 99 on items coloured in shades of orange and blue that looked suspiciously like the colours of the Edmonton Oilers. Wayne has no connection with them, but the inference is there. The only way to fight back is to go to the major retailers and request that they call if anyone tries to market something Gretzky-like. Michael then tries to find a company to put out an official version.

It's killed off some of the pirating, but not all of it. Not by a long shot.

Because there were so many opportunities available, it became important to sit down with Wayne to decide what areas he'd like to concentrate on and what sort of products he'd feel comfortable supporting.

From the start it was never purely a matter of money. You can't just say, "Sure, I like this stick better than that stick because it's worth more money." You have to be honest with people and with yourself. There was a good offer from a reputable firm to produce a Wayne Gretzky signature soft-ball glove. It was turned down. How would it look if Pete Rose endorsed a hockey stick? There was an offer to endorse weight-lifting equipment. But Wayne doesn't do weight work anymore. Who would he be kidding?

You've also got to make sure that you use the products you endorse – all the time. Slip up once and there'll be someone there to see it. Wayne found that out early. He was in a restaurant and absent-mindedly ordered a root beer. A little boy ran right over and said, "Hey! I thought you were a 7-Up man!"

Some of the deals struck were the result of companies coming to Wayne. Others were made by Michael – when he'd actively pursue something of interest that could be of benefit to both parties. With all of them there is a rule that's virtually iron-clad now: no one-year contracts. Make certain the company is reputable, the product good, the money fair to both sides – and sign for three years minimum.

There's good reason for it. Wayne doesn't want to jump from company to company. When 7-Up changed its advertising thrust and moved away from using athletes, dropping people like Wayne, Sugar Ray Leonard, Gary Carter and Tug McGraw, Wayne received a feeler to do one of those "Look who's switched" commercials for another soft drink firm. He refused. 7-Up had been his first major television commercial. It had opened all kinds of doors for him. That's not to say that a couple of years down the road he might not endorse another soft drink. But if the offer came, he'd go to 7-Up and give them first shot at having him back.

Besides, if a person endorses, say, a particular brand of car for one year and at the end of that year, for whatever reason, the company doesn't renew, there's not much chance of a second car company rushing in with an offer to endorse theirs. Michael's approach to a major corporation runs something like this: "We're trying to attach Wayne to major corporations and there'll be only a handful. You come with us now and the opportunity is to be there for decades." Frisbees or cars, the theory applies. Pick the company carefully, sign long-term, and make sure you do everything in your power to make it a great arrangement for both sides.

The longer Wayne plays, the more records he sets, the more his marketability increases. A company in Quebec can issue a press release announcing that it's manufacturing official Wayne Gretzky sheets and pillowcases and *know* that, because of Wayne's name, it's going to be an item in major papers across the country. And if a company like Mattel puts out a Wayne Gretzky doll . . . .

Word about the Wayne Gretzky doll in the orange, blue and white Oilers' home uniform ("For avid fans," the press release said, "his out-of-town uniform, jogging suit and tuxedo are also available.") was big news on a lot of sports pages. Funny news, but big. ("Wayne, I'd like you to meet Ken and Barbie, and Barbie's friend, Midge, and the guy over there with the rifle is G.I. Joe.") Columnists made the expected cracks about a Dave Semenko doll to beat up on any kid who played rough with the Wayne Gretzky doll, and raised other questions:

Would Wayne's clothes fit Dave? Barbie's never did seem to fit Midge.

Would the Wayne doll have a girlfriend doll? After all, she might not like all that time he spent in the factory with Barbie and Midge, even if they were boxed separately.

Would it have extra-long optional fingernails to scratch out the eyes of the groupie dolls?

Would it be one of those new, life-like dolls with full equipment, or would the Wayne doll go through life in neutral? Possible solution: a tiny Wayne jockstrap, sold separately, of course.

And would the Wayne doll be the wetting kind? The *Province* newspaper in Vancouver sincerely hoped not. "If he produced as quickly and as often as he scores goals in real life," it pointed out, "the kids could only play with him in the bathroom."

The doll grew out of a trend noticed in the fan mail. Some seventy-six per cent of the letters were from girls age four to fourteen. Obviously they weren't buying skates and shoulder pads; they must like Wayne because he was Wayne. Mattel Canada called just about the time Michael was opening negotiations with another firm in New York. A three-year deal was struck, with Wayne also agreeing to endorse a small table hockey game in order to make it worth the company's while to bring the figures up to what Michael was asking. The doll is a hit (Mattel U.S. has exercised its option to sell them in the United States), Wayne's happy, Mattel's happy, and so are a lot of little girls. So far, there's been no need for a Semenko doll.

For what seems like the hundredth time that day, Phyllis brings a jug of orange juice to the kitchen table where Wayne, Glen and Brent are about to wolf down their breakfast cereal. Wayne says something about the cereal not containing any sugar. "That's right, Wayne!" Phyllis says brightly.

Brent looks at his mother and gets the giggles, which sets Glen off. Wayne looks at both of them for a second, picks up his bowl of cereal – and carefully pours it over Brent's head.

"*Cut!*" yells a voice from somewhere off to one side.

Phyllis sighs and takes the orange juice back to the counter. The Gretzky family commercial for Pro*Stars cereal, the cereal with Wayne Gretzky on the front of the box, will require at least one more take.

The Pro*Stars project came about because General Mills, after spending thousands of dollars on research, came to the conclusion that they couldn't put a tail on a Cheerio. (Think about it: an O with a tail on it is 9. Two Os with tails and you've got 99. Picture thousands of little hockey players at breakfast, stirring their Wayne Gretzky cereal and making Wayne's number over and over again.) But no matter how they tried, the tails kept falling off. Ninety-Nine cereal, or whatever they might have called it, never made it into the box. But Pro*Stars did.

General Mills liked the concept of a Gretzky cereal and we liked General Mills. There'd been substantial offers from four other cereal companies. Three of them wanted to use Wayne on the box for one year, just to see how it worked. If it hadn't worked, because the cereal didn't catch on, Wayne would have been out of the cereal market. General Mills put together a four-year deal to launch a new no-sugar, whole grain base cereal. Part of the fee involved Wayne endorsing the company. There was a built-in royalty on every box sold, which they said could go as high as four million boxes per year in Canada alone. They also gave us the back of the box where we can launch products like the Wayne Gretzky NHL All-Star sweater, in all children's sizes, with Wayne's name and number on it.

Everything dovetailed so nicely: the family was hired to do the commercial, Wayne got a fee for endorsing the product and a royalty on each box of cereal and each sweater sold.

One of the things Wayne has always tried to do with his outside activities is to get the family involved wherever possible. Keith did two national commercials with him for 7-Up. All three boys appeared with him in advertisements for Jofa, the hockey equipment manufacturer. Wayne had a guaranteed fee, plus a royalty on everything sold, under what was called The Gretzky Collection. A separate contract was built in for the boys, with the money going to the Canadian Amateur Hockey Association in trust so as not to jeopardize their amateur status. For the life of that contract they'll be getting a royalty on the equipment sold. With that one and a couple of others the money becomes pretty substantial, enough to look after their college education should they go that route.

Before we knew any better, people would come to the house in Brantford to do a TV show, set up their equipment, take up the entire day, during which all the regular family routine went out the window, and there'd be no mention of a fee. Then we'd hear that other people doing the same show had been paid for their trouble. Or someone would ask me for some pictures of Wayne as a kid. I'd hand them over and they'd turn up in a totally unauthorized book on Wayne's life. There are about a dozen of those around – again for no fee. We're not trying to be greedy, we're just trying to be sensible.

All of which explains why the limousine pulled up at the house on Varadi Ave. one morning, and took Phyllis and the boys to Toronto. It was time to do the commercial to launch Pro*Stars.

General Mills goes first class. The family stayed in a hotel suite so big Phyllis figured there were more rooms than there were Gretzkys. And the cameras rolled on . . . and on . . . and on. The whole thing took the best part of a day for a commercial that runs thirty seconds. There was a stage set of a kitchen counter and cupboards, with sunlight – as provided by a spotlight behind the set – streaming in through the window over the sink. Wayne had a few lines, Phyllis had a couple, and Brent finished up with something about Wayne liking the cereal because his picture was on the box.

Sounds simple enough. But there's always something not quite right, always a reason to try it just one more time. The boys got tired. When they get tired they get giggly, which explains how Brent got a headful of Pro*Stars. Finally, though, everything was in order for another take. Phyllis returned to the counter, which put her back to the table. She was standing in front of the window looking out into the "sunlight." Suddenly, a head rose slowly into view and a face stared at her through the window. It was Brent. He'd sneaked around behind the set.

"Wanna come outside and play?" he asked.

If the window hadn't been there he might have had his head dipped in orange juice for dessert.

Don't ask me to explain why athletes and movie and TV stars make such a difference in the market place. I work for the telephone company. Whatever it is – "product association," some call it – the experts say it works. They wouldn't be offering the big dollars if it didn't. They're so conscious of it, in fact, that the slightest little thing can set them off.

Take the business of Wayne tucking the right side of his hockey sweater in his pants. As I said, he's done it for as long as he's played hockey. It started out as something we had to do because the uniform sweaters were so awfully big for him. Now it's become part habit, part superstition. In fact, he's actually got a strip of velcro on the inside of his pants, and another on the bottom of the jersey on that side, so it will stay in and look neat. But so what?

So this: Nike had signed a five-year deal with Wayne to endorse its footwear, which is quite a thing when you consider that Nike doesn't manufacture skates or any other piece of hockey equipment. The company had also made a deal with the Oilers in which the company would provide the team with their uniform sweaters, and the sweaters would carry the Nike logo. Everything seemed to be fine. Then Michael received a phone call from the Nike people. Was Wayne angry about something? What was the problem?

Michael was mystified. "What problem?" he asked. "We've got no problem."

"Well, then, why is Wayne doing this to us?"

"Doing *what*?"

"He's tucking in the right side of his sweater?"

"So?"

"So that's the place where we've got the Nike logo – bottom right-hand side. We've got this contract with him, he's endorsing for us, and he's hiding our logo!"

Michael didn't know what to do. Wayne obviously wasn't going to stop tucking in the right side of his sweater, but this was a big client. Something had to be done, and it was. Nike provided the Oilers with new jerseys for 1983-84. The logo is still on the bottom of their sweaters – but it's now on the left side.

It can get awfully complicated. For example, Wayne's company doesn't hold the rights to the Oilers' logo. Every time a company makes a deal with him in which he's to appear in a hockey strip, it also has to deal with the hockey club on the logo. There was a period when the Oilers took the position that because Wayne played for them and they allowed him to meet his off-ice business commitments, they should share in the revenues from that business. On the other hand, we thought they were being unreasonable in dealing with companies on the logo.

Each contract now includes a clause with right of approval on every advertisement. It wasn't always that way, but we soon found out why it had to be. It's something called co-op advertising, and a company acting in all innocence can cause problems you wouldn't believe. Let's say Wayne endorsed a brand of sweatsock, and that sweatsock manufacturer entered into a co-promotion with Adidas. That would result in Wayne's name, or his picture, endorsing a sweatsock with an Adidas jogger while he's under contract to Nike, one of Adidas' greatest rivals.

Couldn't happen, eh?

Well, when Wayne was endorsing GWG jeans, the company came up with a great gimmick: a life-sized cardboard cut-out of Wayne that was so realistic kids were stealing them from department stores. He had a pair of skates over his shoulder, which happened to be the Lange brand. That was fine, because Wayne had no skate endorsement. But eighteen months later, he signed a deal with the Daoust company to endorse a skate boot.

We didn't give it a thought. The GWG campaign had run its course. The cardboard cut-outs weren't in the stores anymore. What we didn't know was that GWG assumed it could still use the ad. As part of a co-op advertising campaign, they passed a cut-out on to The Bay department store, which produced a front cover on its back-to-school flyer featuring Wayne – don't forget, now, the cut-out was so life-like it looked like the genuine article – surrounded by four kids. He's still got the Lange skates over his shoulder – and all four kids are wearing the unauthorized 99 shirts. Fortunately, Daoust understood the circumstances or there could have been a real problem.

Some of the things that happen I find hard to believe. The Neilson chocolate people put out a series of fifty Wayne Gretzky player cards, each with a different photo of Wayne on the front and some information or a hockey tip on the back, inside their Mr. Big chocolate bar packages. In New York, in 1983, collectors were offering $900 for a complete set! Wait till they find out there's going to be forty-nine more to make it 99.

For a while one year Wayne wasn't allowed to increase his life insurance. It seems that a lot of the companies he was representing had taken out policies in his name to protect their investment in him. There were so many policies and so many different beneficiaries, the insurance people thought something was fishy. That's one of the reasons the contracts don't run eleven or twelve pages anymore. By the time you get all the indemnification clauses in, covering the clients in case of accident, they're up to thirty or forty.

I don't want to paint a picture here of some huge, faceless corporation grinding out as much money through Wayne as possible. It just isn't so.

Wayne has become big business, there's no doubt about that. The eight or so major endorsements all run somewhere in six figures each year. An *Advertising Age* article in 1983 stated that "if the world's marketers got together to invent the ideal athlete to endorse products, anyone suggesting an athlete with the credentials and personality of Wayne Gretzky would be accused of pipe-dreaming." But this isn't General Motors. A lot of the decisions are made while we're sprawled on the banks of the Nith having a fishing contest, East vs West, Brent, Glen and me against Michael.

There have been offers from major U.S. marketing firms to take over. Wayne has a different idea. As he grows as a celebrity, or salesman or personality or whatever you want to call it, he wants to keep the circle small. None of this office-in-LA, office-in-New York stuff. He's got one of the three small offices in CorpSport, which is in La Marchand Mansion, a beautiful old historical site in Edmonton that's been newly restored. It's four blocks from his apartment, one block from Michael's. He'll go in at night sometimes and look at the material in three files: Read and Discuss, Read Only, and Sign Only. He's alone, it's quiet, and he can get a lot done.

Wayne understands better than a lot of people the unique position he's in. It hasn't been that long since that first pizza radio commercial in Edmonton. Hockey has given him an opportunity to make a great deal of money outside the game, but there are no guarantees. Statistics in any league, in any sport, tell you that the earning years of a professional athlete are awfully short. Wayne's youth has been a big advantage – but down the road there'll be other young stars coming up, and Wayne Gretzky will be sneaking up on thirty. "Kids play hockey and kids relate to people," he says. "It's tough for kids to relate to thirty when they can relate to eighteen."

Is he the highest-paid player in hockey? It depends on how you look at it, but the first rule is to disregard any figures you see or hear in the media. Neither Wayne nor the Oilers release figures, which are nobody's business. That forces the media to guess, and some of the guesses get outlandish.

The last time Peter Pocklington upgraded Wayne's contract – which, don't forget, is a personal services contract between Mr. Pocklington and Wayne – there was a big story about part of the deal including a shopping centre owned by Mr. Pocklington that eventually would become Wayne's property. It was said to be in Saskatchewan somewhere, likely Saskatoon.

First of all, it wasn't a shopping centre. That part of the contract called for Mr. Pocklington, on or before January 1, 1984, to designate "title to lands and premises located in Canada" of an unspecified piece of property, which he would hold as trustee for Wayne. Mr. Pocklington guaranteed the property to be worth a certain minimum figure when Wayne opted to assume title, and he agreed to pay the difference between that figure and its assessed worth if it wasn't. At one point during the agreement the minimum figure was boosted.

I don't know where the shopping centre idea came up. At the time the deal was signed, the property was unspecified. Technically, I suppose it could have been one square foot of land in Mr. Pocklington's back yard, providing he was prepared to pay that minimum. But do you know what it turned out to be, that shopping centre in Saskatchewan the media were so sure about? An apartment block in Yellowknife.

Close, boys. Close.

As to Wayne's salary and how it rates compared to the rest of the NHL, there are probably some players with bigger base salaries for hockey. If you throw in the potential bonuses, which he's been able to earn every year to date, he'd be right up there with them. But bonuses aren't automatic. They have to be earned. Who's to say he'll get them every season. And things like the apartment block deal are in the future. Certainly there's no one in the game earning more money on the *outside* – but within the game itself, playing hockey and only hockey, is he the highest paid? Who knows?

But that's just scorekeeping. A better question to ask might be, does he *earn* the money he makes, whatever amount it comes to?

Even now there are those who say no. Some people say you'd have to stop and look at how many winning goals are in Wayne's total, how many empty-net goals, how many he scored against inferior clubs. That, they say, is how history will judge Wayne Gretzky.

Oh, really? Stop any hockey fan and ask him how many empty-net goals Gordie Howe scored, or how many times he unloaded on the weak teams in his era. The guy will look at you like you're crazy. Gordie Howe is Gordie Howe, a legend who scored 801 goals over 26 NHL seasons, as big a sports hero as this country has ever had.

The trophies and awards Wayne has won, the records he's set, *prove* that he's performed – and always under pressure; first as the youngest player in pro hockey in the WHA, then as the kid coming into the NHL forced to show the skeptics that his reputation was deserved. But players earn their money on and off the ice. How many people do you think Wayne has attracted to the NHL? How many new fans? How many old fans, who've stayed away for years, were brought back when he and the Oilers upset the Montreal Canadiens in that second playoff year? How much interest has he triggered in the American market which the league has tried so hard to crack: in going for Richard's record and Esposito's record and finally in pursuit of his own?

What people forget is that Wayne doesn't just help sell out his own rink. The Oilers, with Wayne as the big attraction, bring in people wherever they go. The NHL itself proved that in issuing figures based on the 1982-83 season. They showed that the Oilers drew about fourteen hundred more fans per game on the road than the league average.

That translates into roughly $16,370 extra per game for the home teams. And in the NHL those gate receipts are not shared. Over their 40 road games the Oilers played to 94.73% capacity – the highest in the league.

As an example, take the case of the Vancouver Canucks and Los Angeles Kings, who were fighting for third place in the Smythe Division and drew only 9,823 fans when they met in Los Angeles. A week later, when the Oilers played the Kings in the same building, the crowd was 14,578, which meant an extra $50,000 for the Kings. Everyone in the league benefits from the exposure Wayne generates.

And everything indicates that that exposure is only going to get bigger. There's an official Wayne Gretzky Fan Club in Edmonton now. One of the reasons we formed it was the incredible amount of mail he receives. Another was because of some of the things those letters said. A lot of money comes with being Wayne Gretzky – and a lot of responsi-bility . . . .

Chapter 14

SOMETIMES YOU
LAUGH,
SOMETIMES YOU
CRY

"Dear Mr. Wayne Gretzky: Would it be possible
to set up an appointment to see you?
Signed, Your father."

– Letter to Wayne Gretzky, NHL playoffs,
1981-82.

Imagine yourself with a Christmas card list four thousand
names long. Figure out the time it takes to address the
envelopes, insert the cards and lick the stamps. Then figure
out the *cost* of the stamps.

Got it? Good. Now pretend there's a Christmas every
month.

The mail to the Gretzky households – the Brantford
branch and the Edmonton branch – averages four thousand
per month now. During the height of the 1981-82 season,
when Wayne was chasing Phil Esposito's records, it climbed
to between ten and fifteen thousand per month. Almost
without exception each one of those letters is answered in
some form or another.

Most of it is aimed at Wayne and goes to the Oilers' office, but during the summer we'll get fifteen to twenty let-

ters per week in Brantford. They run from requests for autographs, requests for guest appearances at charity or celebrity events, to requests for money. There are some that make you angry and some that tear your heart out. There are fan letters, crank letters, geneology letters, ("We think we're related to you and your family. Here's our family tree. Let us know.") love letters, thank you letters and hate letters. There are letters occasionally, that go straight to the police department.

Wayne can't answer them all. Not personally. The sheer logistics of it are overwhelming. For instance, think about how much time it takes out of a month just signing your name four thousand times. You know how Wayne does it? He goes to his office at CorpSport, and while he and Michael are sitting there discussing business, appearances or his schedule for the next few months, Wayne seldom even looks up. He's paying attention, he's talking, he's absorbing the information – but while he's doing it he's signing pictures or hockey sticks, over and over again: Wayne Gretzky, with 99 written in the tail of the Y.

At home, we receive examples of all the various letters, plus a lot of others from people who just want to compliment us on the way the family has turned out. With Keith now in junior hockey, having played in baseball and hockey tournaments all over the place, we're even getting fan letters for him. If he or Brent or Glen ever turn pro and if what's happened to Wayne ever happens to any of them, we're going to give up and apply to have the Varadi Ave. house designated as a Post Office branch.

We keep posters and a supply of autographed pictures on hand, and answer the mail as quickly as we can. Some of it gets a bit ridiculous. "Thank you for the autographed picture of Wayne. Please send me four more." Those we ignore. But mostly we sit down and write answers, which takes a fair amount of time even with the relatively small percentage we handle. It used to be much worse. Until Michael and the Edmonton office came into being in December, 1981, we handled *all* of Wayne's mail. And even now, with the Edmonton office in place, handling the flood has become virtually a full-time job for several people.

Here's the way it works: the Oilers collect the mail for about a week at a time, then one of two things happens. If the pile gets too large too quickly, they send it to Michael's office by courier. Otherwise, Vickie Moss's mother, Sophie, (Vickie is Wayne's girlfriend) drops by about once a week and picks it up. Usually it's transported in large cardboard boxes or green garbage bags.

Sophie sorts it, either in her home or at the office. She has two ladies who work with her, opening the envelopes, sorting the mail into categories, addressing the return envelopes and inserting the autographed pictures. Among them they read every letter, setting aside any that need personal attention. Sophie then draws a certified cheque from a special account to fill the postage machine – roughly twice a month at $800 a shot – the answers are stamped and sent off, and Sophie heads for the Oilers' office to pick up another batch.

The letters requiring special attention are delivered to Michael's office, about sixty or seventy every couple of weeks. If it's a business letter, Michael handles it; if it's something between a personal and a special request, someone else in the office looks after it. The very personal kind – and there are a lot of them – Wayne answers himself.

The cost of the whole operation you wouldn't believe. Over the years players usually have sent fans small black and white shots, say 3" by 5", provided by their club. With Wayne we wanted to do something special, so we send full colour glossy shots with an action shot on one side and a formal shot of Wayne on the other. Mattel provides the pictures, in exchange for having their company logo printed on the lower righthand corner, and also subsidizes some of the mailing costs. It's a good deal for them, because the surveys show such a large number of the people asking for pictures within the age group the toy company is pursuing. And it's a good deal for Wayne, because bearing the entire cost himself would be just too much to ask.

We get a lot of information from those letters. Every

three months some people at the University of Alberta run a random sample of two thousand letters, breaking them into age group, sex and point of origin. Some of the answers are startling. For instance, just under eighteen per cent of the letters are now from Europe, and fifty-two per cent from the United States. I don't know whether that means every youngster in Canada has now written to Wayne already – going through the mail it sometimes seems like it – whether the American kids are becoming aware of hockey, the Oilers and Wayne at a later stage than Canadians, or whether American kids just like to write letters.

The European letters are expensive both ways, and not just because of the postage. They don't just write. They send pictures of themselves, their school photo or one they've had specially taken, wrapped in cardboard with a request to have Wayne sign that one, preferably "With love . . . ." And of course, once they're signed they have to be carefully rewrapped and mailed back. Sophie's postage machine takes a heck of a beating from Europe. The kids do have enormous faith in the Canadian postal system, though, probably more so than Canadians. They don't know Wayne's address, so they send letters addressed to "The King of Ice Hockey, Wayne Gretzky, Canada", or simply, "Wayne Gretzky, Kanada." I don't know whether it's fame or the Post Office, but sooner or later they get here.

American letter writers tend to be gracious and conscientious. They send stamped, self-addressed envelopes for their picture so it won't cost anything. There's just one hitch: they send American stamps. You can't mail a letter with an American stamp on it in Canada. There's probably a drawer full of American stamps around the office. If we ever open a business in the U.S., we've got the stamp problem licked.

There are lessons to be learned about life from our mail. You learn how lucky you are to be healthy, how lucky you are to have a family with love in it that sticks together no matter what. And you learn that the world is full of people not nearly as fortunate.

Dear Wayne:

It was hard to say who was more excited, the kids or the teachers. Word had spread like wildfire throughout the hospital. Wayne Gretzky and friends were in the building and might be coming to visit the second floor classrooms. Could it possibly be true? The Great One in our very own rooms? The Christmas spirit was already overflowing on the second floor. A visit from Gretzky could blow the roof right off.

An eerie hush fell over the second floor. He *was* walking down the hall. Kids were turning white before our eyes – speechless. Gretzky stood on the threshhold of our classroom. No. 99! The kids sat in stunned, worshipful awe. Gretzky smiled, the ice was broken and an excited babble began to fill the room.

The second floor's very best Christmas present walked down the hall, but the magic lingered for the rest of the afternoon. Santa Claus had to take second star, because of course No. 99 took the first.

Dear Wayne Gretzky:

We are students at Molenaar's Day Nursery. Today we pretended we were blind, and made dot pictures like brail (sic) and brail letters, then we tried to cut, draw and do puzzles with our eyes closed. We all found it very hard. We all are glad we are not blind, and are very happy that on Saturday you raised such a good amount of money to help the blind children. Good luck, Wayne Gretzky. We all love you.

From the children
at Molenaar's Day Nursery.

Dear Mr. Gretzky:

A year and a half ago one of my elderly patients contracted terminal cancer. I asked him how he was managing his discomfort and his fears. His thoughts only seemed to centre around Wayne's on and off-ice accomplishments. He related how great it was going to be to be able to see Wayne play in so many games during the Canada Cup series.

Well, he never made it to the series, but instead of facing his tomorrows with fear and apprehension he always looked forward to the mornings to hear and read how Wayne had made out in those games from the coast.

This ability to make life a little easier for countless people is perhaps Wayne's greatest gift. Trusting that by sharing this experience with you it will alleviate some of the growing responsibilities placed on Wayne and your family, and hoping for your continued success, I am

> Yours sincerely,
> Dr. J. A. Cook,
> Dental Surgeon,
> Brantford.

And then there are the people who *think* they've got troubles. Coincidentally, all those troubles could be cured by an injection of Wayne's money. It could put them through law school, dental school, medicine. Why, it could even cure a broken heart . . . .

Dear Wayne:

You will be very astonished when you get this letter, but you'll understand soon. I don't know any way out of my unfortunate situation so I wrote this letter to you.

TV telecast a little story about you, your family, your career and your salary. They said you will get till 1991 about $50 million (My salary - $900). You are the only one who could help me.

Eight months ago I have met a young girl and next year I would marry this girl but it is impossible because I have so many debts. (U.S. $16,250). COULD YOU GIVE ME THIS MONEY???

You could ask "Why?" and I would answer "Because I don't know anybody who could get so much money like you." I don't know where I could provide U.S. $16,250. Could you HELP me?? PLEASE!

Could you make me a present about the amount? Couldn't you? Or could you loan me $16,250?? I would send you every month $50 til 2012.

Please do it. PLEASE PLEASE PLEASE

I would be already happy if I get any answer from you. Waiting for an answer.

> Uwe,
> Bremen,
> West Germany.

PS: You are holding my life in your hands.

A year or so ago a magazine article on the family made mention of the fact that the fan mail had grown so heavy that Wayne's girlfriend, Vickie, and her mother, Sophie, were handling a lot of it. This did not sit too well with girls out there who had the big crush on 99 – or even with some of the boys who were writing to their hockey hero. Wayne, not personally handling their letters? War was declared –not against Wayne, but against the Other Woman in his life . . . .

Dear Wayne:

No, wait a minute . . . you're not Wayne! Would he grow his hair that long? Aren't you ashamed of yourself, reading the poor boy's personal mail? Why don't you let Wayne read it himself, or is your feminine curiosity killing you to find out what his mail says?

Look out that window! No, not that one, the other one. See the CIA agent snooping around? He just booby-trapped your house. Either stop reading Wayne's mail or poof!, the house gets it.

Get Wayne to send a personal reply or I may cry.

Your fan,
Tim.

Dear Mr. Wayne Gretzky:

Just because everyone likes you doesn't mean that they are all that crazy about your girl friend, too. We wonder where the heck you found that overgrown buffalo.

Don't be angry by reading this, but it's for your own good. Everyone knows that she is trying to use you so she can boost her own career. Good luck with her, but I will be the only one laughing when you guys will be trying to get a divorce settlement.

Dear Wayne:

Getting a personal autograph sent to me was great but next time send yourself in a big box!! And if Ms. Moss gets mad, tuff.

Love from Yvonne.

Dear Wayne, Sophie, Vickie or Sophie's friend, whoever is reading this letter:

The main reason I'm writing you is because I think it's unfair to us fans that you don't give a damn about what happens to the letters you get. You don't even read them, for God's sake. (Sophie, make sure he reads this.)

Remember, you creep, some people do care and they go out of their way to write to say you're a fantastic hockey player or the cutest guy they ever saw. They have dreams, like you. You should at least give them a couple of words of thanks for caring.

How 'bout it? Prove yourself a nice guy, Wayne.

Sheila and Nickie.

Dear Mr. W. Gretzky:

I was told that you sponsor the MS (Multiple Sclerosis) Read-a-Thon. Do you really? Do you give any of the millions of dollars you make to the MS? My mom has MS and do you know the pain she suffers each day? Do you know what it's like to have a mom who can't teach you stuff and can't play with you?

I'm 12 and I've never had any of the things that my best friend has from her mom. Do you really know what it is like to live in a family that the father doesn't give a damn about anybody but himself? Also to live in a family that the mom can't even walk?

I think I'm the only one my mom can trust! Wayne, do you know what it's like to know your mom is going to die before you graduate from high school?

Do you really (support MS research)? Do you give any of the money you make. If you don't you are a #$%%$# money-loving bastard!

If you do give a reasonable amount of money to MS please excuse what I have said above, and please return my picture. By the way, you are a very handsome guy.

Kim.

Dear Wayne Gretzky:

During the summer can you find me a place to run away to, or can you take me to your place? I can't take it here. Every time I say something they yell at me. I told them I wanted to be an ice skater. They told me I wouldn't make it. I told them I was going to be a hockey coach and they said I would never make it. Everything I say, they say I won't make it.

I HATE IT HERE. I HATE IT HERE! I HATE MY PARENTS. I HATE MY PARENTS!

If you took me to your place I would do everything I'm told, I'll do chores and you don't have to pay me. Just think of me as your sister doing your jobs. I'll even take out the garbage for you. I'll dust, vacuum, polish, anything you want me to do.

Please take me in. My parents think I'm a failure.

Your friend,
Cindy.

PS: Write back!
PSS: Don't worry if you don't take me, I'll find some-
where to go on my own. I've been down before and I
HATE IT HERE!

What can you do with letters like that? You can write a personal note, which Wayne does or I do, and tell the kids to
hold on and not to give up because things will get better.
But you can't change their lives for them, as much as you'd
like to. You can only hope that by writing, by communicat-
ing, they've been able to get the problem out, and maybe
taken some of the pressure off.

One thing you can't do. You can't stop thinking about
them. Particularly the poor, brave little ones who've had no
chance at all . . . .

Dear Mrs. Gretzky:

I wanted to write to thank you for your quick response
in sending a photograph of your son to my niece a few
weeks ago. Heather died Tuesday morning after six hard
years of battling with cystic fibrosis. She was a real
Gretzky fan and despite her weak condition she still
watched the hockey games till late into the evening, even
into the last couple of weeks of her life.

Last summer she spent quite a bit of time in Sick
Children's Hospital in Toronto. It was there that her
dream came true and she met Wayne. It was at that time
that your son gave her a wrist watch – something that she
dearly cherished. So when she received his picture she was
really pleased.

Heather was a hero in her own way as well. She had a
very severe case of CF requiring many medications,
treatments and therapies. It was during her stay at Sick
Kids that she reached a starvation state and required a
tube to be put into her abdomen and directly into her
stomach. She was given feedings that lasted 14 hours a
day from that point on. Yet despite all of the pain and

frustration Heather never once complained. She never complained that she couldn't run and play like her friends, or questioned why she was born with such a horrible disease. So, in her own way, Heather was a hero.

So thank you for bringing these moments of joy to little Heather that I will always love and remember with fondness.

Sincerely,
Ruth Bartley.

Mr. Wayne Gretzky:

Please listen. I watched a TV commercial while in Edmonton this season asking for help for children in some far-off country. My grandson's ashes sat at my elbow. He was only two years and seven months old.

Please help the Northern Alberta Children's Hospital. Some day you may need it. A telethon? A $100-a-plate dinner? Your backing could help those struggling volunteers who are trying to get help and surely Alberta has been good to you.

You have shopping malls, influence, prestige to help right there. Please do help – sick children need help more than patrons in a mall, and in the end it is much more rewarding.

If you can ask for help for kids in Timbucktu, how about Alberta kids? They need help, too. It's too late for my grandson. Please help. My pension is enough for me but not much help on such a badly needed project.

Thanks for caring.

A Brantford grandmother.

Wayne does contribute to many charities – more than anyone hears about, including us. A lot of thank-you letters come in with an invoice or tax number, for income tax purposes, for projects or charities that the people who look after Wayne's business know nothing about. Somewhere on the road Wayne has donated an appearance fee or something personal that can be used to generate money for a worthwhile cause. He hasn't told anyone because it's personal. It's just something he wanted to do.

No one can look after them all. There's not that much money in the world. But no matter how much he does, or how well and carefully he conducts himself, there are always those who find fault or want to pull him down to their level . . . .

Wayne Gretzky:

Hi there. I suppose you think this is your regular lies of a fan letter. Will your (sic) wrong. I am a 15-year-old girl who is an avid Canucks fan. I think you are a good hockey player who's (sic) sucsess (sic) has gone straight to his head down to his ankles and back again.

To tell you the truth I think you are a showoff who enjoys as much attention as possible, greedily smiles to magazines and newspapers and enjoys every damm (sic) moment of it. To tell you frankly I hate you with a passion. I think you are ugly and have the grossest body I've ever seen.

Lots of love,
Denise.

PS: Write back and tell me what you think.

Wayne Gretzky:

I may as well spend another 30 cents to my expensive weekend.

In honor of my 50th wedding anniversary I said I'd like to see you play in Toronto as I am an avid hockey fan from away back when they used to play good hockey.

You've become so big-headed that you didn't even have the decency to look up when I asked you for your autograph. Sure you saw me – twice I confronted you and could have touched you. It must be your Polish heritage to make you so ignorant and disrespectful to the elderly.

I had wanted the autograph for an ailing grandson, not for me. I've met Bobby Orr in person. He at least has manners.

Incidentally, you played miserably and was I glad.

Hope you fizz out, big head. Our expenses – please donate to a Boys Club: Room $85, tickets $24, Food $80, transportation $30, stamp .30. Total $219.30. A waste.

Wayne:

How is it that a 19-year-old (20 in a few short weeks) can act like a #$%$ spoiled brat? I'm 19 myself, a university student for two years now, and I don't recall ever acting like you.

Ever since the end of last season I've come close to puking every time I see or hear of you. In a way it's not your fault. The media has built you up to be a superman and I guess, dummy that you are, you believe it. But take a good look at yourself some day and learn some class before it's too late. Most people your age think you're too "great" for your own good.

There's not much you can do about people like that, either, except to hope that they grow up or learn to understand the situation. Take the lady who wanted the autograph. Wayne signs thousands of them. But when he's looking into a crowd and there are a hundred hands waving pieces of paper in his face there's just no way he can get to them all.

Crank letters are a different story. They go into a special file. If that person writes again, the office contacts the police in the person's area just to make them aware of what is happening. If a third letter arrives, the police are notified again and go knocking on the person's door, ordering that the letters cease. They aren't what you'd call threatening letters. There's been only one or two of those. But some of the things they contain are too gross for publication. And you have to be careful.

With the mild letters like the ones above we just send an apologetic letter with a signed picture in it, hope for the best, and console ourselves with the thought that so many people out there do care and do appreciate the effort that's being made.

Mostly you'd have to classify the mail as, well, *nice*. The girls who write from all over the world expressing schoolgirl crushes; the hockey fans, boys and girls who just want to let us know how they feel about Wayne; the adults who write about our family and theirs, the ones who understand a little bit about the pressures on Wayne and on the rest of us – they're friendly people who just want to express that friendship. And they do it in a thousand ways . . . .

Dear Wayne:

If you're free at any time in the last half of May, could you come to a birthday party and end-of-exams party at my place? All my hockey pals will be there and we'd have one heck of a time. You can stay with any of us, you'll have a super time, we'll feed you good food and we'll make sure there aren't any newspaper reporters. Just a good time with some down to earth Wisconsin friends.

> Your friend,
> Craig.

PS: Call collect.

Hi Wayne:

If it's not asking too much could I have something you touched but not a picture.

> Your fan,
> Pauline

Dear Wayne:

I couldn't believe it when I got your autographed picture in the mail! You are such a fox, and definitely the best hockey player in the world.

If you guys come to Philly for a game I'll definitely be there! You are such a FOX! I have millions of pictures on my wall of you – well, not millions, but every one I can possibly find. You're so cute! I know I keep saying that but I can't help it! I'm madly in love with you.

Please write back if you have the time.

Love ya!
Vicki.

Dear Mr. Gretzky:

I got your picture yesterday. I like you better in uniform. My mom likes you better in a suit. If you want to, you can write back.

Your friend,
Ron.

Dear Wayne Gretzky:

I was wondering if you could ask Glen Sather next winter if I could play hockey with you guys. If he says no, that's okay.

Your friend,
Fiona.

Dear Wayne:

If apples were peaches,
And pears were plums,
And if Rose had a different name,
If tigers were bears,
And fingers were thumbs,
I'd love you just the same.

Love always,
Lisa.

Dear Wayne:

Thank you for the autograph that you sended (sic) in the mail for me. I was so happy when I got it.

I just turned 10. If at any time my mother or father

would try to give the autograph away or sell it I will say do not do that, keep it, even. It's valuable.

Sincerely yours,
Micah.

Dear Wayne:

I am a Kings fan and live in LA County. The reason for this letter is to apologise for the way the Kings' fans have been treating you.

Please try to understand. The Kings have been in last place for a while. And when some player comes to town who everyone calls The Great Gretzky you don't take to him so well.

Sincerely,
Maylene.

PS: Keep up the great job, but give the Kings a break!

Dear Mr. Gretzky:

On the autograph you said "In friendship", and I feel I should repay you in some way. I thought money, but I would feel like I was bribing you and what could a millionaire expect from a 14-year-old boy?

So when you're in Boston to play the Bruins I would like to offer you a house to stay at if you have to stay a night because I know you don't mind talking to the press but I'm sure you don't like them following you home.

So when you come to Boston if you don't want to stay at your hotel please write me in advance and I'll set up our extra bed. And Mr. Gretzky, I promise that even if you do or if you don't, either way I won't tell anybody until after you left, because after you leave if you decided to it would be impossible to keep in because you are one (if not the greatest) hockey player of all time.

I know you probably won't because your coach won't let you or you might just not want to but either way will you please return my letter with a response so I at least know you received it.

Your fan always,
Gerry.

Dear Waino:

Thank you for this lovely photograph. I like it very much and I decide (sic) thank you.

"Waino" is yours (sic) petname here in Finland. My petname is Nuni. I hope that you written (sic) me sometimes when you have time. I want learned (sic) English and I hope that I get news (sic) friend and penfriend from elsewhere when (sic) Finland.

I send you my photograph, but it isn't good because I do it myself.

Yours for ever,
Nuni.

Dear Wayne Gretzky:

My name is Janet and I am a Chicago model. I am new here so I have not broken into the market yet (and I'm wondering if I ever will). I have enclosed some pictures of myself so you have an idea of who is writing.

I am a hockey fan first and a model second (a far second). I don't care if I don't eat as long as I have hockey. Good thing, too, since I'm down to $30.

Take care and stay healthy in mind and body. Take a close look at my pictures. Though I have a lot of problems day to day I am a fundamentally happy person. Not many like me around. Keep peace of mind, Wayne.

Love,
Janet.

Dear Wayne:

I'm about the same age as your mother and I think you are a son to be most proud of. You are to be commended for your down-to-earth way of expressing yourself and for your obvious love toward your whole family. You bring tears of joy to my eyes when you speak so proudly of your folks. Oh, how we all wish our young folks to be like you – not the wealth, necessarily, but your sincerity.

Bless you, lad. I love you!

Yours truly,
Donna Mae.

Dear Wayne:

My licence number is GRETZKY. I put your name on all my hockey sticks and named my cat after you.

Good luck!
Danny,
Glen Cove, N.Y.

Hi Wayne:

Being one of your fans since years, and having hundreds of paper clips and photos of you as this is my hobby, being actually in prison and without having a personal one from you, I should gladly appreciate to receive a dedicated one from you that I could use on the first page of my collection if you have a few minutes to mail me one, and if it is not too asking, one of the team too.

Excuse me if I could not go cheer your team up during your regular season as I am behind bars, but be sure I'm always with you guys when your (sic) on TV, or even else, in spirit.

Hope you bring the Stanley Cup home this year.

Yvan.

PS: Excuse my English, I am French.

Dear Wayne:

I live in Anchorage, Alaska, and I am absolutely crazy about you. Anyways, I was wondering if you would like to go to a Sadie Hawkins dance with me at my high school. I

would really love for you to go with me. Even if you can't or don't want to go, will you please write me back?
Thank You!

Love,
Chrissy.

Hello Wayne!

I am a girl 15 from Finland and I like very much of ice-hockey and very much of boys or mens (sic) who play ice-hockey. I think that you are the most beautiful ice-hockey player in the world. Your smile drives me mad! You are our little Peter Pan.

I would be very happy if you sent me your picture. Be so friendly and help me. I really love you.

Satu.

Dear Wayne:

> The 21 year old from Brantford
> Has every possible record.
> He shoots the puck, it isn't luck,
> He sees the holes and scores the goals.
>
> His muscles they are lean and quick,
> These make his moves look smooth and quick.
> The greatest player in orange and blue
> Is also the greatest in good looks, too.
>
> Soon he will win the cup of Stanley,
> In the sport of hockey he is manly.
> He looks great when he's on TV,
> In person he's a real cutee.
>
> His fans will always scream and yell,
> They know he always scores goals well.
> That 99, he's really fine,
> I only wish I could call you mine.

Ann.

Dear Mr. and Mrs. Gretzky:

There were about 25 to 30 fans (at an Oilers game in Montreal, waiting for Wayne and looking for autographs). When Wayne arrived he *ran* into the Forum with a bodyguard! Nobody got his picture nor his autograph. I did, however, get the back of his head (ha ha).

I found out the hotel where he was staying, went there the next morning and waited in the lobby. I saw Wayne getting out of a taxi! My heart started to flip and flop! I asked him if he would sign a picture for me. His answer was "Sure." Then I asked him if I could take a picture of him, and his answer was "Sure. Do you have your camera?"

While I was getting my camera ready another man who was with Wayne told him to hurry up, but your sweet and considerate son said "One minute, this girl wants a picture!!"

Then I asked him "Could I get in the picture with you?" He said "Sure" and put his arm around me while the other man took the picture! Knowing that he was in a rush I kissed him on the cheek and said thank you.

I know that Wayne could have just walked right by me that day because he looked tired on TV and at the game. And that afternoon he had to fly to Buffalo to receive an award as professional athlete of the year.

Now I have such nice memories of him. I think you deserve credit for doing a great job in raising him.

Love,
Kim.

One of the things we've learned, all of us, is that there is a responsibility that goes with being in the public eye. The most casual thing you do can be misinterpreted – and the smallest thing you do can mean so much to someone.

Out of the thousands of letters, this one says it as well as any . . . .

Dear Wayne Gretzky:

You probably won't remember but at your Sept. 15 4 p.m. workout you gave our five-year-old boy, Trevor, a puck. The first one was taken by some older kids so you handed one to him. We have not seen Trev so happy in a very long time.

Last year he had three operations, saw me go through a very difficult pregnancy, was severely disappointed when he got another brother instead of a sister, saw his father go away for six weeks when the baby was only 10 days old, then had to leave all his friends in Prince Edward Island when we were transferred in June. All of this has had a deep emotional effect on Trevor. We appreciate what you did more than you will ever know. Trevor's letter (enclosed) took him all afternoon to write. The words are his own:

Dear Mr. Gretsky: (sic)
   Thank you for the puck. You are the greatest.
   My phone number is .... If you are ever sad, you can call me and I will be your friend.

Trevor.

Chapter 15

WHAT YOU SEE AIN'T WHAT YOU GET

"Two summers ago I'd rather have flown to Vegas than watch my little brother play baseball. Now I'd rather stay home and watch my little brother play ball than fly to Vegas."

– Wayne Gretzky, July, 1983.

Twenty hours after signing his latest contract with Peter Pocklington – the one the media reported could be worth as much as $20 million – and sixteen hours after scoring a hat trick to make it 60 in 49 games, Wayne is standing alone on a stage in the CBC TV studio in Vancouver, staring up at cue cards and trying to sing a parody of *The Devil Came Down to Georgia*. It is not going well.

> *"The Devil came down to Showdown,*
> *He was looking for a soul to steal.*
> *He was in a bind; he was way behind,*
> *And willin' to make a deal . . . ."*

"No, I haven't got the worst voice in Edmonton," he told reporters later. "Tom Wilkinson (quarterback for the Edmonton Eskimos), he's worse than me.

"But not by much," he conceded.

"He said I'll bet your soul
You can't score a goal
With the Devil in the net . . . ."

My son, the TV star. In the middle of the record-breaking 1981-82 season, with so much public interest that there
were fifteen hundred autograph hounds after him in Toronto and it took a wedge of policemen to get him into the
hotel, he's in Vancouver taping the *Paul Anka Show*, sing-
ing and doing comedy commercials. ("Stanley Cup-o-
Soup," he says, pouring it into a replica of the Stanley Cup.
"Tastes great – from the kitchens of Clarence Campbell.") It
takes him two tries. "Aw, I missed the penalty shot in Toronto," he says after the first attempt. "I guess I can miss
this."

The TV show takes eight hours to complete, less meal
breaks. There's also been a CBC radio crew and a local
newspaperman following him around, each doing "A Day
in the Life of Wayne Gretzky." Later, when they're long
gone, the day will end when he slips quietly away for a late-
evening trip to a hospital to visit an acrobatic skier he's
heard about who missed a ramp and is now partially
paralyzed. It isn't a typical day, but it's close.

From the time Wayne really became a celebrity, people
have worried about him, worried that he might burn out,
that he puts too much on himself, that he feels obligated to
accept too many commitments. Two days before the Anka
show, Oilers' PR man Bill Tuele told a reporter friend:
"Wayne's got to stop. He's got to learn to say 'No!' He's getting that pinched look around the eyes. Olga Korbut, the
Russian gymnast, had it, remember? The look that says
you're wearing down. But Wayne will do anything. He
thinks he should. He thinks he *has* to."

Wayne's always disputed that, publicly at least. "This is
the fun part," he told reporters at the Anka taping. "This is
the entertainment. I'm just a country Canadian. To be on
the *Paul Anka Show*, that's an honour. I'm on this earth to
do the best I can. I'm not going to play hockey forever. To

201

do the other things is a thrill. Sure, I'm tired. Tired is part of living."

Four days later he'd be twenty-one years old, and tired was a part of living . . . .

Wayne spent two years running from coast to coast, making what he thought was big money doing public appearances, endorsements, banquets, that sort of thing. And it *was* good money when you think only of dollars. But there came a moment in the summer of 1981 when Wayne realized that there was something more important and far more precious. Something called free time. The clincher was a trip that went Vancouver, Calgary, Regina, Winnipeg and Halifax. He'd spent Sunday in Vancouver and now he was in Halifax doing a radio show at 7 a.m. Wednesday, which was 3 a.m. Vancouver time – the time his stomach, mind and body were still on. "That's it," he told us when he got back to Brantford. "They can have all the money back. It just isn't worth it."

To this day he has trouble explaining it to outsiders. They get a stunned look on their face when he says: "When it comes to the commercial side of it, if I have to work three days for $5,000, forget it."

He's not talking about appearances for good causes. I don't think there are three major charities in the country he hasn't given his support to at one time or another, as spokesman or honorary chairman. He represents four: the Association for the Mentally Retarded, the Christian Children's Fund, the Canadian National Institute for the Blind and the Juvenile Diabetes Foundation. He did a commercial for the RCMP fight against drug abuse, and is involved with other NHL players in another anti-drug program involving kids in schools. He's done commercials for the Lung Foundation and other charities. CorpSport writes forty to fifty letters per week explaining that he can't send money because the precedent would simply trigger a flood. However, those same letters do include autographed items for auction at charity fund-raisers. For charity, Wayne is committed and involved and he wants it that way. But for anything else, there has to be a limit.

"A guy phones from Vancouver and says he'll give me $10,000 and two first-class tickets from Brantford to speak at a Saturday night banquet. When Dad or Mike says no, he says, 'Are you *crazy?*' Well, it's two hours' work, but I have to leave Brantford Friday for Saturday and I can't get home before Sunday night, so where does he get that two hours business? If it's not $10,000 for two hours' work, I just tell Mike or Dad to say no. I know it sounds silly . . . but time is more precious than dollars."

How serious is he about this? Well, he's often asked by corporations to appear at a luncheon. Just have lunch with them, that's all. Just be there, or even go fishing – for $20,000. Almost without exception he says no. He's turned down a $10,000 fee just to appear at a shopping centre opening. Time is precious – so precious that he once paid $15,000 to go for a walk.

We'd just come back from a trip to Russia. The plane trip had wiped us out. We got home and fell into bed. In two days Wayne's tennis tournament opened in Brantford – and Wayne was supposed to drive in to Toronto the next day to film a commercial with the Mattel people. They'd booked an arena, their crews were hired, everything was ready to go. Except Wayne.

"I can't do it," he said when Michael phoned to remind him. "Tell them I'm sorry, but I'm burned out. Tell them I'll pay whatever it's cost this time, and set it up for another day."

When he woke up the next morning, he drove to the farm, took out a fishing rod, and went for a walk by the Nith, all by himself, just recharging his batteries. The bill from Mattel was $15,000. He didn't catch even one fish. But for Wayne it was worth it. He'd bought himself a little slice of time.

Things are better organized now. Summers are planned

ahead. The major companies, for whom he does endorsements or commercials, are sent a schedule of the days he'll
be available and are requested to send Michael their six
choices in order of preference. They're all in by the end of
February, laid out on a chart and juggled so that they can
all be done in one trip back and forth across the country.

It has to be done that way, because there isn't really that
much time. The two weeks after the season ends are for
total rest. With the Stanley Cup playoffs continuing
through mid-to-late May (assuming the Oilers make the
final), that rest period ends in the first or second week in
June. Then it's directly into the summer schedule, with
holidays squeezed into whatever time comes loose. But extra
things keep coming up. (Wayne's personal training for this
past season's Canada Cup, for instance, started July 15.)
And before you know it the Oilers are opening camp again.

Most summers Wayne tries to get away, but it's getting
harder every year. A couple of years ago, he flew to Martinique, figuring he could just relax because no one there
would know him. He got off the plane, headed for a cab,
and saw a little native boy in the street playing a game that
looked like hockey – using a Titan stick with Wayne's
signature on it! He went into a restaurant that night and saw
someone reading the current issue of *Sports Illustrated*. His
picture was on the cover.

Another time, Michael and Wayne drove from Vancouver to Seattle, with some people from Nike, to film a
commercial in an ice house – Wayne standing on a six-foot
block of ice shaped like the Nike "swoosh" logo. They
stopped for a bite to eat at a McDonald's outside Bell-
ingham, Wash. In thirty seconds Wayne was surrounded by
kids. Fortunately, we have a system for going to
McDonald's. It revolves around one sentence.

"Eat first," he said. "Sign later."

Obediently, the kids went back to their tables. As Wayne
ate his Big Mac and fries, he felt a hundred pairs of eyes on
him. He finished, wiped his mouth with his napkin, and

nodded his head. They flooded over the table, and he spent the next half hour signing his name.

Guess what's a big thrill for Wayne. Getting a haircut. Because if he changes the style just a little bit, there are a few days in there when no one recognizes him, and he can walk the streets in peace.

Okay, you say, but it's the same for all the NHL stars. But it *isn't*. For one thing, most of them play for teams in American cities where the marketing opportunities for a hockey player aren't so great, because hockey in the U.S. isn't a game of nation-wide interest. For another, Wayne's accomplishments have put him off by himself in the eyes of the people who make the decisions on who's marketable and who's not. Mike Bossy, for instance, is a superstar playing for a Stanley Cup champion team. And yet, unfortunately, there aren't very many Mike Bossy commercials.

Wayne is grateful for the opportunities. What concerns him is that his situation gives a distorted picture of what those opportunities are.

"I wish they had a players' association for endorsements," he said once, "because I'd like to be president on behalf of the guys in the NHL, and the kids who'll be coming in – especially for kids.

"An agent says, 'Come with me and I promise I'll make you $50,000 off the ice for doing practically nothing.' It doesn't happen. Kevin Lowe of our team works extremely hard at it. He does banquets, he has his own radio show – he might be making more off-ice than ninety-nine per cent of all the other athletes in Canada. That's because he devotes time to it – hours and hours and hours – and plans ahead for the day when he won't be playing. But when an agent says to a kid, 'I'll get you $20,000 and all you'll have to do is wear their skates,' that's a lie. There are no free rides. Companies want more for their investment than that. I know better than anyone. I spent two years flying all over the country proving it.

"At eighteen or nineteen it's not going to affect you. I did it and I loved it. It was fun. If I had it to do over again I would. But nobody tells them about the time and the cost. If I say I'd rather spend a day at the farm with my Grandma than go somewhere and make $20,000, they laugh. They can't believe it. But it's true – and if they're as fortunate as I've been, when it comes to the opportunities, the day will come when they will feel the same way. Nobody tells them. And somebody should."

Amen. And while we're at it, let's get somebody to give a course on how to pick an agent and what to look out for. There are a lot of good agents out there, but there are also a lot of sharks. For a boy just coming out of junior hockey at seventeen or eighteen, it's all too easy to make the wrong choice.

You take the business of an agent's percentage of the contract he negotiates. Some take five per cent, some take up to ten per cent – but that percentage is of the *entire* amount of the contract, and that's not logical.

Any first-round draft pick knows he's going to get big money. He could get a large percentage of that money all by himself, just by walking through the general manager's door. Why should an agent get a percentage of that? A far more sensible approach would be for a boy and his father, or friend or adviser, to go in, negotiate for as much as *they* can get, leave without signing, and *then* go to an agent and say, "They've offered me this much. I'll give you a percentage of anything you can get me *over* that figure."

Think about it. Why should an agent get a split of something you'd be able to get for yourself without him?

If I was asked to advise a young player about to turn pro, there are a few other things I'd warn him about.

* Have *everything* in writing. Never let an agent get away with saying, "Don't worry. I'll take care of that." If you get the wrong kind, the person he looks after first is himself. Ask the players who've lost their life's savings.

* Be sure it's ironclad, before negotiations start, as to whether or not your agent is getting a percentage of your

signing bonus. To me, bonuses are the monies a player receives for achievements during the season – but unless that's clearly defined in the contract "bonus" could mean *all bonuses, including the one for signing.*

* Find out in advance who pays the lawyers' fees, the accountants' fees, and all the other fees you're liable to find on the agent's bill, if the responsibilities aren't down in black and white. Better still, use your own lawyer and your own accountant. With good people in those areas, you might not even need an agent.

* Demand monthly statements.

* Before you agree to give power-of-attorney to an agent or anyone else, be sure you're totally aware of what the term means and the dangers that can go with it.

* Remember that it doesn't take many five-per centers to take twenty-five per cent of your earnings.

Those are a few of the basics. To a boy just starting out as a professional, in awe of the National Hockey League, and all excited about playing with and against the stars he's watched for years, those basics can be awfully important. It can even be the difference between whether you keep your money – or someone else does.

The difference between what has happened to Wayne and what has happened to other hockey stars today is that they are hockey stars, and Wayne is a *celebrity*, just as Gordie Howe is still a celebrity. Howe's playing days are over, but he still can't walk down a street without someone stopping him for an autograph. Wayne has become sought after by people outside the game, the ones the magazine writers are always calling the Beautiful People who live in the Fast Lane. Case in point: the Gretzky portraits.

Leroy Neiman, who has gained an international reputation for his portraits of athletes, followed Wayne around for several games making sketches. The three hundred copies issued, available only in Canada, all but sold out in six months at $2,200 each. In the U.S. you could now get $5,000 if you had one to sell.

Pop artist Andy Warhol followed with his Gretzky portrait, unveiled December 12, 1983, at a party in New York. He did six originals (which Associated Press described as "each looking a bit like a badly-exposed colour photo negative"). One went to Wayne, the others were put on sale at $35,000 each. In addition, three hundred prints of one of the paintings were offered for sale at $2,000 each. Wayne received a fee plus royalty on posters made from one painting, which were distributed world-wide.

Only a handful of athletes – people like Willie Shoemaker, Jack Nicklaus, Joe Namath, Muhammad Ali, and Kareem Abdul-Jabbar – have been painted by both Warhol and Neiman. Somehow, Wayne has caught the imagination of the American star set. And while Wayne has come to accept the fact, and enjoys the situations and the friendships, he still hasn't gotten over the surprise that it should be that way.

One night he was in Los Angeles to play in one of those celebrity pro-am tennis tournaments, where people bid for the right to play doubles with the celebrity of their choice. There was Wayne in the same room with John McEnroe, Bjorn Borg and a handful of other top-notch pros, when a local entrepreneur named Bob Franks announced that he had just paid $7,500 to play tennis with Wayne. "I want to play with the greatest athlete in the world," he said, then headed for the kitchen and returned with magnums of champagne for every table.

"Oh, it was flattering, all right," Wayne said later. "But sitting with all those great players around and having him pay that much to play with me – I didn't know where to put my face."

Singer Billy Joel phoned once when Wayne was out. He wanted to come to his tennis tournament in Brantford and asked Wayne to call him back. Wayne was actually afraid to. This was *Billy Joel!* and he was only Wayne Gretzky of Brantford, Ont. He never shows it, but there are still times when he feels slightly out of place.

One of the major things taken into consideration in planning Wayne's summer schedule is to make it as much fun as possible. If you can't have fun when you're twenty-three and on top of your world, when can you? So when the invitation came to go to California, stay on the beach and do some personal appearances, the immediate answer was "Why not?"

Wayne's a soap opera fan like his mother, his sister and his brothers. He knew that if he did a spot on *The Young and the Restless* the critics would pan him. He was willing to do it for the enjoyment and the learning experience. As for the critics, he simply said, "I didn't score a goal my first time on the ice, either."

And there were side benefits. He appeared on a TV special, *The Best of Everything*, in which Hollywood stars modelled designer clothes. Actors like Paul Newman and Lee Majors were there, but the pre-program advertising centred around Heather Thomas, a young actress who appears with Majors in his show *The Fall Guy* – and Wayne Gretzky, hockey player, Edmonton Oilers.

They filmed the show, but Wayne had to skip the black tie dinner and dance that evening, which was also being filmed to insert in the program. He had a rather important prior commitment. A year earlier he'd won the American Academy of Achievement Award. This year an actor who'd met Wayne in Buffalo was to be one of the winners and he had requested expressly that Wayne be the one who presented to him. So Wayne finished filming the TV show in Los Angeles and hot-footed it to San Diego for the awards presentation that night.

It made for a crazy, hectic day. But would *you* want to disappoint Burt Reynolds?

The sports awards are another thing entirely. He treasures each of them, big or small. No athlete ever gets tired of winning. From trophies to cups to new cars (six at last count), they'll always be remembered. Each of them has a story to go with it, but none as wild as the one that goes with the *Sports Illustrated* Sportsman of the Year Award for 1982.

Outside of competition trophies themselves, this is probably the most prestigious, highly-publicized sports award in the U.S. Part of the reason is that the magazine lets the suspense build up through November and December, and somehow manages to keep the choice of winner from becoming public knowledge until the day the issue announcing it comes out.

We knew *SI* would go to any length to keep the winner's name secret. We'd even been warned that if the word got out any time up to within three days of publication, they'd switch and go to their second choice. That year I believe it was Herschel Walker, the Georgia running back who had won the Heisman Trophy as the outstanding player in college football.

But we underestimated the trouble they'd go to in making sure there was no leak at their end . . . .

The award is announced in the magazine's year-end issue. Actually, Wayne knew he'd won it on November 12. People from the magazine had given Michael the word – and the warning – that day at a meeting in New York. The next trick was to get photos taken, including the cover shot, in the middle of a hockey season in which Wayne was setting records and attracting media like flies to honey everywhere he went, without tipping their hand.

This is how they did it.

First they flew a man into Edmonton who spent three weeks checking out the Northlands Coliseum and figuring out what equipment might be needed. Then they rented the Coliseum on November 29 – overnight.

The film crew flew in, waited until the Coliseum closed, and went to work. The boards were blacked out, the lighting set. But Wayne wasn't there. He'd played in Detroit the night before and was on his way home. However, Michael is roughly Wayne's size and colouring. He would do.

They sneaked him into the rink at 3 a.m., and he was there until 10 a.m. They dressed him in Wayne's clothes, Wayne's uniform, everything, just to test the lighting. Then they started taking shot after shot.

When they were finished, they took down the lights, cleared the boards, removed every trace of their visit, and flew back to New York. There they developed all the pictures of Michael in the various clothes and poses, and picked the two they thought might make the best cover shot. Then they set a date and rented the Coliseum *again* from 7 to 9 a.m., flew the crew back to Edmonton, duplicated the lighting and backdrop of the first visit, hustled Wayne into his strip, positioned him precisely where Michael had been for the two shots, and snapped away. Then they flew home, still undetected.

There was one problem, though. While all this was going on, Michael was trying his best to look innocent. The media were growing suspicious. Suddenly four former NHL superstars – Phil Esposito, Bobby Hull, Bobby Orr and Ken Dryden – were following the Oilers everywhere they went. *SI* had them there on secret assignment. The thrust of the cover story would be Gretzky as seen through the eyes of four of the game's all-time All-Stars. But Michael couldn't say that – and if the real reason got out, Herschel Walker was Sportsman of the Year.

He did the only thing he could. He lied. He told them the four were there to do a special story about Wayne – for the Oilers. They bought it, *SI* got its cover picture, and Wayne got his award.

Estimated cost of that one cover picture: $80,000.

The episode had an interesting sidelight. The Wayne Gretzky on the cover of the magazine didn't look quite like the Wayne Gretzky who received the Grecian Urn trophy between periods of a game in Edmonton December 22. On the cover of the magazine, his hair was longer – much longer then he ever let it grow. But at the time he was pursuing the NHL consecutive-game point record. Hockey players are not short on superstitions. As long as the streak was alive, he would not trim his hair or shave off the slight moustache that had appeared on his upper lip.

But he looked scruffy. So, for the sake of appearances, he shaved off the moustache for the photo session. And when he broke the record and ran the streak to 30 (the record he pushed to 51 games last season), he decided enough was enough. The morning he arrived in Los Angeles for a game that night, he went out and got a haircut.

That night, the Kings shut him out . . . .

Strange things happen to you when you're in the public eye, things over which you don't have any control. Your name gets associated with some product or project, and the fact that the name is there makes the whole thing look legitimate, whether it is or not.

For Wayne, that's becoming a problem. For instance, how do you think he felt on November 2, 1983, when an RCMP officer knocked on his door and asked him what he knew about his investment in a pirate ship?

We'd heard something about it two weeks earlier – a call to CorpSport from a man in Pennsylvania who'd heard Wayne was in on some investment in Europe. He wanted to warn him to get out because it looked like nothing but a scam.

About two hours after that, I got a call from Gus Badali. Did I know anything about an investment Wayne had made in some ship? Something about a forty per cent investment in some kind of pirate ship in Europe. The FBI was involved and about $600,000 had been put into it by other investors and now the money had disappeared and they're trying to get it back; then they'd heard from a guy in Trenton, N.J. that the investment had been made on Wayne's behalf by his father, Walter Gretzky, and the FBI will be in touch with the RCMP, and . . . .

"What are you talking about?" I asked. The FBI? The RCMP? A *pirate* ship? "Phone the FBI!" I insisted. "*Do something!*"

That night I reached Gus again. He told me not to worry,

it was just some guy trying to pull a shakedown or something. Wonderful. The FBI and RCMP might be after my son, but don't worry. The next morning, I tracked down Wayne, who was staying with friends in the southern U.S. He knew nothing about it. He remembered being called once a long time ago about an investment in a ship, but he'd just said to send the information to the office in Toronto.

"You didn't sign anything?" I insisted. "You're sure?"

"Dad," he said patiently. "Even if I'd signed anything it wouldn't have mattered. I was under age. And you know I'd never sign anything without talking to you first, especially something that big."

"Well, if you *knew* about it, why didn't you say something?"

That's when he gave me one of the facts of life as he was now living it.

"Dad," he said, "something like this happens to me almost every day. There are always offers and people with ideas who want me to get involved. What good would it do for me to call you every day with another one?"

Eventually, I got Ian Barrigan involved in Edmonton. He started checking, phoning the man in Pennsylvania and talking to the RCMP. And we found out what it was.

It was a pirate ship, all right. Not a movie pirate ship. Not an Errol Flynn kind of pirate ship, roving the seas and knocking off merchant ships. A genuine pirate ship positioned off the coast of Europe, beyond the jurisdiction of communications governing bodies, "pirating" radio signal space and programming without restrictions of any kind and making good money selling advertising time. And Wayne Gretzky of the Edmonton Oilers was rumoured to be a major investor, but no one knew for sure.

Then the RCMP officer came calling on Wayne. He was very nice about it. He assured Wayne it was a routine call, made at the request of the FBI, who were conducting an inquiry. Wayne told him what little he knew, referred him to me, and I did the same. Ian had a lengthy meeting with the RCMP officer a few days later. We were assured that

Wayne was in no way implicated, that none of his money was invested in the ship. Just like that, it was a dead issue.

But there was a sequel.

Apparently someone still thought he was involved. A lawyer from somewhere in the U.S. wrote Wayne a nice letter congratulating him on being one of the new investors in the ship, pointing out that he (the lawyer) had been working on the project since 1981 – and enclosing a bill for services rendered, requesting immediate payment "so that an unpleasant collection effort will not be necessary."

The bill was for $113,575. Ian turned it over to the RCMP. I hope that somewhere out there the man is holding his breath waiting.

That's one side of being a celebrity – the down side. But stardom, or fame or whatever you want to call it, can also help make nice things happen . . . .

It was June, it was hot, the air conditioning wasn't working, and we had people stacked in our house like cord wood.

Wayne and Vickie were there, my sister, Sophie, Charlie Henry and his son, Peter, plus the family, plus a guy who didn't have a hotel room – a pilot friend of Wayne's who'd flown in from Louisiana. Naturally, Wayne had said, "No problem. Stay at our house." The guy had been there for two days, sleeping on an old couch we'd pulled out in the basement, because that was the only space left, when Phyllis suddenly realized she didn't know who he was. She was introducing everyone in the room to another mob of people who'd arrived, and when she got to him she had to stop and ask, "By the way: What's your name?"

It's been that way every June at our house for the past four years – "What is this, a Holiday Inn?" Phyllis asked me once. "I swear next year I'm going to put a desk in the front hall so people can register as they come in the door!" – and all because Wayne walked in one day in 1981 and said:

"Dad, I want to hold a tennis tournament. Nothing huge or anything. Just a little, fun tennis tournament and maybe invite a few friends. How about helping me set it up?"

"Sure," I said. After all, what was so tough about a tennis tournament? You booked the courts, you made the draw, you told everybody what time to be there, maybe dug up a prize or two. Things like that couldn't take up much time. Like Sam McMaster used to say, a piece of cake . . . .

The Wayne Gretzky Celebrity Tennis Tournament actually was born at 4 a.m. late in the 1980-81 hockey season during one of those late-night bull sessions between Wayne and Charlie Henry. Wayne wanted to do something for Brantford, something that would be good for the city and that the city would support. He and Charlie were just sort of kicking it around.

"What are they short?" Wayne asked.

"Well, the CNIB needs help," Charlie said.

That was all it took. Everyone in Brantford grows up with an awareness of the problems of the blind. The W. Ross MacDonald School for the Blind in Brantford was the second such school established in Canada. It's been there since May 1, 1872, offering classes and training for the blind, and doing research into diseases of the eye. Wayne knew some of the people there, sighted and unsighted. One of the first things he did, when he turned professional, was to establish a scholarship fund there each year for the boy judged to best combine classroom ability and sports participation. He's always had a special feeling for the handicapped, partially I suppose because he grew up with an awareness of his Aunt Ellen's situation with Down's Syndrome, and later through his close association with Vickie's brother, Joey Moss, who has the same affliction.

So, they would do something for the blind. The city recognized the problems of the blind as well or better than anyone in the country. The support would be there. The question was, what was the best way to go about it?

"How about a tennis tournament?" Wayne suggested. "You know, get some sports people together, maybe one or two TV celebrities, charge admission to watch them play, hold a fund-raising banquet to award the prizes . . . something like that?"

"Sounds good," Charlie said. And we were off and running.

I don't think any of us had any idea what we were getting into. This was going to be a quiet little local tournament. We'd raise a few dollars to aid the blind, people would have some fun along the way, and if it worked out we'd do it again next year. If someone had told me Cheryl Tiegs, the best-known model in the world, would play in two of the first three tournaments, or that we'd reach the stage where celebrities from Hollywood would be phoning and asking if they could *please* get an invitiation to play, or that we'd wind up having trouble keeping the field to the maximum thirty-two (because we've only got one portable court) without offending anyone, I'd have told them they'd been standing in the hot sun too long.

How could anything like that happen? This was Brantford, Ont., population 74,800. Why would a lot of world-famous people come to a quiet little tennis tournament? What we didn't understand, I guess, was how much of a celebrity Wayne had become in his own right, particularly after the '81-'82 season. If Wayne Gretzky was holding a tennis tournament then it wasn't quiet or little. It was an Event. It was a Place to Be.

Wayne chuckles a little these days about how it worked out. Because while he had the idea and threw himself into it, he also had a long list of hockey and business commitments for the summer. He couldn't be around much for the actual work that went into organizing it. Guess who that left? "I sort of started the engine, handed Dad the wheel and jumped off the boat," he tells people now. "Whenever Dad and I have a disagreement about something concerning it now he says, 'Okay, we'll change the name to *Keith* Gretzky Celebrity Tennis Tournament!' "

It is true that the organization part of it falls to me and a committee of Brantford volunteers. It's also true that it's become a twelve-month job. But don't kid yourself about which Gretzky is the key ingredient. You think people would be phoning from Hollywood to play in the *Walter* Gretzky Tennis Tournament?

Strangely enough, there are still people who don't understand that. A sponsor actually came up to me once and asked: "Walter, what does *Wayne* do for the tournament?" I couldn't believe it. The only answer going through my mind was, "If you're that stupid, you really don't *deserve* an answer." Fortunately, Murray Angus, our tournament chairman, was there. He could tell I was upset and jumped right in.

"Do you realize what the payback is for Wayne?" he asked. "Do you have any idea how many events he has to go to in order to repay all these celebrities for coming to *his* event? It takes up a good part of his entire summer. So let's drop it right there."

Murray doesn't mess around.

We've had sponsors from the beginning, and they've been great. For example, Nike equips the competitors from head to toe. Wilson Sporting Goods gives every celebrity a new tennis racquet and tennis balls. They get bags loaded with things like golf balls, shirts, good gifts of all kinds. One year everyone got a jacket.

We don't pay anyone to come, but from the second they arrive until the second they leave they're treated like royalty. So, naturally, they all want to come back – which presents a problem: we raise the bulk of the charity funds from the banquet and we need fresh faces each year to keep the public interest up. But how do you tell someone who's looking forward to returning that this time there's no room on the draw?

We also have to be awfully sure that the people we advertise as being in the tournament and at the head table actually get there. Someone who pays $60 for a ticket may be doing it just to see his favourite entertainer. If that entertainer isn't there, we've got a dissatisfied customer who might not buy next year. But we've been quite lucky. To most of the celebrities, a commitment is a commitment.

Jamie Farr, who starred as Cpl. Klinger in the *M.A.S.H.* TV series, has become a good friend of Wayne's in the past few years. He's also a devoted hockey fan who lives in the Los Angeles area. What with his new *AfterM.A.S.H.* TV series in the works and all the other projects he's into, he is extremely busy – but he'd made arrangements to clear the weekend of the 1983 tournament. Naturally, he was one of our big cards when it came to advertising. He'd been super about it, even doing some radio tapes urging people to get out and give their support.

Four days before the tournament, he had to cancel out. When he phoned to tell us, he was really upset. We told him to forget it, that we understood. But he wouldn't. He insisted that we set up a phone call from CKPC Brantford so he could make *another* radio tape to be played periodically over the next four days. In that tape he apologized to the people of Brantford for being unable to make it, urged them again to support the tournament, and promised to be back some day to take part in one. Jamie Farr is a professional.

The tournament is big now, the costs incredible. Air fares run about $14,000, accommodations $5,000, civic centre and banquet hall rental $12,000 – the list goes on and on. We make money every year. For the first two years it went into research for the blind. Funds from the 1983 event were used to purchase machines to play the "talking books" to the blind – two hundred and fifty-seven units at a total cost of $45,000, distributed across Canada, all with money raised through the tournament.

You wouldn't think it would be all that time-consuming to set up a one-day tournament and a banquet. But with people coming from all over, and the publicity involved because they're all celebrities of one sort or another, we found we'd grabbed a tiger by the tail. We've got our own phone line now on a permanent basis. The Post Master General even issued us a special box number (Box 99, Brantford. Wonder where they ever came up with a number like that?). The committee pitches in, and for the last two years I've been able to get time off work.

That first year, though, we had no idea whether the tournament would even live, let alone grow. All we could do was plan it – frantically, that first time, because we did it from scratch in a couple of months – and hope the people showed up. As it turned out, we had no cause to worry.

Bobby Orr was there. He came at his own expense, refusing to accept even the air fare. Father Costello and Father Quinn of the famous Flying Fathers' hockey team are there every year. They drive up from the Detroit-Windsor area, and it took three years for us to coax them into accepting enough money to buy their gas.

You find out right away that athletes and celebrities are just like any other group. Some care, some don't. A man like John Allan Cameron, the Maritimes TV personality, is so delighted to be a part of the tournament he'll do anything to help. Once he drove in from Toronto, picked up Keith and Murray, took them to Kitchener to do a talk show promoting the tournament, and brought them back. Then there was the celebrity who picked up his airline ticket, tried to cash it in, and came to the tournament by car.

The tournament gives us a real chance to study people. You learn quickly that, charity event or not, everything had to be done on a strictly business basis, written down so it can be pulled out later. A verbal agreement to purchase doesn't always work. Some of the people you're dealing with seem to feel that because it's a charity event with some sponsorship, they might as well make a little money on their own. Unless it's written down, the price you get on the bill isn't always the one you got verbally.

You can read a lot about people from the hotel bills they leave behind. This is a charity event, remember. Air fares, room rental and meals are our responsibility. All incidentals are theirs. You look at the extras on some of those bills – the room service tabs, the liquor – and wonder what makes some people tick. By then, though, it 's too late. All you can do is shake your head and put the individual's name on a list – the list of those who won't be asked back.

But those are isolated incidents. Mostly we get people – athletes and celebrities alike – who are concerned with coming in, helping raise the money and entertaining the people, while having a good time themselves. If they're singers, they sing at the banquet. When you think of the fees they charge for doing a show on stage or TV, we pack a lot into that $60 banquet ticket.

Just look at some of the names on our guest list over the first three years: Don Cherry, Bobby Riggs, Cheryl Tiegs, Gloria Loring, Alan Thicke, Lover Boy (the Vancouver rock group that's among the most popular in the world), Anne Murray, Robert Walden (a wonderful man who played Rossi on the *Lou Grant* TV series), Karen Baldwin (Miss Universe of 1983), Eric Fryer (who played the title role in *The Terry Fox Story*). We got them because Wayne has come to know them and they've come to know him. We've gone from wondering whether anyone would come, to wondering how we're going to tell a bunch of famous people they can't come this time because there's no room.

Just a simple little tennis tournament, Wayne said. Look after that for me, will you, Dad? Well, we've done it, and it's been fun, and we'll keep doing it. Expenses are going up, though. For one thing, there's the sign Phyllis threatens to have made to hang outside the door. "Hotel Varadi. No Vacancy!"

So many good things happen when you're a star athlete. But the theory that everything gets thrown your way for nothing just doesn't stand up. Why, even free cars can cost you.

When Wayne tied Dionne for the scoring title as a rookie and didn't share it and was declared ineligible for the rookie-of-the-year award, Peter Pocklington presented him with a new Ferrari as a sort of consolation prize. It was his on a three-year lease – but because the use of a car was a gift, although Mr. Pocklington was paying for the lease, the

Tax Department counted its value as income to Wayne. So he wound up paying taxes on the $60,000 car for three years and then, when the lease expired, he paid another $25,000 to buy it.

You also have a heck of a time getting cars you win across the border, when the All-Star game is in the U.S. Sometimes it gets to be such a pain you wonder if it's worth it. I know I wondered after he won one at the 1983 All-Star game on Long Island. A New York paper even quoted me saying, "Just what we need. Another headache." I should have guessed what would happen.

When Michael got to his office the next week, there were three telephone messages asking him to call back, all from someone in the New York area whose name he didn't recognize. The guy had what he considered a great idea.

"I read about Gretzky's problem with the car," he said. "I'm prepared to fly to Edmonton at my own expense and take that car off his hands. I'll drive it home and he never has to see it again."

Michael declined with thanks. We'd never had the car anyway. Wayne took cash instead.

Naturally, the family follows the car stories with interest. The car Wayne won as NHL player of the year in 1981-82 sat in our garage for a year until Keith was old enough to drive. Now it's his. Kim's got the car in Los Angeles that came with the player-of-the-year award for 1982-83.

Glen and Brent can hardly wait. As Glen puts it: "Wayne, the garage is empty. Now *mine* can sit in there until *I'm* old enough to drive!"

Chapter 16

GRETZKY? ARE YOU ONE OF *THE* GRETZKYS?

"Sometimes – not often, but sometimes – I'd find myself wishing my last name was anything but Gretzky."

– Kim Gretzky, 1983.

There was the day Kim got into the cupboard when she was very small and tasted the oven cleaner. Peeled the top layer off her tongue, and if Phyllis hadn't been there in a hurry, rinsed her mouth and gotten treatment for her, heaven knows how badly she'd have been hurt.

There was the morning five-year-old Wayne ran into the house, bolted under his bed and quivered there, while Phyllis answered the door to an angry man who explained that the boy who'd just ran into the house had thrown a rock at his car.

There was the day that three-year-old Brent found the heavy lights for my photo equipment on my bed, turned them on, crawled under the bed – and was still there when the bed caught fire. Fortunately, he was pulled out in a hurry.

There was the evening I was reading the paper in the living room, Phyllis was making dinner, and Glen came through the kitchen door crying because a bee had bitten him in the ear. "Go see your Dad," I heard her say. As he came into the living room I reached out, without looking up, to give him a hug and pulled him down onto the chair. Then I lowered the paper and darn near passed out.

I barely recognized him. His face was puffed up and blotchy white. I was so scared I don't think anybody ever got to a hospital that fast. I practically threw him into the car. When we got there, Glen's face was so swollen they checked to make sure his breathing was all right. Then they called in a doctor who gave him a shot of penicillin. Glen immediately broke out in blotches all over his body.

By this time I'm shaking like a leaf. I rushed him to our own doctor, who was waiting. Glen was allergic to penicillin. Phyllis knew, but I didn't. The upshot was that Glen started taking injections for immunity to bees. It was going to be a permanent thing: one injection per month, forever. It went on for a couple of years, until we found a specialist who ran tests to see what bees he was allergic to. There was just one – the yellow jacket. The specialist told us that if Glen took one injection per month for a year, there was an eighty-five per cent chance he'd build up an immunity. He did it, and it worked. I think he got the immunity about the same time I stopped shaking inside at what might have happened.

It seemed that everyone had a turn. In the summer before Wayne went to the Soo to play junior "A", we took the family to visit my sister, Jennie, and her family on their tobacco farm in North Carolina. They had a few horses, and we went out into the pasture to get the one the kids could ride. But there were too many of us. Someone must have moved suddenly, because the horse bolted, kicked out with both hind feet – and caught Brent squarely in the back.

He flew forward, the wind knocked out of him. I guess he was only partly conscious. He wasn't wearing a shirt, and there on his back we could see scratches all along his spine where a hoof had caught him. He wasn't seriously hurt, but if he'd been standing another inch closer to that horse . . . .

I mention these things to point out that life in our household isn't just sports. Wayne sets records and the phone rings and people want interviews. But everyday life goes on, just as it does everywhere else. We have the laughs and the problems and the narrow escapes that face every family sooner or later. And there are thousands of families who have several children involved in sport and have to run in twenty directions at once, making sure they all get to where they're supposed to be. The differences – opportunities and stumbling blocks – are there because Wayne is Wayne, hockey is hockey, and if you're going to have a superstar in the family, you'd better be prepared to have people watching your every move.

On balance, I think it's been great for all of us. But it's hard to really know how it's affected the kids. There have been a lot of pluses: trips to Europe, a chance to meet sports heroes and TV and movie celebrities, opportunities to do commercials.

And there have been minuses for them too. Kids need to be accepted for themselves, and when you've got a famous brother, sometimes it's hard to be sure in your own mind whether people want to be friends because you're you or because your brother is Wayne Gretzky.

It's been funny, sometimes, watching the way the kids react in public. For instance, when someone asks for Glen's autograph, he'll look up and say, "What's the name, please?" Brent will go up to someone and say "Hi! I'm Wayne's brother!"

They're all different. Phyllis went to pick up Keith at the airport, when he came in from working at a summer hockey school in Penticton, and said he looked like he'd just reached in the laundry bag and put on whatever he pulled out without ironing any of it. Pick Glen up and he'll look like a million bucks – sports jacket (collar up), sunglasses, burgundy *leather* tie.

Glen may turn out to be the sharpest of them all, in more ways than one. When Wayne's home, Glen will follow him around the house watching him dress, seeing how he combs his hair, how he puts his shoes on, everything. And he'll ask him, "How do I get my hair to look like that?" He may also be the best at school. "Glen's the brains in the family," Keith once told a reporter. "He makes up for me. He's smart and he works hard. He brings the books home. We used to bring 'em home, too – but Glen *opens* them."

There are drawbacks. The entire family hasn't been together for Christmas since 1977, the last one before Wayne turned pro. That bothers Wayne. Last Christmas, he flew Glen and Brent to Edmonton to spend a few days with him and shipped them home Christmas Eve. He misses them. Don't forget, it's not been that long since he was a kid himself.

When we sat down to do this book, one of the first questions that came up was: "What effect has this had on the kids?" The truth is, that's difficult for parents to answer. Do you ever *really* know what your children are thinking and feeling?

So we decided to ask them. Without Phyllis or me sitting there making them self-conscious. Instead, Jim Taylor took them aside one by one, put a tape recorder in front of them, and asked them to go to it. (Brent was excused on two counts: (a) he was a bit young for it and (b) no one could figure a way to get him to sit still that long.)

Listen, then, to three views of what it's like to grow up as a Gretzky . . . .

Kim

"It used to bother me, being known as Wayne's sister. Not that I was left out, because I never was. My parents gave me whatever I wanted within reason. It was just that everything was built around hockey and I didn't *play* hockey. I guess that's why it hurt so much when I had to give up track, because it was something I was doing for myself, by myself.

"My Dad helped me a lot when I was training, just like he helped the boys. He'd be there to time me, to encourage me, to watch me run . . . . You know, my father will *never* slow down. He doesn't push us, he pushes himself. It's enough to give us ulcers worrying about how he treats his. It's been good for him. He enjoys it. It's just that he works himself up a lot. Yes, he worries me . . . .

"I guess when there are no kids left he'll be a little bit nuts for a while . . . . Hey! Can't you just see my Dad as a grandfather? That would really be something. He'd love it, and the kids wouldn't be spoiled. Not very much they wouldn't . . . .

"You know, reporters keep asking me what's different about our family and when I say 'Nothing' they just look at me funny and ask again. They won't believe me. They ask and ask. The money didn't change anything, really. It just got more hectic around here with people knocking on doors looking for pictures and autographs and things . . . . If there was a difference it's that people suddenly expected more from you. Not athletically – not from me, anyway – but in school. And I've never gone to a school Wayne attended except public, and I was out of there before he turned pro . . . .

"Swell-headed? Well, maybe Glen and Brent for a bit because they were so young and so much happened so quickly. And if they were it didn't last. Living this way just became part of their lives. They accept the fact that there are going to be people around all the time and a lot of noise and publicity. It's the way things are . . . .

"Keith . . . Keith is just Keith. He'll never change. Stubborn as anything, but I think being away from home bothers him more than he lets on, just like I think Glen doesn't let on to anyone how much it bothers him that he might not be able to play pro hockey. You know, I remember once when he was small and a reporter asked him why he hadn't started skating until he was six when the rest started when they were two or three. Glen started to cry, and Dad had to answer the question.

"I might be wrong with Glen, it's just a feeling – but with Keith I'm sure. He's phoned me a couple of times in California just to talk. With Wayne away from home so young, I guess Keith and I got pretty close even though there's four years difference . . . . Wayne used to kid the two of us. I remember once he came to us and said if we'd help him clean all the junk off the back yard he'd tell us a secret. So we rushed out and did it, and he said there was a man coming to put in a pool. Actually, he just wanted the yard cleared so he could do the lawn . . . .

"Keith stands up for Keith. He's proud of Wayne, he loves him, but he is *Keith* Gretzky first, not Wayne Gretzky's brother. If he makes it to the NHL he wants it that way, on his terms, for what he's done, not who he is . . . . I'm proud of Wayne. Very proud. I'm like Keith. I want to be recognized as Kim Gretzky, too. When I went to California to school it was partially to take a business course and partially to get off and start a life of my own. But it didn't work, because down there they know me, too. Maybe it's the name. There aren't too many Gretzkys. And when they started showing the 7-Up commercials in California that didn't exactly help . . . .

"The important thing though, is that as a family we're close and always will be. Mom gets frustrated sometimes at so much going on and Brent and Glen will fight and Dad will rave about the phone bills – but we're close. We love each other. It's like I keep telling those reporters. There's nothing different about us at all . . . ."

Keith

"Guys take extra runs at me. That doesn't bother me. It happens to any good hockey player so it's kind of a compliment. But they take the extra cheap shot, too. I guess that goes with being a Gretzky . . . . All you can do is tell them to shut up. Well, maybe once in a while you can do something else, give them the stick or something. But not often.

"It's a little bit like the recognition when you're not playing hockey: they take the extra shots, some of them, they expect more from you. You just live with it. Like, maybe I was drafted a little bit because I was considered a good hockey player and a little bit because I'm a Gretzky. I don't know, and it doesn't matter. I'm playing, that's what matters.

"Moving away from home, playing in Windsor, was rough at first. I wasn't playing much, for one thing. That changed, though, after Wayne Maxner took over as coach in December, and living there has been easy because I'm staying with great people, Eddie Mio's Mom and Dad. It's like another home.

"The NHL? The thing is, I've got to grow. I only weigh 155 and I'm not tall. It hasn't been a problem yet, but I have to grow. I worked out during the summer and we do weight training once or twice a week. I think it will be all right.

"I don't know how it would work out for Glen or Brent, being the third or fourth Gretzky. It might depend a lot on what I do. If I make the NHL and have a good career, then the heat would really be on the next one who came in. If I don't, if there's just Wayne, it might not be so tough . . . . Besides, Brent wants to be a goalie. He doesn't play there, but he wants to be. Crazy – but he wouldn't be compared to Wayne then, would he?

"The NHL's my goal. I've never wanted to be anything but a hockey player. Being Wayne's brother . . . well, there are a few disadvantages sometimes, but mostly it's been great . . . . What will I do if I *don't* make it? Wow, that would be a hard, hard question. I don't even want to think about it."

Glen

"Sure, I want to play pro hockey if I can. If I can't, I'd like to be an actor, but maybe that's just a dream. I'm a teenager already and with acting I think you have to start at five or six. Or an agent, maybe. I see how Mike Barnett does it. He travels all over the world, knows a lot of movie stars.

Maybe some day I could have my own company. But acting more than anything, if I can make it . . . .

"My feet? Oh, sure, they hurt. They hurt a lot. They hurt almost every practice. I don't say anything. What's the use? Nobody can do anything about it. I just sit down for a minute on the side boards, take a rest until they feel better.

"Feel sorry for myself? Not exactly. The odd time I wish I had . . . you know, the physical things to play hockey the way I'd like to. But I've never given pro much thought. It would be nice, though . . . .

"The guys on the other team try to hit you a lot more, try to run at you and hurt you more than the rest of the team just because you're a Gretzky. I noticed it when he started playing in the NHL. They really tried to go after me then. They say stuff like 'Where's your crying towel?' and 'You suck, Gretzky.' It bothered me at first, but I know a lot more about protecting myself now and I can outskate some of them sometimes. Mostly I just ignore it and try to play my game.

"Yeah, sometimes you feel left out, but I think that happens to every boy once or twice. The part I don't understand is at school. I'll be in the cafeteria and guys who think they're cool and hate sports will come up and say, 'You're just a Gretzky' and shove you out of line. Or in gym at team games they'll try to hit me, I think because they're jealous or something.

"Sometimes it gets to be a drag (being known as Wayne's brother). It gets boring sometimes with reporters. They expect someone as good as Wayne. I think there's even more pressure now. They talk like we've had more time and Wayne to teach us so we should do even better. Like they expect Keith or Brent or me to score 50 in 29, not 39, or 250 points instead of 212. And he does help us. He'll see our game and sit afterwards and tell us something we should or shouldn't do. Or when we've been watching him, he'll say, 'Did you like that move? Have you tried it?' But *he* doesn't expect us to be another him. He just wants us to learn and have fun, and that's all I want to do, too.

"Spoiled? We've travelled, which is fun. We've seen some of Europe and Russia, and played showdown against Russian kids. You know what happened once in Moscow? We were in the gym and Wayne spilled a fruit drink and about a hundred cockroaches swarmed out from under the wall. It got pretty scary.

"Oh, yeah, spoiled. Well, we get equipment: skates and things like that. But we don't get free dressers or beds or lunches or pop or ice cream. We still have to work as much as other kids. And the hockey is still fun.

"Tell you something nice about Brent? Let's see . . . well, it's good to have someone around to beat up every morning . . . ."

There they are, the three who've lived with the situation longest. For Brent it's really just beginning, but he's come to recognize the signs, particularly in the 1982-83 season as he grew to an age where he was more apt to notice.

As he lined up for a face-off once in a game that had grown extremely physical, Brent mentioned to the referee that this was pee wee hockey and bodychecking wasn't allowed. "Listen Gretzky," the referee snapped, "you're not in the pros yet."

Once, as we walked out of the arena behind a boy and his father, after a game in London, we heard the boy crowing about how he'd "really decked that Gretzky." Brent nudged me, looked up, and grinned. Because it wasn't just the boy who was pleased. The father was happy, too. "Yeah, I saw that," he told his son. "It was great."

Then there was the tournament game against Waterloo, when Brent scored both Brantford goals in a 2-2 tie. All through the game one of the rival coaches had been on Brent's back, using foul language in what looked like an attempt to rattle an eleven-year-old kid. The referee heard it all, but instead of handing out an unsportsman-like conduct penalty or throwing him out, he just told Brent not to pay any attention. "He's just trying to get your goat," he said.

Brent's coach, Brian Eadie, confronted the other coach in the hallway after the game. It quickly became a shouting match, and nearly grew into a fist fight.

Then there was the game in the 1982-83 season when Brent was benched in the third period. He was on defence and wasn't playing as well as I've seen him play, but his team was leading 3-2 and he'd set up two of the goals. He was on the ice for the third and on the bench when the other team scored both its goals. That made him a plus three. Then, late in the second period, he took the puck behind his own net, started a rush up ice, but had it poke-checked away before he got to his blue line. The puck went into a corner, and the other team wasn't able to capitalize. No goal resulted from the play, but it had been a misplay on Brent's part, no question.

But he didn't get back on the ice until the final minute when the score was tied 3-3, which was how it ended.

After the game, our parent rep spoke to the manager upstairs and asked why Brent hadn't been used in the third period. The reply was that "Brent just wasn't his usual sharp self."

I walked over and asked if Brent had run his mouth off at the coach or something.

"No," he said. "Brent just wasn't sharp tonight. He got poke-checked and lost the puck."

"Did they score a goal on it?" I asked. I was really puzzled.

"No."

"And that's why he didn't play in the third?"

"Yes."

Well, he was the manager. But until the play on which Brent had lost the puck, he was plus three. The other team had scored twice, which meant that somewhere, someone else hadn't been sharp either. There'd been two mistakes. But no one else was benched. The theory seems to be that if it's someone else who makes a mistake, well, that happens. If it's Brent, well, it had better not happen. He's a Gretzky.

Yes, Brent's getting his taste of it just as the others did.

But you know, I don't think it will bother him much. He's too bouncy to let anything get to him for long. He's thinking, though. He's always thinking.

Last Christmas Eve, he was about to board a plane from Edmonton, after he and Glen had been visiting Wayne. When he said he wanted to sleep on the plane so he'd be in shape for Christmas, Wayne suggested he take a Gravol. Brent was horrified.

"Oh, no!" he said. "There's no way I'm getting on drugs!"

For all of them, the benefits of life as a Gretzky far outnumber the problems. Take Brent, for instance: if he wasn't a Gretzky, how would he ever have met his Soviet buddy, Vladislav Tretiak . . . ?

Chapter 17

MISSION TO MOSCOW

"Vladislav Tretiak and Wayne Gretzky. Two giants on the same ice. When they worked, there was electricity in the air!"

– Charlie Henry, 1983.

It looked like your typical street hockey "showdown," the kind you see wherever kids gather for pick-up games – whether it be on the road or in the rink: two boys taking turns shooting at a goaltender, seeing who can beat him more often.

Keith, Glen and Brent lined up in turn, each competing with a shooter and a goaltender his own age. The competition was keen. The other kids cheered. There was a lot of laughter. It was pick-up hockey, Canadian style. Then the big kids came out to play: Wayne Gretzky and a player in a red uniform with CCCP on the front, playing showdown against a goaltender named Vladislav Tretiak – and the streets and rinks of Canada were a long way away.

We were at the Red Army Sports Club in Moscow, courtesy of the Soviet Union and Filmsport Canada Inc., a Winnipeg-based company, which was filming a one-hour show for a TV special starring the Gretzky family. The idea, according to the Filmsport release, was to "focus on the humanistic qualities of sport and the role sport plays in the promotion of international goodwill and understanding. This theme will be projected through the life of Wayne

Gretzky, his relationship with his father, mother, brothers, friends, and one of his fiercest rivals on the ice and good friend away from the hockey arena, Vladislav Tretiak."

Translation: the whole family, plus Phyllis' mother, Betty Hockin, Vickie Moss and her mother, Sophie, and Charlie Henry and his wife, Nan, were part of a party of twenty-five including film crew, getting an expenses-paid chance of a lifetime to see Moscow. We landed at Sheremetyeve International Airport on June 28, 1982, and before we left for home on July 5, we had packed in enough sightseeing and memories to indeed last a lifetime.

The idea of the film itself was a good one: Soviet players of all ages were to be shown during their training sessions with Vladislav (or Vlad, as we were all soon calling him) as the instructor and commentator, with Mr. Skvortsov of Gostelradio on the ice as translator. Our boys would watch the drills, then try them themselves. I'd use our boys to show the Russians some of our training techniques and drills, and then they'd try them. The viewer would get a good comparative look at the two systems, the boys would learn, and everyone would have a good time. It worked out perfectly.

One difference in approach really stood out. Watch the Soviets the next time they're on television. When they try to go around a man, they depend on sheer speed. Then watch the good NHLers like Gilbert Perreault, or Denis Savard, or Wayne. It's not just speed. They use the deke, the stick-handling, the dropped shoulder.

I did one drill with the Russian boys, getting our boys to go through pylons by dropping a shoulder one way and going the other. It's something I've taught each of them from the beginning, so they had no trouble. The Russian kids tried it, at first found it difficult because it was so foreign to their own approach, then gradually caught on. When they did it, they'd grin and nod and really get excited. It made for some great film.

Wayne says he remembers looking at Brent standing

there in his new equipment, with the best of everything, looking over at the Russian boy, the same age as Brent, with the battered skates and the second-rate equipment, and then watching the drills and wondering if maybe we don't over-coach and over-teach.

"I mean, how much can you teach a ten-year-old?" he said later. "There's only so much he's going to take in. Do the basics – that's all they do over here. You see a ten-year-old team in Canada and all you hear is 'Shoot! Stay on your wing! Forecheck! Dump it in! Up and out!' The Soviets get all their ten-year-olds on the ice and say 'Play shinny. Grab the puck and go.' That gives them the skating, the puck-handling. It's fascinating to see how well they handle the puck.

"They're told, 'Take the puck and put it in the net. Don't stay on your own wing. Don't forecheck. Just get the thing and go.' My three brothers handle the puck very well. The Soviets had five or six kids from each age group there, and every one of them handled the puck as well or better than my brothers. They scrimmage and go all over the ice. Tretiak is out there with them laughing and screaming and having fun with them. You watch the same things in our rinks and you hear, 'Dump it in! Shoot! Knock his head off!' It's dumb and it's boring."

We'd taken a lot of extra things with us, suitcases full, in fact: as many pictures of Wayne as we could (he was asked for autographs there almost as much as he is at home, but from a crowd that averaged out a little bit older, in their thirties and forties), plus copies of the CAHA once-a-year hockey book, which we had trouble getting in. Apparently the Soviets frown on people bringing books into the country. And gum, lots of gum. If we'd left everything else at home and filled the suitcases with gum, we still wouldn't have had enough. Everyone, the kids, the doorman at the hotel, everyone, wanted gum.

We'd also brought some extra hockey equipment in sizes

to fit our three boys. We passed some of it out to the Russian boys during the drills and it was like they'd just found buried treasure.

And it wasn't just the boys. Anatoli Firsov, the legendary Soviet star who was coaching their junior team, accompanied Vlad everywhere he went. Firsov and Charlie Henry became quite good friends. One day they went out for a skate, Charlie in his new Daoust skates and Firsov in a scruffy-looking old black pair that had obviously been through the wars. Charlie offered to let him try his skates, and wound up giving them to him. A couple of days later, he tried to borrow them back, just to go for a skate. Firsov said no, that was not possible. The skates were not here.

"Where are they?" Charlie asked.

"On farm," Firsov said. And the farm was forty kilometers away. Anatoli had effectively buried his treasure.

When we weren't on the ice training, we were seeing Moscow and doing some socializing. Again, the little differences stuck out.

For instance, Tretiak and Firsov were almost always our constant companions during the trip. The kids, particularly Brent, just worshipped the Soviet goaltender. They'd pick us up each morning at the Sovietskaya Hotel – but they'd never come in. They'd wait for us outside in the street. This was a tourist hotel and those were the rules. Tretiak was a Soviet hero, but he couldn't set foot in that hotel.

We were well treated, although the boys didn't care for the food and didn't really hit the meals until we turned up at one of our frequent visits to the Canadian Embassy. Then they really hit those hamburgers. Personally, I got along fine. There was plenty of buttermilk, just like the old days at home. Once, though, after a particularly late night, we had a craving for some down-home Canadian food and wound up at an Embassy staff member's house, munching peanut butter and jam sandwiches! Home is a lot of little things.

We played tourist, of course, did Red Square, saw the incredible Moscow Circus, and watched one of the most impressive sights ever: the changing of the guard at Lenin's Tomb. Wayne saw it more than any of us. One night he couldn't sleep, so he wandered down to the lobby at about 1:30 a.m., found Charlie (who never sleeps), and they walked until 8 a.m. Every time they passed through the square on the hour, they'd stop and watch the guard change.

It wasn't all fun, though. We were filming seven or eight hours a day and there was a certain amount of frustration. There was also a feeling that we were on display, that we were representing our country and had to be extra careful in everything we did or said. That's why I was so proud of Wayne when he got a chance to display some international diplomacy.

We were in a group including Canadian Ambassador G. A. H. Pearson and Serge Pavlov, then Minister of Sports for the Soviet Union. Mr. Pavlov spoke through an interpreter, making conversation with every member of our group, but showing special interest in Wayne. One thing he mentioned was that they didn't like Bobby Clarke in the Soviet Union because of the rough type of hockey he played. He referred specifically to the slash across the ankles of Valeri Kharlamov during the 1972 Team Canada-Soviet Union series. He then asked Wayne: "How do you feel about him, especially when you're one of the type of players we have in the Soviet Union?"

Wayne didn't hesitate. He just smiled and said, "You have to remember that Bobby Clarke, like the players in the Soviet Union, is a fierce competitor, and one of the reasons he's so admired by the Canadian and the American sports fan is that, unknown to some people – and possibly even to your people – Bobby Clarke is a diabetic. Yet at no time has he ever used that as an excuse when he hasn't performed up to par or his team hasn't won. He's become an inspiration to people with handicaps, proving they can be overcome with hard work."

Canada 1, Soviets 0.

There were restrictions we found annoying, and in a way a little bit frightening. There was a guard at the hotel door twenty-four hours a day and if you didn't have a card you didn't get in. Cameras are viewed with suspicion. They have a tower in Moscow like Toronto's CN tower that offers a great view, but I had to check my camera at ground level before I could go up. I wanted to take a picture of a Russian guard at the Embassy and was told by our guide that I couldn't, "because a lot of the guards don't like it." It annoyed me – I told the guide that anywhere in Canada or the U.S. a soldier or policemen will give a tourist a smile and pose for a picture – but on the way out of Moscow heading for the airport I got back at her. As the bus moved along, I leaned down beside her and began taking pictures through the window. She didn't say a word, just stared straight ahead. I know it was rude on my part. I was just trying to get a point across. I think I did.

But people are basically the same no matter where you are, and the people of Moscow made the memories good for us. Tretiak and Firsov, for example, were especially good to the boys, and I can still see Vlad's wife, Tatiana, beaming proudly each time he was asked for his autograph.

We were supposed to go to Tretiak's apartment for dinner, with the crew filming the evening. He'd invited the entire family, but we'd been warned in advance that the apartment wouldn't be big enough for all of us. To avoid any possible embarrassment on the Tretiaks' part, it was suggested that we send word that the kids would be there but that Phyllis and I couldn't make it.

Vladislav insisted. Finally, we said no, but added that if the boys went we'd be happy, impressing upon him how good it would be for them to be able to go home and say they had dinner at Vladislav Tretiak's home. Vlad, of course, understood that.

Vladislav Tretiak. A great athlete, but more than that, a great person. When he came to the airport to say goodbye, there was a scene I will never forget.

Brent was upset at leaving Vlad. When it was time to board, we looked around and couldn't find him. Finally, Vlad spotted him, crouched behind the equipment bags, his eyes a little bit teary. He scooped him up into his arms, gave him a big hug, and said goodbye. Brent even managed a smile. And there's no need to ask the name of his favourite Soviet hockey player. That name will never change.

As this is written, a special target looms mere months away. The Russians are coming to Canada, along with other hockey nations, to renew the Canada Cup competition. For Wayne, the Stanley Cup has always been the No. 1 goal – but the Canada Cup is a close, close second.

He first played the Soviet Union in the Junior World Cup competition in 1977 at the Forum in Montreal. He was sixteen, and he almost didn't make it. Ernie "Punch" McLean, one of the Team Canada coaches said he had reservations. "He's a great young player," he said, "but does he have the strength to take it in the rough going?"

After McLean criticized his play in an exhibition game against Sweden, Wayne admitted he thought his chances of making the team were slim. "Maybe they'll say it's my age," he said. "If they do, it's a poor excuse."

He was young, no doubt about that – so young that he visited the Montreal Canadiens' dressing room as though it was a shrine, and asked the trainer where Guy Lafleur sat. "Right there," the trainer pointed, "between Pierre Larouche and Steve Shutt."

"Boy," Wayne sighed. "Those are sure two lucky fellows."

Then he went out and won the tournament scoring championship with 8 goals and 9 assists in 6 games. He was also named to the first All-Star team at centre, but the TV sets for the two most valuable players on the Canadian team went to Ryan Walter and Rob Ramage. I never quite figured that out.

Team Canada lost 3-2 in the big game against the Soviet Union after being up 2-0. The Soviets went on to beat Sweden 5-2 for the title.

The next time Wayne faced the Soviets it was as a member of the WHA All-Star team, playing on that line with Gordie and Mark Howe against touring Moscow Dynamo. The WHA swept the series, 4-2, 4-2 and 4-3. Later, the Oilers would beat a Russian touring team in Edmonton. Then came the 1980-81 Canada Cup series. Everyone remembers that. People called it a national shame as Team Canada was whipped 8-1 by Team Russia in the last game. Everyone forgot that Canada had won the first two meetings. The way the competition was set up the last game meant everything and the Soviets ran away with it. But there wasn't a player on that Canadian team who didn't vow that there'd come another day.

For Wayne it came at a time when he'd rather have been somewhere else. He hadn't planned to play for Team Canada in the 1981-82 world championships in Finland. He'd planned to be with the Oilers in the Stanley Cup playoffs. But the Los Angeles Kings had stunned them in the first round, taking the series 3-2, and the next day Wayne and Paul Coffey were off to Finland. It was a disappointment, but it also led to one of the most moving moments in Wayne's hockey career.

As the tournament ended, Darryl Sittler was named Team Canada's most valuable player and presented with a wrist watch. Right there in the rink, with the crowd looking on, he skated over and tried to give it to Wayne. "Take this," he said. "It should be yours."

Wayne didn't want it, of course. Darryl had played exceptionally well. The selectors had chosen him. But as Wayne said to me later: "What a man he was to come over and make the offer. A man like that, whom I respect so much, to do a thing like that . . . ."

He won't forget his friend, Darryl Sittler – nor his friend, Vladislav Tretiak. The last time they met on the ice, they were surrounded by laughing kids from two countries for a television film. Each Gretzky boy was wearing a Team Canada sweater from the 1972 series. When the series was over, they stripped them off and exchanged sweaters with their Soviet showdown opponent. They were looking forward to another Canada Cup meeting this year, but Tretiak has since retired. There'll be another Soviet goalie, another Soviet showdown. Who knows, maybe Vlad will be there as a coach. But Gretzky *versus* Tretiak, never again. I'll bet they both feel sorry about that.

Chapter 18

WE'RE STILL JUST THE GRETZKYS OF BRANTFORD

"I don't know what I'll do when the boys leave and I don't have to drive them all to games. I'll probably join the Big Brothers."

– Walter Gretzky, 1983.

I came home after making presentations at an afternoon basketball tournament at St. John's College and found a big, dark blue Cadillac in our driveway with a ribbon around it. The licence plates looked familiar, which figured – the last time I'd seen them that morning they'd been on my station wagon.

"Phyllis!" I yelled as I came through the door. "My station wagon's sitting out there and somebody's switched its plates to . . . ."

There were two strange people sitting in the living room.

"Don't look at me," Phyllis said. "I had nothing to do with it." The kids had scattered, heading for cover. It was April 23, 1983, our twenty-third wedding anniversary. So far, it didn't look too promising.

The strange man introduced himself and his wife. He had a Cadillac dealership, and he was handing me a set of keys. Suddenly, it hit me: *Wayne*. It had to be Wayne! He was in Edmonton, but it still had to be him. He'd traded in my station wagon, had the plates transferred and had arranged to have it delivered gift-wrapped while I was away. This man was going to drive away my old station wagon and leave me a *Cadillac*! It was so thoughtful of him. It was such a wonderful gesture.

It was *terrible*!

How was I going to get to work? I couldn't drive that thing. Walter Gretzky, driving to the Bell in a Cadillac? What would the other guys say?

Maybe it wasn't too late. The next day I phoned the dealership. Maybe I could buy back the station wagon. That thing would go anywhere. Just throw all the hockey gear in the back, jam in a bunch of kids and take off . . . . "Hello? . . . Oh. Well, thanks anyway."

They'd sold it. They'd sold my station wagon. The Gretzkys had a Cadillac. Well, it was a prestige car, all right. And I was really proud of Wayne for remembering and being so generous. But it sure wasn't any Blue Goose . . . .

The Blue Goose was a '65 Chevy, and there probably wouldn't have been as many White Tornado stories without it. Bob Hockin had a station wagon and I had the Goose and between us we'd take about three-quarters of the Steelers. I'd drive those cars over 200,000 miles, mostly between arenas, and when one was reduced to junk, I'd buy another one.

It wasn't unusual for us to get stuck or to stall, which could be a problem because I never was one to leave for some place with time to spare. Wayne used to kid me sometimes: "Dad, it'll be nice when I get to junior hockey. I'll always be on time, because you won't be driving."

The car would stall or seize up or go low on oil and we'd be standing there on the highway in the middle of winter and I'd say, "Wayne, when I get my big, black, shiny Cadillac . . . ." Then we'd coax it back to life and nurse it to the arena one more time. It became a kind of family joke. "Boy, when I get that Cadillac . . . ." But I was always kidding. What would I do with a Cadillac?

We drove the Goose everywhere. Sometimes, driving

home late at night from an out-of-town tournament with the snow blowing outside and the heater keeping us warm inside, I'd start to feel sleepy. So I'd tell one of the kids to comb my hair, or just use his fingers and scratch my head, and we'd go the rest of the way like that. Close moments. You remember times like that. Now Wayne was a success. He had the money, he remembered the old days, and he wanted me to have that Cadillac. That made it the nicest present a man could get.

I also remember that Phyllis sold the Goose when I wasn't looking. I came home one day and it was gone. It was the Cadillac story all over again, only this time there was no other car.

"Phyllis, where's the Goose?" I demanded.

"Here's your $25," she said. "I called the wreckers. They towed it away."

Boy, was I mad. The Goose was only ten years old. Couldn't have had more than 180,000 miles on her. I could have squeezed out at least another 40,000. Woman didn't know a great car when she saw one . . . .

The two station wagons that followed the Goose were special, too. I had enough money to pay for part of the first one. The other $3,000 I borrowed from Dad. He was pretty sick at the time. When I tried to discuss how I'd pay it back, he just looked at me and said, "Don't worry about it." He knew there wasn't much time left.

The second one – the one Wayne wound up trading in on the Cadillac – just showed up. Wayne was home and he'd taken Kim out to buy her a car for her seventeenth birthday. They were gone for hours. When they finally got home, Wayne handed me a set of keys.

"Here, Dad," he said.

"What's this?"

"Go outside and see," he said.

I went out the front door and just about fainted. There wasn't one new car in the driveway, there were two: Kim's Firebird, and a station wagon.

"Whose is that?" I asked suspiciously.

"It's yours, Dad," he said. "I want you to have it."

He'd gone out to buy one car and come home with two. Just like that.

I'm not saying Wayne's success hasn't changed things. Of course it has. What we've tried to do is make sure it doesn't change *us*. Wayne is so generous, so determined that nothing is too good for the family, that sometimes it's not easy.

After his first year in the pros, Wayne came home for the summer, walked in one day and said, "Mom, I've got just the house for you."

"What do you mean, a house?" Phyllis asked.

"Just a beautiful house," he said enthusiastically. "Up by the Mowat's. We've got to go look at it today."

"How much is it?" she asked.

"Oh, it's only $100,000, and you'll really like it."

"Wayne," she said, "we already have a home."

"Oh, no," he said. "This is a nice *big* home, just for you and Dad and the kids."

Phyllis gave me the news that evening. We didn't want to hurt Wayne's feelings, but we told him that for now we were going to stay in this house. And for a while, that was it.

In the summer of '82, he came in again. This time he had Stan Posavad with him. Stan was the manager when I coached a junior "B" team. He was also a real estate salesman.

"C'mon, Dad," Wayne said. "We gotta go."

"C'mon where?" I asked suspiciously. My son who wanted to buy us a house is standing there with a real estate agent and I shouldn't be suspicious?

"C'mon," he insisted. "There's something we're going to see."

Well, Phyllis and I piled into the car with them and off we went to this exclusive part of Brantford, a development full of homes worth $200,000 to $300,000. We looked around and it wasn't for me. Little tiny back yard – I didn't even want to get out of the car. But we got out and wandered around while Wayne bubbled about how nice it was up there, how the air was so fresh and clean. Then we went home. That night, Phyllis and I had a little talk.

"You want to live up there?"

"Not me."

"Me neither. But we have to do something before he picks out a lot, builds a house and comes home one day, hands us the front door keys and says, 'Here's your house.' "

Phyllis had an idea. Wayne was just heading off to Martinique for a holiday. She knew where there was a building lot. We'd buy it, tell Wayne we're going to build on it some day, and stall him off. Brilliant.

We bought it, and phoned him in Martinique. He was really excited. "When do you start building?" he asked. Oops!

All we were trying to do was stall. How could we make him understand, without hurting his feelings, that this was our home, that it might not be anything fancy, but it belonged to us.

Phyllis came through again.

"What we'll do," she said, "is build an addition. We'll have it done before he finds out, and then he'll know we're staying."

The next time he asked when we were going to start building our new house on our new lot, we told him the following summer. Meanwhile, we made arrangements to start converting our house to a split-level. The builders started in November and finished in January. Of course, Wayne found out eventually, and wound up paying for it. He loves it, too. He just hadn't realized how much could be done to the old place.

And we came to an understanding.

"Why were you so determined to buy us a house?" I asked him.

"For you and Mom," he said. "I just wanted to do it for you."

"Wayne, thank you," I said. "But if you really want to do something for us, just promise you'll remember one thing: the rest of the kids may never ever be as fortunate as you are. If they ever need any help, you look after them, and you'll have done everything in the world you could do for us."

He'd have done that anyway. Knowing that makes it even nicer.

We could move, but the people who buy the old house wouldn't be getting full value. They could only buy the building and the rink in the back yard, if they cared to flood it. The memories would all go with us.

Everything happened so quickly. We're through the 1983-84 season now and Wayne's a veteran pro at twenty-three – but only six years ago he was a seventeen-year-old kid getting by on his $24.01 a week playing junior hockey. Since then, he's met the President of the United States. ("I remember telling him one time that the Lord gave you two eyes and one mouth and you should keep two open and one shut," Gordie Howe said. "Years later he told me he'd just met the President and had followed my advice.") He's been to Hollywood, become a celebrity and put hockey numbers on the board people thought were impossible. The family has ridden private jets and gone to Moscow as guests of the Soviet government. We've met people we'd seen only on television, and had them in the house.

Sometimes we talk about it, Phyllis and I, thinking back over what's happened since the days we first decided that Wayne had to get out of Brantford if he was to have a chance at a normal life. That's a joke, too, of course. His life is a lot of things, but normal it isn't. And while Wayne's running all over the continent, at the house on Varadi Ave. we try to live an everyday, ordinary life.

Despite the problems we had with a few people in Wayne's days in minor hockey, Brantford has become very proud of him and has shown it in all kinds of ways. There are the street signs proclaiming the city the home of Wayne

247

Gretzky; there's the arena named after him, and the cornerstone on the addition to St. Mark's ("This cornerstone laid by Wayne Gretzky, 1979.") where our family always went to church and Sunday school. At least, Wayne always went. Brent would say, "No Sunday school today, Wally. *Practice!*"

Even now we hear about things he's done that we didn't know about, things that tell us the respect is there. Eddie O'Leary of the *Expositor* was remembering one the other day:

"The Pittsburgh Penguins used to train in Brantford. The year Wayne scored the 378 goals, I was sitting in the rink watching them work out and Wayne asked me if I could get him into their dressing room. He'd be what - ten or eleven?

"Jack Riley was manager then and he said fine. He was really interested in seeing this kid who scored all the goals. The Penguins were just super, particularly guys like Ken Schinkel. They talked to him, spent time with him. It was one of the first times he'd ever come into contact with pro athletes. I think it stuck in his mind, how they acted toward him, and now that he's called on so much, he has a great respect for the responsibilities that go with being a star.

"A couple of years ago, he was home and I asked him if he'd visit the Brantford Boys and Girls Club with me. 'No problem,' he said. They had twice the number of kids that night than they usually had, even though there'd been only a couple of hours' notice. Wayne autographed books and pictures for about forty-five minutes, then grabbed a stick and played floor hockey with them. All of a sudden they were on the same level. I think sport today, with all its problems, needs a Gretzky. I just don't think enough people really believe the kind of guy he is."

We hear Wayne stories in all sorts of places. Once, when the Oilers had a brief break during the 1982-83 season, we flew to Palm Springs with Wayne. We were up near the front of the plane, Phyllis sitting next to him. When she went to the back of the plane to the smoking area, one of the stewardesses approached her.

"You must have paid extra for your seat," she said.

Phyllis didn't know what she was talking about.

"Don't you know who you're sitting next to?" the stewardess asked. "That's *Wayne Gretzky!*"

"I know," Phyllis said. "He's my son."

She couldn't believe it. Phyllis was getting a big chuckle out of it. Then another guy asked: "Gretzky? Is he a football player?"

Then there's Charlie Henry, talking about being with Wayne and Brent and Peter Pocklington at the Conservative convention, when Mr. Pocklington was running for the party leadership.

"Peter brought Wayne into the delegates' tent," he recalled. "Someone started yelling 'GRET-zky! GRET-zky!' and pretty soon everyone was yelling it. Pocklington was so startled he stopped shaking hands."

"Gosh," a guy suggested, "maybe Wayne should have run."

"He'd have won," Charlie said. "He'd have won."

He was kidding. I think.

And my sister, Sophie, telling us that Wayne's fear of flying, which has received so much publicity over the last couple of years, may have started before he ever flew.

Sophie's husband, Jack White, worked for Air Canada in Toronto. Wayne visited them when he was about six, and Jack and Sophie took him through a passenger plane as it sat on the runway.

"Go ahead, Wayne, sit in one of the seats," Jack suggested. Wayne just shook his head. Sophie says he was chalk white. He wasn't going to sit in that airplane, even on the ground. And he didn't.

We've never figured out what started the discomfort Wayne feels about flying. Hypnotism helped for a while.

Now he takes Dramamine to settle his stomach, but it can't settle his mind. If he ever decides to retire early, flying might be the big reason.

We're no different from anyone else – once you overlook the fact that we might open the door and find a radio or TV crew, that people sometimes go through our garbage looking for souvenirs, and that once, when Brent got mad at Glen and put one of his brand new boots in the middle of the road, a car screeched to a halt, a hand reached out and grabbed it and the car roared off.

Of course, there is Morris . . . .

Morris is a family member you haven't met – Morris Gretzky, a cat who thinks he's a dog.

Morris is Brent's cat. Brent can do anything with him. Sometimes he throws him around his neck and wanders around the house wearing him like a fur. Morris never moves. Cats are supposed to be independent, but at bedtime Brent just yells, "Morris! We're going to bed!" and the darned cat just follows him up the stairs like a puppy.

This past winter, Morris had to go to the vet. For a while we thought we were going to lose him. Brent was crushed. Every day, sometimes two or three times a day, he'd be on the phone. "Hello? I'd like to inquire about a patient. How is Morris Gretzky . . . ?"

Glen didn't exactly try to cheer him up. After Phyllis took Morris to the vet, she came home to find Glen holding a service for the cat – complete with bread, wine and candles on the table.

The doctor couldn't quite figure Morris out. But then, he didn't know Brent. "Mrs. Gretzky," he told Phyllis, "I think your cat is spoiled. He'll eat, but only if I feed him by hand. We might have to feed him intravenously."

I could just see it: Morris lying in bed, one paw stretched out sideways, the tube coming out of it and running up to a tin of Nine Lives. Before it could happen, Morris got better.

He came home, we got the bill, and then *I* was sick. Brent felt a lot better, though. He had his dog back.

Morris got back just in time to discover that the kids had bought two goldfish: Miss Vicki and Big Wally. Morris thought this was just fine.

The kids put that bowl everywhere to keep it out of Morris's reach. At one point Glen had it on the floor in his closet with the door shut. But before Morris could figure how to slide the door back and have some lunch, there was a death in the family. Big Wally died.

Glen decided on a church funeral. He got one of Kim's old cosmetics compacts for a casket and gave Big Wally a memorial service. When I got home the compact was on the table surrounded by flowers, and Glen was sitting there with a scarf around his neck like a priest's vestments. It was orange. The message of hope it bore read, "Go, Oilers, Go!" As I came through the door, he looked up and said, "Come, my son. I will comfort you . . . ."

You see? We're just an ordinary family. We've got one boy who's a hockey star, three who'd love to be and will give it a shot, and a girl who wants to have her own day care centre because she loves working with kids and does it well. Our kids scrap and make up and scrap again. We argue about tying up the phone and I beef about the phone bill. That runs anywhere from $400 to $800 a month because there are so many things going on, and all three kids who are away phone home a lot, always collect. I get my cheque from Bell in one hand and give it back to them with the other. It's an ordinary house on an ordinary street. We didn't know when we bought it that it would become a sort of landmark, the Home of the Great Gretzky. We didn't know there'd be a particular Great Gretzky. We think they're all great.

The Great Gretzky . . . .

John Herbert, a reporter for the London *Free Press*, says he was the first one to hang the nickname on Wayne. But Cam Martindale, who taught and coached Wayne at

Greenbriar School and has followed his career closely, recalls seeing it on the school walls before he ever saw it in the paper. It was when Wayne was in Grade Eight and the school was getting ready for the annual staff-vs-senior boys' basketball game. The kids dreamed up some interesting names for their players and splashed them on posters all over the school trying to psych out the staff: Marvelous Martindale, Tiger Taylor, Stompin' Stamer, Sogs Sovereign – and Great Gretzky.

It would be only right, I think, if the nickname did come from someone in Brantford where Wayne grew up. He lives in Edmonton now in his six-room, two-level, seventeenth-storey penthouse with the security system, the special key you have to insert in the elevator control panel to take it past the sixteenth floor, the fake name on the mailbox and the secret code on the buzzer. (He thought he'd moved in undetected. The second morning he was in the place, the night after he'd scored a hat trick, he picked up the newspaper at his door. On the wrapper the paper boy had scrawled, "Great game last night, Wayne!") He has all those things and I guess in a sense he belongs to the whole country now.

But in his mind, home is Brantford and the farm and the river and his family. And that's one mark that's carved in the book to stay.

Chapter 19

LET'S HEAR
IT FOR
BRAINWASHING

"Never strangle your kids. It's not good for them."

– Walter Gretzky, 1983.

Coaching any sport at kids' level is a matter of teaching fundamentals. Later on, as they get into more competitive leagues, the professionals can take over and polish certain skills or put players in positions that require specialization. But in the formative years, the most important thing a coach in any sport can do is strip the game to basics and concentrate on two things – fundamentals and fun.

As a hockey player I was never that good. I started at fourteen, played junior "B" for five years, scored quite a few goals, and even got a tryout with the Toronto Marlies' junior "A" team. Once, when I was talking about it, I mentioned to Wayne that I had just gotten over chickenpox when I had the tryout. He never lets me forget that. I'll be arguing about something he did in a game and he'll grin and say, "How many goals did you score in the NHL, Dad?" Then he'll stop as though he just remembered something and say, "Oh, yeah – I forgot. It was the chickenpox that stopped you, right?"

It was the Marlies, though, who taught me what I wound

up telling Wayne – and later the other boys. They told me I was too small, too light and not rough enough. I weighed about 130 then, and I wasn't tall. Heck, I'm only 5'9" now. So I told Wayne from the start: "Never assume you're going to be a pro hockey player. I'm small, you're small. It might not matter how good you are. Always be prepared to be something else." He always did, too, even though hockey was No. 1. He was going to be an architect, an engineer and a hundred other things. That was fine with me. I knew how scouts think, and how many things can go wrong. As the other boys came along, they got the same word: give it your best shot if you want to, but *never* at the expense of everything else. I think it sank in; I hope it did. There are a lot more kids who want to play in the NHL than ever make it, no matter how hard they work. It's one of the saddest lessons they have to learn.

Over the years as Wayne developed and the other boys started playing, and stories got around about the back-yard rink and the Gretzky family, people got the idea that there must be something in the family genes that produces athletes, or that at the very least I must be some kind of supercoach or tyrant of a parent whipping his kids to the top. Well, I never coached that much – the one year with Wayne and one in junior "B", plus a little lacrosse and baseball – but along the way I formed some definite opinions on the way it should be done when it comes to kids.

The first is to keep it simple. It's something Canadians tend to overlook. We get too complicated. You get some coaches who'll take a kid just beginning to learn the game and say, "You're a defenceman, so you only go as far as the blue line and no further." Well, that might or might not be sound defensive coaching, but I know one thing it does for sure: it strangles the kid. It puts hobbles on him. Kids should be encouraged to be creative on the ice, to try to think things out and do what seems to be the right thing.

Howie Meeker, the hockey analyst, was speaking one night at a sports celebrity dinner in Brantford. He said he'd seen two bantam teams in Toronto that played better positional hockey than a lot of professional teams. "There's just one problem," he said. "They went up and down the wings like they were on a string. By the time they're eighteen or nineteen none of them will be playing pro because they've learned nothing else." We place so much emphasis on a set style and organization that the kids get very little chance to develop individual talents.

Hockey is five things: puck-handling, thinking, skating, checking and desire. If you've got those five you can be a hockey player. And at a young age I'd put those first three skills in about that order.

You take Brent. He started playing when he was five, and has been playing rep hockey since he was seven. He's always been a goal scorer. He has the natural ability, the deke. And the reason the deke works so well is that he's always out there practicing it. You'll find that about a lot of great hockey players. When a Mike Bossy wheels and shoots in a fraction of a second and always seems to know where the net is and which corner is open, and an announcer calls it "instinct" or "natural ability," what you're really seeing is instinct and natural ability honed and perfected by hour after hour and year after year of practice. I have my own word for it. I call it brainwashing.

People marvel at Wayne's anticipation, his ability to always show up around the puck. "He disappears," they say, "and then he shows up where the puck is." That's not quite true. He doesn't go where the puck is, he goes where it's *going to be*. And that doesn't surprise me at all. Why should it? It's common sense.

There's always been a theory that you can't teach anticipation. I've never bought that. I think you can. It's all part of teaching a boy how to think when he's on the ice. Try this drill with your boys, the way I ran it with mine.

First, show the wrong way. Stand at the blue line against the boards and shoot the puck toward the corner, so it will go around the board behind the net to the far corner. Most kids will chase it around the boards, which is where it's been. They're following it.

Now show the correct way. Shoot the puck the way you did the first time, only after you shoot, cut across the front of the net to the other corner. Unless someone stops it en route, that's where the puck will be when you get there. Do it once and it's an exercise. Do it a few thousand times and it's "uncanny anticipation."

What it does for a boy is to teach him to think on skates. In order to develop that anticipation, he has to do the mathematics: given the velocity of the puck, the speed at which it's travelling and the direction it's going, it should wind up right about *here*. And if your calculations are right and no one's stopped it first, that's where it will be.

Brainwashing. Doing something again and again, until the pattern of it is imbedded in your mind to the point where you don't have to think about it. You just do it.

The other aspect of anticipation is figuring out what the opposing player is going to do with the puck. Work with your own teammates long enough and you develop a knowledge that tells you pretty much how each of them works, and what he's likely to do in a given situation. But the opponent, that's a different story. But there are clues.

Watch a defenceman bringing the puck up ice. Watch where he looks. Chances are the last man he looks at before he looks down at his stick is the player who's most likely to get the pass. Wayne got to the point where he could time it, break between the two defencemen for the interception, and have a good chance at a breakaway.

We worked in the back yard on fundamentals. Still do, with the other boys. I'd show Wayne the right way and the wrong way. For example, take a boy who's a left-handed shot skating in a circle to the right. The wrong way is to tuck the right arm into the chest. He'd try it and find he had no control over the stick or the puck, which would slide right off the end. Then I'd show him the proper way, right arm out, up, and toward the right. The control is there and you could go in a circle forever.

256

Brent's like Wayne, a good skater with a skating style similar to Wayne's. He'll do the odd thing that will make me do a double-take, he looks so much like Wayne at that age. And he's really got that deke down, dropping the shoulder or the head to go around someone. Again, it's something that was taught and worked on.

We had pylons on the ice – staggered, not in a straight line, because how often are the players you're trying to beat going to be in a straight line? So you skate toward one pylon, drop a shoulder, head fake to the right and go to the left. Sometimes you don't have to move the puck to fake, just the head or shoulders. If a kid doesn't learn that at a young age he'll never learn it. I really believe that. Learn it early or it's gone.

But if you can get the deke down, if you can handle the puck and stickhandle, you can make up for the fact that you're not a good skater. Wayne was always good at it. Strangely enough, I believe that's one of the reasons he never got to be a good skater at a young age, and why people say he's not a good one now, although he's a lot faster than he gets credit for being. He never had to be fast. He could deke the same kid three times just standing still. And he thought the game out so well, he never did a lot of unnecessary skating.

Or take passing the puck. Passing is a team sport. Kids shouldn't be taught to pass just for the sake of passing. If two of you are going up ice and there's no pressure or no advantage to passing, then don't pass. You might make a bad pass or the other guy might not take it properly, so by keeping the puck you're eliminating two possible mistakes. If there's a guy in the clear, even slightly ahead of you up ice, or in a better possible scoring position than you, you *automatically* pass it. But never pass just for the sake of getting rid of it. That's why you'll see Wayne go one way, spin, and go the opposite way. There's no one open or in a better position.

There's one catch. If you keep the puck like that, don't lose it. Your mother might be in the stands and someone will yell, "Lady, your son is a puck hog!" And her boy may be benched for not passing the puck.

There's nothing magical or mysterious about things like that. They're basics, as basic as keeping your body between the puck and the player checking you. The problem is that some coaches get so involved in teaching kids the advanced hockey, they forget to show them the basics that will allow them to perform all the tricky things they're trying to teach. It's getting better, though, now that coaching certification programs are available for all levels.

Mind you, it's not easy. One of the things you can't afford to forget is that you're dealing with kids, and kids tend to take you literally. A coach on Brent's ten-year-old team told one boy after a game, "Boy, you were really out in left field today." The boy went home and told his parents the coach had given him heck.

He repeated what the coach had said. "And you know something, Dad?" he added. "He didn't even know we were playing hockey. He thought we were playing *baseball!*"

Another thing that always bothered me about minor hockey was the equipment. It wasn't being produced for little kids, it was being produced for little adults. The manufacturers knew who was buying it; they'd just forgotten who'd be *using* it.

I've always believed that in order to play the game, you have to feel as though you were part of it – part of the puck, part of the stick, part of everything. To me that meant the lightest equipment possible. But here we were, Canadians, supposedly the world's leading authorities on hockey, and at one time you couldn't even buy kid-sized sticks. They were skating around using an adult's stick they could barely wrap their hands around. That's why I used to shave down the shafts of Wayne's sticks, as well as cut them down. I carried a hacksaw in the equipment bag. Sticks were $7 each and there I was cutting and chopping them. But it was the only thing that made any sense.

A friend of mine named Carl Charlton coached a house

league team of ten-year-olds and sometimes I'd help him out. One day he spoke to a boy who was using a stick that was miles too long for him.

"Hey, son, we've got to get that stick cut down for you," he said. "Get it done for next practice, okay? You'll be able to stickhandle a lot better and play the game the way it's supposed to be played."

"Oh, I can't do that," the boy said.

"Why not?"

"Well, we've only got one stick. I have to share this one with my older brother."

And pads, that's another story. I've never understood the reason for all the bulkiness at the front of shoulderpads. Enough pad to cover the shoulder sure, but out front? It would help, maybe, but how can you play hockey? And shinpads – they stick out so far that when kids do a cross-over they trip themselves. Consequently, the boys have always used the lightest equipment possible, even if I've had to doctor it myself. Even now Wayne just wears a little cup over the shoulder with no chest padding, which proves my point about coaching: what you teach a boy, what he gets accustomed to, is exactly what he'll use and what he'll do later on.

Skates? I always got them "rockered," taking the long, flat blade and curving it. The process has to be done slowly or the blade becomes like soft iron and won't hold an edge, but when it's done properly you've really got something.

Picture a rocking chair. The parts that touch the floor are bowed slightly so the front and back ends are in the air. That's an exaggeration, but it should give you the idea. With the skate blades "rockered," you have slightly less blade on the surface of the ice. It costs you a little bit in speed, because there's less blade against the ice when you push off, but you gain in that it allows you to make much sharper, quicker turns.

And then there's the skate boot itself, which is far more important than it sounds.

Watch Wayne when he turns. Most players lean over. Wayne does, too, to an extent, but when he turns quickly, watch his ankles. He just flops his ankle over. In all the things that have been written about Wayne I don't think anyone's noticed that. In fact, he turns more on one ankle than the other, so the leather on that one has to be more flexible. He'd have a terrible problem skating in a moulded skate.

Two or three years ago he was having trouble when he turned. He'd make the sharp cut and just fall down. I knew what it was. He'd start the turn, the ankle would go over, the leather would touch the ice and down he'd go. So off we went to the Daoust factory to get a new set of boots. You could see the difference. The old boot was very wide. Tip it, as Wayne did flopping his ankle, and the leather hit the ice very quickly. Now he's fitted specially with a narrow boot, which gives the ankle more room to bend without touching the ice.

There's something else that's different about Wayne's skates. He's got a bone that juts out slightly on the outside of his left foot. Daoust actually built a little cup into that boot to allow space for the bone so it wouldn't be rubbing.

Unfortunately, minor hockey players haven't signed deals with skate manufacturers. Dear old Mom and Dad have to pay the shot. But getting the right skate and boot is one of the most important parts of the preparation. They don't necessarily have to be the most expensive, they just have to be right for the one who's wearing them. The economics of buying equipment creates another problem. A lot of parents shopping for skates will buy, thinking in terms of making them last through next year, too. As a result the skates are too big, the boy can't skate properly, and therefore can't make the best use of his own abilities. In the short term it cuts costs for the parents, but in the end it's the boy who pays.

The gloves you know about. We bought the white ones because we were in a hurry, and because they were flexible and light enough that Wayne could feel the stick through them and have a better awareness of the puck. All the way through minor, junior and pro hockey he stayed with the lightest possible glove, and even had a way of making them lighter.

From the time he was six, he'd take the strings out of the sides of the gloves so his hands could move around inside. He's got a funny up-and-down way of moving his wrists, and with the strings in he couldn't do it, so out they came. It meant sacrificing a little protection, but he never got hurt. Then in his first year of pro, he spent all his time with bruises on the inside of his wrists. That was enough for Glen Sather.

"Get the strings back in there," he said.

For a while there was a compromise. Sather had Wayne wear pads on his wrists. But the strings never did go back in and eventually the padding went out. Old habits are hard to break.

Proper instruction, proper practice, proper equipment. For good coaching and the best results you need all three. But there's a fourth ingredient. Unfortunately, it can be the hardest to find: proper people.

Equipment today is tailored to all age groups. Coaching has improved tremendously over the years. The certification program has helped to raise the standard. But the certificates say the people holding them have passed the tests and know what and how to teach. They don't say anything about the people themselves.

We've been fortunate in our family to be associated with some outstanding coaches – or, rather, outstanding people who happened to *be* coaches. People like Phil Hatcher, who was so instrumental in getting Kim started in track; Al Springall, who was Wayne's first minor baseball coach; and Dick Martin, Wayne's first hockey coach and the first man to spot the potential he had. Remember, that first tryout was open to all the ten-year-olds in Brantford. Wayne was four years younger than most of the others, the smallest boy there. But in all that mob, Dick spotted him and signed him.

I can still remember the day Wayne first went out for baseball. At the time you didn't just register and play, you had to make the team in your area. I'd told Wayne I'd get him to tryouts as soon as they started, but he missed the first couple because we didn't know they were on. Wayne was six and some of the boys were ten or eleven. I didn't think there was any way he could make it, but I didn't want to let him down. So I asked Al if he'd just let Wayne come to a couple of practices, so he'd at least have the satisfaction of knowing he'd tried. "Sure," he said.

That night Wayne told me, "I'm going to make the team." I explained that the odds were against it, but he was sure. About two weeks later, he rode his bike to practice because I was working late. When he came back, he rode up the driveway full speed, steering with one hand and waving a certificate with the other. "See?" he yelled. "See? I *told* you I'd make the team!"

The point is, Al could easily have said he was too late, too small, too far behind. But he gave him a chance to try. He cared about the individual. That's what coaching is all about.

It's not always that way. I've seen junior hockey coaches who carry twenty-four kids on the roster and sit five out every game. Can they say they care for the individual? Prior to the '82-'83 season, I set up a family photo session in Toronto with Collegiate Sports. It was part of an ad campaign and you just don't throw those things together. So I set it for early September, knowing there wouldn't be much in the way of practice at that time, except for some land training. As it turned out, Glen missed a practice. When he explained why the next day, his coach said, "Which is more important – practice, or having your picture taken? It better not happen again."

He needn't have worried. Right then, he was no longer

Glen's coach. Glen dropped down to the "B" team, where he was happy all season. To me, minor hockey at that age is participation and enjoyment. I wanted no part of a guy who came on like a dictator.

You get some coaches who say, "You've got to be tough out there – *tough!*" A lot of kids misunderstand. They think tough means ramming a guy into the boards from behind or cross-checking him. As long as you've left somebody lying on the ice that means you're a tough guy. At one time, before they took the body contact out of minor hockey, you'd get a lot of big guys who manhandled little guys physically, even to the point of fist-fights.

I've got my own definition of "being tough out there." I always say to the kids, "You want to show how tough you are? Go into the corner first and come out with the puck. Anybody can ram somebody from behind or put a stick to him or, if you're bigger, manhandle or slug him. It doesn't prove a thing. But if you can go into that corner first with someone chasing you and breathing down your neck, and come out with the puck, *then* you've shown how tough you really are.

I once saw a coach split a team of fourteen-year-olds into two groups, one along each blue line. First, he told them to put down their sticks. Then he explained what he wanted them to do. They were to skate full speed at each other, with each boy ramming into the one opposite him. No slowing down. The man wanted full-out collisions. "We'll see how tough you guys really are," he said.

That's not toughness, that's stupidity. Minor hockey officials should take coaches like that, line *them* up at the blue lines and let *them* run into each other.

Then you have the coaches who think only about their sport, their team.

I've always believed a youngster should play as many sports as possible. Hockey is a winter game. Baseball is for the summer. There are definite seasons. Switching from one to the other gives a boy a fresh outlook, fresh enthusiasm.

Hockey's a great game, but it would get awfully boring if it went all year. Yet that's what some coaches seem to want.

Come February, when the boys are in the thick of hockey playoffs, the baseball coach will call indoor practices. The season doesn't start for three months, but his team is going to be *ready!* The word gets out: "If you want to make this team, be at the practices." The kids are caught in the middle. They can't miss baseball practice, but they obviously can't skip their hockey playoffs. Or the same thing will happen in reverse. The hockey coach sets dry-land training just when baseball season is getting down to the crunch. It's ridiculous.

To me a season is a season. If you start it, you finish it and no one – coach or parent – should expect anything less. When that season is over, then you should be free to step into the next sport without any penalty or word from the coach. It's only logical. We're dealing with kids here, not professional athletes. It doesn't always work out that way.

There's something a lot of parents forget about the people who coach their kids. Outside of school teachers, coaches probably spend more time with those kids than anyone outside the family. Because they're coaches who've been players themselves, most of them, and have the ultimate say in when, where and how much a boy or girl plays, they are in a position to exert tremendous influence.

People take great care in selecting their babysitters. They join Parent-Teacher associations to keep an eye on how their children are being educated. But for one or two games or practices a week, plus weekends, they turn the same boy or girl over to a man or woman some of them have never so much as met.

There are two other groups parents should keep an eye on when it comes to minor sports: their children, and themselves.

Give yourself an education some time. Walk around the stands in a rink and check out the children. Watch them. Listen to the language.

Wayne is used to being booed. It's something every athlete faces. It's a little bit silly – "If I'm paying $15 for a ticket, I'll cheer for my team," he says. "I might yell a little bit at the other one, but I don't understand how a guy can waste his time booing." – but it's a fact of life. What shatters him is the *kind* of booing he gets.

"I'll be along the boards and there'll be kids seven, eight or nine years old *swearing* at me. Some of the things they're yelling you wouldn't believe. And their parents are sitting right there doing absolutely nothing about it. In fact, some of them are *encouraging* them. Do they think they're hurting us? If I'd done that my father would have picked me up and dragged me home. But first there'd have been an awful *smack!*"

He is right about that. And when it happens, no matter how many people are around, there *should* be a smack. You can teach more than hockey in a rink. If you don't, you're cheating your kids. Again, we're talking about a small minority. Overall one of the big reasons the system works is the support of the parents. But there are some, however few, of the other kind. Even one is too many.

Chapter 20

EPILOGUE: A FEW WORDS FROM 99

"Every year I send my Dad two return airline tickets to Florida. They won't go. I keep saying, 'Relax! I've made it now. Enjoy it.' 'BS,' he says. 'Now I have to worry more.'"

– Wayne Gretzky, 1983.

This is my Dad's book. That was the understanding from the start. But he left something out. He told you about the rest of the family. Now I'd like to tell you about my Dad.

I've heard all the stories about how he pushed me into hockey and kept me out in the back yard practicing because he wanted me to be a star in the NHL. But my Dad never put pressure on me; *I* put pressure on me. All he ever said was, "I don't care what the outcome is. It's good to win and I want you to do your best, but as long as you prepare and do the job to the best of your ability that's all anyone can ask for." If he knew that I *hadn't* prepared or *wasn't* ready, then he would question me.

And he had a right to, because at the time he was putting a lot of money into me. We don't realize it as kids, but minor hockey is expensive. We're doing it for fun, but he was sacrificing a lot of things around the house to allow me to play hockey. All he wanted in return was my best – always. And he's never quit wanting it.

Picture this: we're on Long Island, down 3-0 in the '82-'83 Stanley Cup final against the Islanders. It's the day before Game Four, we're practicing, and I'm sort of going through the motions. Dad's come down for the games and he's watching me. When I came off the ice he was waiting.

"Why were you practicing today?" he demanded.

"Because everybody had to," I answered.

"Well, you wasted your time," he said, "because you didn't give it an effort."

I walked away. Things were bad enough being down 3-0. And I forgot about it.

Dad didn't. We lose the last game, the season's over, and now it's May and I'm at the farm with Dad. It's hot, and Grandma's watering the garden. My Dad looks at me, looks at her, looks back at me and says:

"See! She's seventy-nine and she's still working, and you're in the playoffs and you're not even *practicing*!"

There's not much doubt that hockey caused his ulcers. He worried about everything. The night before tournaments, he couldn't sleep. It's not that he's so bent on winning, it's just the way he is. For instance, I can honestly say I've never worried much about what's said or written about me. I didn't have to. Dad worried enough for both of us. It used to influence him in dealing with me. He'd hear somebody at the rink say, "That Gretzky's hair is too long," and he'd tell me, "Cut your hair." Then, finally, he realized that there are so many people out there, you can't keep them happy.

My Dad is really something. He said once that he's just a man who works for the phone company, but that now he's had to become a little bit of a lawyer, a little bit of an accountant, a little bit of a marketing man. And that's true, because he oversees everything I do on and off the ice. He makes sure they're not working me too hard. I mean everybody – my agent, my marketing people, everybody. When he feels someone is pushing me too hard, he steps in and tells me. That leaves me a choice: keep going, or agree with my Dad and slow down.

He *is* a man who works at the phone company, but now he reads every contract I have from top to bottom – hockey, endorsements, everything. I guess the bottom line is that he's looking out for me. I'm not saying everybody else isn't, but he doesn't care about anybody else. He's looking out for Wayne Gretzky and Wayne Gretzky only. It's been that way for as long as I can remember. And because he's a man who cuts things down to fundamentals, he's developed a great instinct for seeing problems before they come up.

He looked at a contract I'd signed with a skate manufacturing company and told me I was heading for trouble. I had two separate endorsement contracts, one with Daoust to endorse their 301 model skate boot and one with Perfecta to endorse their skate blade. Daoust doesn't manufacture skate blades, only boots. Dad read the contract and said there should have been a clause in it stating that I'd endorse the boot only when it had the Perfecta blade on it. And as it turned out, he was right. Daoust sold a big order of the 301 boot with a different brand of blade attached. So there I was, endorsing a skate boot carrying the blade of a company in direct competition with Perfecta people whose blade I wear and endorse. Eventually we got it straightened out, but for a while there I was losing an endorsement and both companies were unhappy. And Dad had seen the possibility as soon as he read the contract. "Walter might not have much formal education," Michael says, "but he probably has the equivalent of a Masters in business and before we're all done he'll probably have his doctorate."

Now, of course, I'm getting older and more capable of making the big decisions for myself, and people have said it might make for difficulties between us. But that's silly. My Dad and I fight and argue over everything – what I do on the ice and off. I hope I'm lucky enough to have the same relationship with my son: that he'll respect what I tell him and realize I'm trying to do what's best for him, without being afraid to stand up and give his side of it.

I agree with my Dad ninety-five per cent of the time, not

because he's my father, but because he's older and a heck of a lot wiser than I am. There's still that little percentage when I'm sure I'm right, and I have to make a stand and go against his opinion. I think it was hard for him the first time it happened. But that doesn't mean that the next time I'm caught up in a situation, I won't be turning to him. I may wind up doing it my way, but when I'm sixty I'll still be listening to him first. Why wouldn't I? In the crunch, he's always been there . . . .

When I was nine or ten, Dad and I would play catch in the back yard maybe twenty minutes every night. One day I decided what we really needed was a pitcher's mound. Down at the end of our street there was a vacant lot covered with rocks and stuff, so I went down there with the wheelbarrow and a shovel and loaded up. I was wheeling it up the driveway when Mom came out the door.

"Where do you think you're going with that junk?" she said.

"Back yard," I said. "Build a pitcher's mound."

"Oh no, you're not," she said.

Well, I knew my Mom meant business. But I also knew my Dad. I just left the wheelbarrow in the driveway and waited for him to come home from work.

"Where you going with that?" he asked.

"Back yard," I said. "Build a pitcher's mound."

"Sounds good," he said. He went into the basement, nailed a couple of boards together for a slab and helped me build the mound. It was there for eleven years.

He loves that back yard. It's a rink in the winter and a baseball bullpen in the summer, and it's just become a part of us like the house and the farm and Brantford. When I turned pro and got some money, I went to him with what I thought was a great idea. "Dad," I said, "I'm gonna put a swimming pool in the back yard." "Are you *crazy!*" he asked, and went away shaking his head. Needless to say, we do not have a swimming pool.

Maybe it's because I've had some success, but people keep

looking at my parents as though there's some sort of secret formula for producing Wayne Gretzkys that they've stumbled on. We laugh about it sometimes. Take, for instance, the business with the rink in the yard.

In 1979, I told a reporter for the Toronto *Sun* that my Dad and I would be on the rink for hours a day. And I was quoted, accurately, this way: "Honest to God, it was so cold I'd come in the house crying." Now I can just see a bunch of kids coming in crying and hearing their Dads say: "Get back out there! Wayne Gretzky froze. He's sitting in a penthouse in Edmonton. Where the heck are you?"

But they miss the point. They say to me, "You practiced four hours a night," and I say, "Yeah, I guess I did." But looking back at it, I wasn't practicing. If I'd thought I was practicing I'd probably never have done it. I did it because that was what I had fun doing. I never thought, "Well, I'll practice four hours today because if I do that, I'll have a chance to make the NHL." It never entered my head. We did it because we enjoyed it. Other kids were staying out there skating a lot longer than I did and they didn't make it. You can't say, "If you do this you'll make the NHL." It just isn't true. I'd skate for three or four hours and come in, and my Dad would say, "Had enough, eh?" and I'd say, "Yeah," and the next day I'd be out doing it again.

Oh, I cried, all right. Chilblains. Every kid who ever stays out in the cold, then comes into a warm house, gets them. When your feet warm up it hurts and itches like mad. But I don't remember the crying. I remember the hot chocolate, and my Dad's big, strong hands holding my toes to make the cold go away . . . .

And now I'm in the National Hockey League and the money's good and the opportunities are great, and people look back to the days of the back-yard rink and tell their kids, "Do what Wayne Gretzky did. Look how hard he worked. Look how long he practiced." But the one doesn't necessarily follow the other. You won't make the NHL if you *don't* practice, but there's no guarantee you'll make it if you do.

I did a lot of other things, and that's important. I played other sports, I swam – for a couple of years I crocheted. Got pretty good at it, too. I read somewhere that Jacques Plante, the famous goaltender, crocheted as a hobby, so I tried it. Made my Mom a purse, did a rug. (*"Look, son, Wayne Gretzky crocheted and he's in the NHL. Now pick up that crochet hook!"*) I still try to do a lot of other things. I didn't sing on *The Paul Anka Show* because I plan to be a singer, or appear on *The Young and the Restless* because I want to be an actor. They were new things to try. Hockey can't be everything. I'll keep trying things that look interesting or challenging, looking ahead to the day when hockey will be over and I'll need something else.

The pressures are getting bigger, I know that. I've found myself getting less and less patient, snapping not at outside people so much, but at my family. I have a shorter fuse these days and I know it's not going to get any better.

You know the only place I can go to get away from it during the season, the only place I can totally relax? On the ice.

When I play hockey, there's nothing on my mind but the game. I know players whose off-ice activities affect their on-ice performance; they have off-ice problems and can't shake them when they play. The ice is where I get away. Sometimes I chuckle to myself. I walk in the dressing room, pick up a ping pong paddle, play a game, tape up four sticks and go out and play. You have this one thing to do and there's no one bothering you to do anything else. It's great. The games are always the best part. The work comes with the rest of it.

That's the thing about what my Mom and Dad have done. They don't have the games to relax in. I had the easy part. So did Kim and Keith – and Glennie and Brent have it now. All we had to do was play. Equipment, transportation, arrangements – they took care of them all. It makes me wonder sometimes: what kind of a father will Wayne Gretzky be . . . ?

There's no way my son's leaving home at fourteen.

There was this little guy, twelve years old, in St. Catharines a while ago, whose father was going to send him to Toronto. My Dad told him the Ontario Minor Hockey Association wouldn't let him do it, and he was right. The boy wound up being suspended. I guess the bottom line would be whether or not they were sending him to learn to be a professional hockey player. My parents sent me to get away and live a normal life. If I became a pro hockey player, good. But if I became a good human being and came out normal, that was what mattered. You don't send your kid away from home at eleven or twelve or thirteen or fourteen and say, "You go there and learn to be a hockey player." That's not right.

At fourteen, I thought going to Toronto was the greatest thing in the world, and it turned out to be the best thing that could have happened to me – but if there was one thing I could do over again, I'd like to be able to say I lived at home until I was eighteen or nineteen. I guess you can't have your cake and eat it, too.

If I'm lucky enough to have a son and he's lucky enough to play hockey, I hope I'll watch him play, let him play, encourage him to win, give him all the support I can – and if he doesn't win say, "I'm sorry," and stop to buy him an ice cream cone. In one respect I'm different from my Dad. I won't be on the phone at night arranging exhibition games or losing sleep worrying. I'm going to be in this game from the time I was six until who knows. When I quit, I just want to walk away from it. But I'd love my son to know the joy of playing it.

A lot of the trouble and confusion in minor hockey is caused by parents, well-meaning parents, who want to have it both ways.

Some parents say kids should play for fun, and that's

great. And they say kids should go out there and everybody should play, and that's great, too. Then they say kids should go out and, win or lose, leave the game there when they go home. That's wonderful. And there's a place for that. The way minor sport is set up, if you want to be content with that level there's a place for you. But if you *want* to be the best, if you *want* to be under pressure at that age, if you *want* to win every day, there's a place for that, too. And there should be.

If you're my son I'm going to say to you, "You're playing on this team and you're going to do the best you're capable of doing, and you're going to learn to do what you have to do to win. But if you lose, that's fine. Learn from it, leave it there, and go home and live your life. When you go back again, try to learn from your mistakes, but you still want to win.

"That's the way I believe you should be brought up, because if you are, then win or lose it's going to carry into your school, into your job and into your life. You should want the feeling inside that says, 'Damnit, I'm gonna be the best. Our team's gonna be the best.' That's the feeling you've got to have."

There's room for kids whose parents don't want them under pressure, who think it's bad for them. There's house league hockey. And there's the other side where there's pressure, where the team is expected to win. Where I get mad is when the coaches of the pressure-situation teams try to bring the good players down to the average rather than encouraging the average ones to lift themselves to the level of the good ones. They do that because they're afraid of causing dissension. That was where my problems in minor hockey started. I had coaches, some of them, who wanted me to be an average hockey player. If I had a team with an exceptional player on it, I'd be saying to the others, "Hey, watch what he does, and try to learn to do it yourselves." If they can't do it, that's fine. But they've tried, and in trying they've probably done better than they thought they could.

It's a question of pushing yourself to your best. My Dad

always said, "I don't expect you to do what you can't, but I expect you to do the things I know you can." Take school. He knew I was good in certain subjects and not so good in others. If I did well in one of the poor ones, that was great. But if I did badly in one he knew I could handle, that was uncalled for. Everything hit the fan.

The other thing to remember is that no kid, no matter how good he is in minor hockey, can say for sure that he's going to make the NHL. Too many things can happen. And if there was one piece of advice I could give to those who do get a chance to turn pro it would be this: if you can't play in the NHL, go home.

My brothers could be in that position and I'd tell them the same thing. Glennie, for instance. No one worked at it harder or wanted it more, but it could be hard for him. Deep down I think he knows it and is preparing himself for other things. If he did make it to the pros and was a borderliner, I'd tell him to forget it, as I would have. Because when NHL teams open camp saying all positions are open, they're lying. If I played two years in the minors and hadn't made it, I'd have no qualms about saying, "Thank you very much. I enjoyed it, I learned a lot, and what I learned most is that I have to get a job or go back to school."

I have been very fortunate. All my life I've been surrounded by a family that loves me. And I've played the game I love.

Hockey is so much *fun*. You know, maybe it's just as well that I live in a penthouse. If I lived at street-level in Edmonton, the winter would come and I'd look out the window at the kids playing road hockey, and before you know it I'd be out there with them and there would go my game that night.

Some day if I'm lucky, maybe I'll take my son out on the ice at the farm, or play with him on the rink in the back yard in Brantford. And when he comes in, crying a little because his feet are frozen, I'll hold his toes and make the cold go away, just like my Dad did for me.

Appendix

Wayne Gretzky Career Statistics

			Regular Season					Playoffs				
Season	Club	League	GP	G	A	PTS	PIM	GP	G	A	PTS	PIM
1975-76	Nats	Jr. B	28	27	33	60	7	n/a	n/a	n/a	n/a	n/a
1976-77	Nats	Jr. B	32	36	36	72	35	n/a	n/a	n/a	n/a	n/a
1976-77	Petes	Jr. A	3	0	3	3	0	—	—	—	—	—
1977-78	Greyhounds	OHA	64	70	112	182	14	13	6	20	26	0
	Jr. totals:		127	133	184	317	56	—	—	—	—	—

(n/a: Not available.)

1978-79	Indianapolis	WHA	8	3	3	6	0	—	—	—	—	—
1978-79	Edmonton	WHA	72	43	61	104	19	13	10	10	20	2
1979-80	Edmonton	NHL	79	51	86	137	21	3	2	1	3	0
1980-81	Edmonton	NHL	80	55	109	164	28	9	7	14	21	4
1981-82	Edmonton	NHL	80	92	120	212	26	5	5	7	12	8
1982-83	Edmonton	NHL	80	71	125	196	59	16	12	26	38	4
1983-84	Edmonton	NHL	74	87	118	205	39	19	13	21	34	12
	WHA totals:		80	46	64	110	19	13	10	10	20	2
	NHL totals:		393	356	558	914	173	52	39	69	108	28

Stanley Cup, 1983-84

Game 1
Oilers 1 at Islanders 0

First period – No scoring. Penalties: Lowe (O) 8:40, Potvin (I) 11:34, Hunter (O) 14:09, Potvin (I) 14:51, Jackson (O) 15:47.

Second period – No scoring. Penalties: Dineen (I) 11:52, Jackson (O) 1:55.

Third period – 1. Edmonton, McClelland 3 (Hughes, Hunter) 1:55. Penalties: Hunter (O) 9:06, Jonsson (I) 15:42.

Shots on goal by:
Edmonton   10   12   16 – 38
New York   14   12   8 – 34
Goalies: Edmonton, Fuhr; New York, Smith, Melanson.

Game 2
Oilers 1 at Islanders 6

First period – 1. New York, Trottier 7 (Bossy, Boutilier) :53;
2. New York, Gilbert 5 (LaFontaine, Persson) 5:48 pp; 3. Edmonton, Gregg 3 (McClelland) 15:06; 4. New York, Gillies 8
(Kallur) 18:31. Penalties: Anderson (O) and Tonelli (I) :09,
Huddy (O) 4:14, Hughes (O), Jonsson (I), D. Sutter (I) 6:29,
Huddy (O) 8:51, B. Sutter (I) 9:12, Jackson (O) and Gilbert (I)
12:11, Jonsson (I) 12:52, McClelland (O) and D. Sutter (I)
minors and majors 15:42.

Second period – 5. New York, Trottier 8 (B. Sutter, Flatley) 4:52;
6. New York, Gillies 9 (Potvin, Bossy) 16:48 pp. Penalties:
Jonsson (I) 5:37, Anderson (O) 16:05.

Third period – 7. New York, Gillies 10 (Trottier, Boutilier)
17:04. Penalties: Messier (O) and Dineen (I) minors and majors
6:52, Gretzky (O) 8:30, Semenko (O) 15:16, Lumley (O) and
Dineen (I) majors and game misconducts, Linseman (O)
minor, major and misconduct, Gilbert (I) double minor, major
and misconduct 17:25.

Shots on goal by:
Edmonton   12   6   5 – 23
New York   12   9   5 – 26
Goalies: Edmonton, Fuhr. New York, Smith.

Game 3
Islanders 2 at Oilers 7

First period – 1. New York, Gillies 11 (Flatley, B. Sutter) 1:32;
2. Edmonton, Lowe 3 (Anderson, Lindstrom) 13:49. Penalties:
D. Sutter (I) and Linseman (O) 2:27, B. Sutter (I) 6:30, Mc-
Clelland (O) 8:49, Jonsson (I) 10:59, Fogolin (O) 14:32, Gilbert
(I) major, Jackson (O) major, Flatley (I) double minor, Gregg
(O) 15:16, Tonelli (I) and Linseman (O) 17:53.

276

Second period – 3. New York, Gillies 12 (Trottier, Bossy) 2:53 pp; 4. Edmonton, Messier 6 (Fogolin) 8:28; 5. Edmonton, Anderson 6 (Huddy, Gretzky) 19:12; 6. Edmonton, Coffey 7 (Hughes, Linseman) 19:29. Penalties: Hunter (O) 1:55, B. Sutter (I) 3:34, Pouzar (O) 10:00, Trottier (I) and Pouzar (O) 14:22, D. Sutter (I) and Fogolin (O) double minors 17:53, Melanson (I) and McClelland (O) 19:37.

Third period – 7. Edmonton, Messier 7 (Hughes) 5:32; 8. Edmonton, McClelland 4 (Lumley) 5:52; 9. Edmonton, Semenko 5 (Kurri, Gretzky) 9:41. Penalties: Pouzar (O) 6:16, Anderson (O) 6:56, Morrow (I) and Anderson (O) 14:19, Melanson (I), McClelland (O) 19:37.

Shots on goal by:
New York   10   8   8 – 26
Edmonton   11   12   17 – 40
Goalies: New York, Smith, Melanson; Edmonton, Fuhr, Moog.

Game 4
Islanders 2 at Oilers 7

First period – 1. Edmonton, Gretzky 10 (Semenko, Kurri) 1:53; 2. Edmonton, Lindstrom 4 (Anderson) 3:22; 3. New York, B. Sutter 4 (Gilbert, Morrow) 14:03; 4. Edmonton, Messier 8 (unassisted) 17:54. Penalties: Nystrom (I) 4:41, Potvin (I) and Lumley (I) 13:20, Langevin (I) major 15:53, Morrow (I), Kurri (O), Gretzky (O) 17:31, Lowe (O) 18:25, Linseman (O) major 18:51.

Second period – 5. Edmonton, Lindstrom 5 (Messier, Coffey) 5:21 pp; 6. Edmonton, Conacher 1 (Hughes) 7:58; 7. Edmonton, Coffey (Kurri, Semenko) 10:52; 8. New York, Flatley (Gillies, Persson) 19:44.

Third period – 9. Edmonton, Gretzky 11 (unassisted) 14:11. Penalty: Huddy (O) 6:36.

Shots on goal by:
New York   7   7   7 – 21
Edmonton   16   10   12 – 38
Goalies: New York, Smith. Edmonton, Moog.

Game 5
Islanders 2 at Oilers 5

First period – 1. Edmonton, Gretzky 12 (Kurri) 12:08; 2. Edmonton, Gretzky 13 (Kurri) 17:26. Penalties: Edmonton bench (served by Lindstrom) :47, Flatley (I) 4:09, Persson (I) 7:43, D. Sutter (I) 18:47.

Second period – 3. Edmonton, Linseman 10 (Gretzky, Huddy) 0:38; 4. Edmonton, Kurri (Coffey, Anderson) 4:59. Penalties: D. Sutter (I) 4:19, Semenko (O) 10:22.

Third period – 5. New York, LaFontaine 2 (Flatley, Gillies) :13; 6. New York, LaFontaine 3 (Gillies) :45; 17. Edmonton, Lumley 2 (unassisted) 19:47. Penalty: Flatley (I) 16:45.

Shots on goal by:

New York	8	6	11 –	25
Edmonton	9	5	9 –	23

Goalies: New York, Smith, Melanson; Edmonton, Moog.

1984 Playoff Scoring Leaders

	G	A	Pts		G	A	Pts
Gretzky, Edm	13	21	34	Flatley, NYI	9	6	15
Kurri, Edm	14	14	28	Linseman, Edm	10	4	14
Messier, Edm	8	18	26	Trottier, NYI	8	6	14
Coffey, Edm	8	14	22	Naslund, Mtl	6	8	14
Gillies, NYI	12	7	19	B. Sutter, NYI	4	10	14
Bossy, NYI	8	10	18	Bellows, Minn	2	12	14
Anderson, Edm	6	11	17	MacInnis, Cal	2	12	14
Reinhart, Cal	6	11	17	Hughes, Edm	2	12	14

Wayne Gretzky's NHL Awards

First All-Star team: 1981-82-83-84.
Second All-Star Team: 1980.

Hart Memorial Trophy (NHL most-valuable player to his team): 1980-81-82-83-84.

Art Ross Trophy (Leading scorer, regular season): 1981-82-83-84. (Tied Marcel Dionne for scoring title in 1980. Dionne awarded trophy on basis of most goals scored.)

Lady Byng Trophy (Sportsmanship and gentlemanly conduct combined with a high standard of playing ability): 1980.

Lester B. Pearson Award (NHL's most-valuable player as voted by players): 1982, 1983, 1984.

Emery Edge Trophy (Player who appears in minimum 60 games and leads NHL in plus-minus statistics, in which player gets a plus when on ice for an even-strength or shorthanded goal by his team, and a minus when on ice for even-strength or short-handed goal by opposing team): 1984, Plus 76.

Wayne Gretzky's NHL Records

Career

Highest goals-per-game average: .905.
Highest assists-per-game average: 1.41.
Highest points-per-game average: 2.325.

Single Season

Most goals (92) 1981-82.
Most assists (120) 1981-82.
Most points (212) 1981-82.
Most assists, one playoff year (26) 1982-83.
Most points, one playoff year (38) 1982-83.
Most three-or-more goals games (10) 1981-82: One five-goal game, three four-goal games, six three-goal games. 1983-84: Four four-goal games, six three-goal games.
Most short-handed goals (12) 1983-84.
Most goals including playoffs (97) 1981-82 (92 league, 5 playoff).
Most assists including playoffs (151) 1982-83 (125 league, 26 playoff).

Most points including playoffs (234) 1982-83 (196 league, 38 playoff).

Most goals by centre (92) 1981-82.

Most assists by centre (125) 1981-82.

Most points by centre (212) 1981-82.

Most goals in first 50 games of season (60) 1981-82.

Most consecutive games, one or more assists (17) 1983-84.

Most consecutive games, one or more points (51) 1983-84.

Most assists, one game, in first NHL season (7): Edmonton, Feb. 15, 1980, in 8-2 win over Washington.

* – Most assists, one game (7) (with Billy Taylor, 1946-47 Detroit Red Wings).

* – Most goals, one period (4) (with six others).

* – Most assists, one period (4) (with 19 others).

Playoffs

Most points, one playoff year (38) 1982-83.

Most assists, one playoff year (26) 1982-83.

* – Most shorthanded goals, one playoff year (3) 1982-83 (with three others).

* – Most shorthanded goals, one game (2): Edmonton, April 6, 1983 in 6-3 win over Winnipeg (with two others).

Most points, one game (7): Calgary, April 17, 1983, four goals and three assists in 10-2 win.

* – Most goals, one period (3) (with 16 others).

* – Most assists, one period (3) (with 29 others).

* – Fastest goal from start of period other than first (9 sec.): Edmonton, April 6, 1983 in 6-3 win over Winnipeg (with six others).

All-Star Game

Most goals, one game (4) 1983.

* – Most points, one game (4) 1983 (with four others).

Most goals, one period (4) 1983.

Most points, one period (4) 1983.

---

* – Shared.

Other Awards

Officer of the Order of Canada, 1984.

Sports Illustrated Sportsman of the Year, 1982.

ABC's *Wide World of Sports* Athlete of the Year, 1982.

Associated Press Athlete of the Year, 1982.

Chicago Tribune Athlete of the Year, 1982.

Sporting News Man of the Year, 1981.

Sporting News Player of the Year, 1980-81-82-83-84.

Hockey News Player of the Year, 1979-80, 1980-81 (with Mike Liut), 1981-82, 1982-83, 1983-84.

Victor Award (excellence in your sport in North America) 1980-81-82-83.

American Academy of Achievement Award (honouring worldwide excellence in your chosen field) 1982.

Canadian male athlete of the year, 1980-81-82-83.

Charlie Conacher Award (humanitarianism and community service), 1981.

Seagram Seven Crowns of Sport Award (dominance in your chosen sport), 1981-82-83-84.

Vanier Award (awarded annually to five outstanding young Canadians by Canadian Junior Chamber of Commerce), 1982.

Dunlop Award (North American professional athlete of the year), 1983.

Acknowledgements

Walter Gretzky and Jim Taylor wish to acknowledge, in
conjunction with the Big Brothers of Metropolitan Toronto,
the following corporations for their support of a special
fund-raising event associated with this book.

Bell Canada
Black's Cameras
Butterfield and Robinson Travel
CN Tower
Commonwealth Holiday Inns of Canada Limited
General Mills Canada, Inc.
Gulf Oil of Canada
Hayhurst Advertising Limited (Sports Division)
Hiram Walker & Sons Limited
Hockey Hall of Fame and Museum
Labatt Brewing Company
Mattel Canada, Inc.
Mediacom, Inc.
Nordair Limited
Philips Information Systems Limited (Micom System)
Ridout/Chateau Gai Wines
Seven-Up Canada Inc.
System 4 Limited
The Royal Bank of Canada
The Westin Hotel – Toronto
Toronto Transit Commission
Travelers Canada
Treasure Tours (Canada) Limited
William Neilson Limited

MAR. 5/86

WAYNE GRETZKY reaches the 1300TH POINT MARK, IN his 7TH SEASON IN the N.H.L.

MAR. 7/86

WAYNE GRETZKY SETS N.H.L RECORD FOR ASSISTS IN A SEASON, 136

MAR. 18/86

WAYNE GRETZKY SCORED his 50TH GOAL FOR the 7TH STRIGHT YEAR.

MAR. 25/86

WAYNE GRETZKY reached THE 200TH POINT MARK, IN A SEASON: FOR THE 4TH TIME IN 7 N.H.L SEASONS.

APRIL 2/86

PAUL COFFEY TIES BOBBY ORR'S record for goals by A defenmen AT 46, IN A SEASON.

APRIL 2/86 PAUL COFFEY SETS NEW N.H.L RECORD FOR GOALS BY A defenmen IN A SEASON AT 47.

APRIL 4/86

WAYNE GRETZKY TIES his N.H.L RECORD FOR POINTS IN A SEASON 213, WITH his 160 ASSIT.

APRIL 4/86

WAYNE GRETZKY SETS NEW NH.L RECORD FOR TOTAL POINTS IN A SEASON. 213

APRIL 6/86

WAYNE GRETZKY finished 1985/86 SEASON WITH 215 POINTS NEW N.H.L. RECORD.

APRIL 12/86

MIKE BOSSY SET N.H.L PLAYOFF RECORD FOR GOALS AT 83.

APRIL 30/86

CALGARY FLAMES ELEMINATE THE EDMONTON
OILERS IN THE 7th GAME OF THE SMYTHE
DIVISON FINALS; by 3 TO 2 SCORE.
STEVE SMITH SCORED INTO HIS OWN NET
AT ABOUT THE 10 MINUTE MARK OF THE
THIRD PERIOD TO GIVE CALGARY THE LEAD.

MAY 14/86

CALGARY FLAMES ELEMINATE the S.T LOUIS
BLUES, IN 7 GAMES from the PLAY offs
SCORE 2-1

MAY 24/86:

THE MONTREAL CANADIENS eleminate
The CALGARY FLAMES IN 5 GAME.
TO WIN THE STANLEY ~~~~~ CUP
FOR THE 23rd TIME: (1985-1986.

The 1985/86 CON SMYTHE trophy
WINNER IN THE PLAYOFFS IS

1985 - 1986
N.H.L. SEASONS END.

MONTREAL SETS NEW RECORD FOR championsh
IN NORTH AMERICA AT "23" beating
the NEW YORK YANKEES AT 22.